POLITICAL PHILOSOPHY NOW

Chief Editor of the Series:
Howard Williams, University of Wales, Aberystwyth

Associate Editors:
Wolfgang Kersting, University of Kiel, Germany
Steven B. Smith, Yale University, USA
Peter Nicholson, University of York, England

Political Philosophy Now is a series which deals with authors, topics and periods in political philosophy from the perspective of their relevance to current debates. The series presents a spread of subjects and points of views from various traditions which include European and New World debates in political philosophy.

POLITICAL PHILOSOPHY NOW

Carl Schmitt and Authoritarian Liberalism

STRONG STATE, FREE ECONOMY

Renato Cristi

UNIVERSITY OF WALES PRESS • CARDIFF • 1998

© Renato Cristi, 1998

British Library Cataloguing-in-Publication Data
A catalogue record for this book is available from the British Library.

ISBN 0-7083-1440-6 cased
     978-0-7083-1441-8 paperback

All rights reserved. No part of this book may be reproduced, stored in a retrieval system, or transmitted, in any form or by any means, electronic, mechanical, photocopying, recording or otherwise, without clearance from the University of Wales Press, King Edward VII Avenue, Cardiff, Wales CF10 3NS.

The right of Renato Cristi to be identified as author of this work has been asserted by him in accordance with the Copyright, Designs and Patents Act 1988.

Reprinted 2018

Typeset by Action Typesetting Ltd, Gloucester
Printed and bound by CPI Group (UK) Ltd, Croydon, CR0 4YY

Contents

Acknowledgements		vii
Introduction		1
1	Crossing the Rubicon: Schmitt and the Nazi Revolution	25
2	Political Romanticism and the Catholic Counter-Revolution	53
3	Freedom and Authority: *Complexio Oppositorum*	79
4	Hegel contra Schmitt	96
5	Sovereignty and Constituent Power	108
6	The Constitution of Political Liberalism	126
7	Hayek contra Schmitt	146
8	The Concept of the Political	169
9	The Bridge over the Rubicon	179
Conclusion		200
Appendix: Carl Schmitt, Strong State and Sound Economy: An Address to Business Leaders		212
References		233
Index		243

TO THE MEMORY OF MY FATHER (1909–1997)

Acknowledgements

I owe special thanks to Howard Williams who first suggested that I write a book on Schmitt and supported me throughout with rich insights and stimulating comments. My colleague Leo Groarke has been a wellspring of good advice and intellectual camaraderie.

I am indebted to many colleagues and friends who gave me the benefit of their enlightened conversation and correspondence: Benjamín Arditti, Heiner Bielefeldt, Frank Deppe, David Dyzenhaus, Peter Erb, Richard Gervais, Montserrat Herreros, Thomas Hueglin, Ingeborg Maus, Helmut Quaritsch, Piet Tommissen, George Urbaniak and Patrice Vermeren. Over the years, Karen Scott and Amy Menary, from Interlibrary Loans at Wilfrid Laurier University, scoured the libraries of North America in search of the literature on Schmitt that I required. I should like to thank Ceinwen Jones at the University of Wales Press and the copy-editor, Jane Robson, for their efficiency and support during the preparation of this book.

A note of thanks also to Ingeborg Maus, Piet Tommissen and William Scheuerman who furnished copies of important publications that I was unable to locate. I owe thanks to Joseph Kaiser, for his permission to translate and publish 'Strong State and Sound Economy', Schmitt's address to the *Langnamverein* conference in 1932 which appears as an appendix to this book. The original draft of Hayek's *Law, Legislation and Liberty*, which he presented at a seminar held in 1970 at the University of California at Los Angeles, was given to me by Francis J. Pelletier, who attended that seminar.

Early versions of chapters of this book appeared in *Canadian Journal of Political Science*, *Canadian Journal of Law and Jurisprudence*, *History of Political Thought* and *Owl of Minerva*. Joseph Velaidum helped me with the translation of Schmitt's text and the preparation, for my personal use, of a concordance of the three versions of Schmitt's *Der Begriff der Politischen*.

For generously supporting the research involved in this book, I am grateful to the Social Sciences and Humanities Research Council of Canada and the Research Office at Wilfrid Laurier University.

My most personal debt of gratitude is to my wife Marcela who made many sacrifices while I was researching and writing this book.

Introduction

A state which is strong can adopt a more liberal attitude
(Hegel, 1991: 295)

I

Present-day German conservatism has inducted Carl Schmitt into the Hall of Fame of political thought. He has been elevated to the rank of classical political thinker (Wilms, 1988), with a stature comparable to that of Machiavelli or Hobbes. Furthermore, since the fall of the Berlin Wall, a reawakening of the conservative movement has propelled Schmitt's work to the very centre of the discussion. The much talked about Carl Schmitt Renaissance (Koenen, 1995: 2; Maus, 1994: 2) has been fuelled in large measure by the political climate of ideas in Germany.[1] 'Whoever wants intellectually to take contemporary German conservatism seriously is bound to discuss Carl Schmitt' (Mehring, 1992: 13).

Conservatism thought is, first and foremost, a national phenomenon (Greiffenhagen, 1979: 611).[2] True to this conservative trait, Schmitt's work bears a distinctively German trademark. This is an author fundamentally determined by one particular national circumstance – the German revolution of 1918–19, which brought the demise of monarchical legitimacy and the promulgation of a liberal-democratic constitution (compare with

---

[1] The discussion of Schmitt's work has produced an enormous body of literature. The secondary literature mentioned in the massive biographical study by Andreas Koenen, which includes mostly German material, is composed of more than 2,500 titles (Koenen, 1995). For German jurists and political philosophers the case of Schmitt has acquired proportions comparable to that of Heidegger (ibid. 1).

[2] Conservatism traces its intellectual roots to the reaction against eighteenth-century Enlightenment rationalism by authors like Burke, de Maistre, Haller and Gentz. It is to be expected, then, that conservative thought should naturally tend to avoid abstract philosophical considerations and not show much interest in matters that rise above national or regional situations.

Holmes, 1993: 37). Schmitt's most important work, his *Verfassungslehre*, is a constitutional law treatise, which is basically the commentary on a text – the Weimar constitution (Schmitt, 1928). To some its spare and clear prose may appear to 'glow incandescently' (Holmes, 1993), but this does not alter the fact that this is a scholarly interpretation of a constitutional document that ceased legally to exist more than sixty years ago. Why, then, has Schmitt's theory of the state and the constitution,[3] sustained mainly by labyrinthine legal arguments and nourished by German constitutional history, sparked so much interest in continental Europe, and most recently in the English-speaking world?[4] Is this interest fuelled solely by the fact that he gave constitutional and legal advice to the Nazi regime from its very inception which helped to define its revolutionary stance? Or is there still something of theoretical value to be learnt from his intellectual work?

The depth and breadth of the work produced by Schmitt is atypical of a constitutional theorist. His analyses of the Weimar constitution as a positive constitution were the front-line of a much broader campaign aimed against the German revolution of 1918–19 and its liberal and democratic principles. This campaign was driven by conservative convictions backed by metaphysical and political artillery. The matrix of European conservative

---

[3] Early, in his *Die Diktatur*, Schmitt used succinct expressions like 'die Staats- und Verfassungslehre' (Schmitt, 1921: p. xi) and 'die konstitutionelle Staatslehre' (ibid.: 44), which integrated the theory of the state and the theory of the constitution into one discipline. Later, in his *Verfassungslehre*, he sought to distinguish them, in accordance with liberal constitutionalism and its methodical avoidance of the political. He thus defended the view that the theory of the constitution had to be taken 'as an independent domain ... that required to be studied in itself' and kept separate from a 'general theory of the state (politics)' (Schmitt, 1928: p. xii). At the same time, he acknowledged a difficulty with liberal constitutionalism, namely that it tended to reduce the whole constitution to the liberal *Rechtsstaat* aspects and did not take into account its political aspects (ibid.: p. xiii). In view of his own revaluation of the political, Schmitt compromised and included in his own theory of the constitution a limited study of 'the theory of state forms in general, and the theories of democracy, monarchy and aristocracy in particular' (ibid.: p. xiv). The synthetic formula 'theory of the state and the constitution', seeks to capture the real proportions of Schmitt's compromise and is closer, in this respect, to his earlier usage in *Die Diktatur*, which will reappear in later works (compare with Schmitt, 1932a: 19).

[4] Interest in Carl Schmitt, spear-headed by Joseph Bendersky, George Schwab,

thought is to be found in the vicinity of modern revolutionary movements – the English revolutions in the cases of Hobbes and Locke, the French revolution in the cases of Burke, de Maistre and Hegel, the 1848 European revolutions in the cases of Marx, Kierkegaard and Donoso Cortés. Much inspired by the thought of these authors, Schmitt followed them in tying his personal and intellectual destiny to a revolutionary event that coincided with the pattern of modern revolutions. Like revolutionary England, the German revolution sought to secure a sanctuary for the protection of individual rights and to confirm the rule of law or *Rechtsstaat* as constitutional keystone. Like revolutionary France, it procured the abrogation of monarchical legitimacy and the affirmation of popular sovereignty by an explicit appeal to the *pouvoir constituant* or constituent power of the people. Like revolutionary Russia, it demanded and obtained a recognition of the obligations of the state towards the welfare of its citizens. The German revolution also saw the brief ascent of radical socialist factions whose aim was a soviet-style system of government.[5]

In the wake of his counter-revolutionary predecessors such as de Maistre and Burke, Schmitt decided to settle accounts with the revolution in Germany on the constitutional front. This was the single endeavour that defined his entire intellectual strategy. The revolution had deposed monarchy and abolished the monarchical principle. Schmitt feared that this would lead to the demise of the

---

Paul Edward Gottfried, Ellen Kennedy and the TELOS group, coincided with a conservative revival in the 1980s (compare with Schwab, 1988; Haselbach, 1988). In the case of the TELOS group, the critique of Schmitt has meant the appropriation of some of his conservative ideas with the intention of developing a leftist *Realpolitik* (compare with Piccone and Ulman, 1987). In the 1990s, a new generation of scholars, which includes Peter Caldwell, David Dyzenhaus, Stephen Holmes, John McCormick, William Scheuerman and Richard Wolin, has taken up the study of Schmitt in order to generate the antibodies needed to forestall the rise of anti-democratic liberalism in Canada and the United States. Attention has also been paid to Schmitt in Britain. Recently, Perry Anderson has included Schmitt, together with Leo Strauss, Friedrich Hayek and Michael Oakeshott, as a member of 'the quartet of outstanding European theorists of the intransigent Right whose ideas now shape ... a large part of the mental world of the end-of-the-century Western politics' (Anderson, 1992: 7).

[5] As Bendersky notes, when the monarchy collapsed Schmitt's anxiety stemmed 'from the specter of a dictatorship of the proletariat ... [He] wondered to what extent the left might succeed in destroying the institutions of the Second Reich and in revolutionizing the social order of Germany' (1983: 195).

state. Like Hobbes, his entire intellectual production was marked by a radical defence of the state.[6] The battleground of his choice was the Weimar constitution and the institutions that grew under its shade. A multifaceted scholarly formation that added philosophical substance and literary style to his enormous juristic acumen determined the breadth of his critique of the constitution. His ability to sustain this critique through the years was the result of combining a continuous allegiance to his central strategic aim with a pliable tactical itinerary, which he accommodated to the changing political circumstances.

To declare Schmitt's conservative critique of Weimar liberal constitutionalism as his overall strategic aim seems to me uncontroversial. The same may be said of his conservative distaste for democracy and socialism. As far as I know, there is no dispute concerning Schmitt's conservative aims and credentials. What is open to controversy is the nature of the tactical fulfilment of that strategy. During the Weimar republic he chose, for example, to defend the inviolability and integrity of the Weimar constitution *qua* absolute constitution. He did so by arguing against those who, like Gerhard Anschütz, interpreted its article 76 as granting the legislator an unconstrained and open-ended power to reform it (Anschütz, 1933). According to Schmitt, the Weimar constitution *qua* absolute constitution was defined by liberal-democratic principles. The legislator could not, within the scope of its constitutional power, reintroduce monarchical legitimacy or transform its republican set-up into a soviet-style system. At the same time, Schmitt defended an interpretation that strengthened the role of *Reichspräsident* at the expense of parliament. He was ready to extend dictatorial powers to the *Reichspräsident*, powers that, short of destroying or abrogating the constitution, gave him the ability to suspend substantial parts of it. This illustrates the

---

[6] Rumpf notices that Schmitt shared with Hobbes a common concern – the need to bolster the authority of the state (compare with Rumpf, 1972: 109). And Bendersky acknowledges that 'from his earliest writings under the monarchy, the state has remained the crucial element in Schmitt's thought. Only the state can guarantee the basic human and societal requirements of order, peace and stability, which are requisites for freedom and cultural development' (1983: 285). Emphasis on order and stability is typical of conservative thought. But to require order and stability as the condition of freedom is the hallmark of conservative or authoritarian liberalism.

challenge faced by Schmittian scholars when they try to chart the ambivalences of his positions, the twists and turns of his commando tactics, which involved, at one point, open collaboration and straightforward defence of the liberal and democratic elements of Weimar's constitutional regime. This challenge can only be met if Schmitt's theory of the state and the constitution is assumed to be his strategic baseline.

The argument expounded in this book seeks to define the scope and assumptions of Schmitt's theory of the state and the constitution and the pivotal task it addressed – securing the state's autonomy and independence. Only this would shore up and strengthen the power and authority of the state. A strong state, however, did not imply cancelling civil society's own independence. If totalitarianism means that the state ultimately assimilates and metabolizes civil society, at no point of his intellectual development did Schmitt espouse such a totalitarian view. On the contrary, he thought that an autonomous state would prove its strength by affirming the freedom and autonomy of civil society. This is a keystone of Schmitt's theory of the state and the constitution. At one point during the Weimar republic, Schmitt publicly stated his dual affirmation of a strong state and a free economy, which neatly encapsulates the aim and scope that defined his theory of the state and the constitution.[7] My choice of the motto 'strong state and free economy' as the subtitle of this book is intended to highlight this. In order to adjudicate between the opposing claims of a sovereign state and a free civil society and harmonize their interests, Schmitt appealed to the distinction between the substance and the exercise of sovereignty, developed by medieval philosophers like D'Ailly and Gerson (Schmitt, 1921: 44, 193). This distinction, mentioned only in his early Weimar production, provided him with the definitive model for the

---

[7] Lutz-Armen Bentin believes that it was Johannes Popitz who originally formulated the Schmittian notion of a free economy in a strong state. It was also Popitz who first brought Schmitt in contact with German industrial circles and made arrangements for the conferences he delivered at the *Langnamverein* (Bentin, 1972: 125). According to Nicholls, Popitz helped to 'pave the way for Hitler' (1994: 43). His Manchester liberal views on the economy were clearly expressed at a conference organized by the Friedrich List Society and held at Essen in October 1929. There Popitz 'waxed eloquently on the sufferings of the wealthy in Weimar and impressed upon his listeners the necessity of giving the upper classes economic security' (ibid.).

operation of a strong state. Normally, the exercise of state sovereignty was juridically ordained and was thus limited. But the substance of its omnipotence was unlimited and remained in a state of latency, waiting to be roused in exceptional circumstances. Schmitt's emphatic affirmation of the sovereignty of the state was due to what he saw as the weak state that had resulted from the revolutionary abrogation of the monarchical legitimacy in Germany. A convinced etatist and anti-monarchomachist, Schmitt followed Hobbes in judging that only the strongly decisive state could avert the possibility of a civil war. Its strength could be measured by the capacity to identify friends and enemies and draw between them clear adversarial lines. Once order was re-established and normality returned, the exercise of state sovereignty could again be juridically determined. The normativity of a legislative state could replace the stark *raison d'état*, the political reason of an absolute prince. Only contempt for the reality of the political would allow one to pretend that a system of legality could sustain itself and maintain no reference to a substantive order of things. If liberalism were to be identified with this apolitical view, Schmitt was a unswerving critic; if liberalism were to restrict its apoliticism to the sphere of civil society, and acknowledge the necessity of a sovereign state that retained the monopoly of the political, Schmitt would not object to conservative or authoritarian liberalism.[8]

Schmitt's conservative thought found in the critique of liberalism a continuous line of argument. That critique can also be said

---

[8] In 1936, Schmitt used the formula 'authoritarian liberalism' to characterize the constitutional systems prevailing in the nineteenth century. He rejected those systems, arguing that National Socialism had been able to supersede the old encrusted concepts that properly belonged to 'an authoritarian liberal world' (Schmitt, 1940: 231). It seems to me that prior to his involvement with the Nazis Schmitt would not have objected to that formula as a description of his system of ideas. It was the formula used by Hermann Heller, for example, to define the views espoused in his 1932 *Langnamverein* address (Heller, 1933: 295–6; compare with appendix). Only by assuming that the notion of 'authoritarian liberalism' is an oxymoron, can McCormick say: 'just because Schmitt's Weimar work is not latently Nazi, does not mean that it is not authoritarian or antiliberal' (McCormick, 1994: 647, n. 25). Or Mouffe say: 'there is, however, no doubt that it was [Schmitt's] deep hostility to liberalism which made possible, or which did not prevent, his joining the Nazis' (Mouffe, 1993: 121). For an early account of the plausibility of a conservative liberal position, compare with Friedrich, 1955.

to have provided a unifying theme to the entire German conservative movement. It would be a mistake, though, to assume that antiliberalism signified the presence of a monolithic line of argument reflecting uniform political assumptions. On the contrary, two lines of argument should be discerned in the thought of German conservatives. The difference between these two lines of argument may be illustrated by reference to the dispute between two eighteenth-century French schools of historical thought. This discussion pitted Germanists against Romanists; that is, those who saw the French political tradition as stemming from feudal institutions against those who saw it determined by the absolute rule of Roman emperors (Meinecke, 1922; Mathiez, 1930; Keohane, 1980). The actual intention of the Germanists, represented by Fénelon and Boulainvilliers (*thèse nobiliaire*), was to shore up the autonomy of the nobility and their feudal *puissances particulières* in an age characterized by a strong, centralized monarchy. On the contrary, Dubos, representative of the Romanist school, defended an absolute monarchical regime (*thèse royaliste*). This bifurcation in French thought, in the decades following the French revolution (Mannheim, 1971: 177ff.), is equally discernible in the case of Germany. Here one can detect a nationalist strand of thought, which favours an authoritarian system of government, strongly centralized and with access to the totality of political power, and a corporatist strand which envisages countervailing social powers. These are supposed to offset the excessive centralized control that has been placed in the hands of the state. Nationalism and social corporatism thus constitute the two major themes which form the basis of conservative arguments against German liberalism.

The advantage Schmitt had over most of his conservative predecessors and many of the contemporary ones was that the German revolution of 1918-19 did not take him by surprise; he was ready and waiting for it, steeped as he was in the counter-revolutionary writings of the conservative tradition of thought. He was even prepared to unmask those who claimed to serve the conservative counter-revolutionary cause but, in his own mind, had betrayed conservatism. (The first edition of his book *Political Romanticism*, a study of the political thought of Adam Müller and Friedrich Schlegel, was published early in 1919.) In 1921, when he published his *Die Diktatur* (*Dictatorship*), he was able to identify, for the first time, what would become his main counter-revolutionary weapon. This was not so much a principle or an abstract idea, but a concrete institution inscribed in the very core of his adversary – the Weimar constitution. Schmitt saw in the dictatorial faculties that its article 48 conferred on the *Reichspräsident* a procedure to dilute the revolution's democratic design and to restore the strong authoritarian state that had been gratuitously dissipated by the revolution. When in 1928 he published his *Verfassungslehre*, this was much more than a systematic, scientific treatise on constitutional legislation. In spite of his reassurances to the contrary, his constitutional treatise was also a political tract.

In 1930, his interpretation of the constitution bore political fruit. President Hindenburg installed a presidential regime, based on Schmitt's reading of article 48, which introduced an authoritarian system of government. With the establishment of a strong state, grounded on constitutional guidelines, Schmitt finally convinced himself that he had reached a *modus vivendi* with the Weimar constitution. He could even feel loyal to it, or his interpretation of it. When it seemed that the Nazis would undermine it, he publicly objected to their plans. It seemed as if after having built his bridge over the river Kwai, he was now ready for its defence. During the next three years Schmitt's efforts were aimed at bolstering the ramparts of that constitution. He thought that the only protection rested on a strong state headed by a strong *Reichspräsident*. More to the point, the defence of the constitution meant joining forces with General Schleicher, Hindenburg's Minister of Defence, who seemed most favourably disposed to bolster the idea of a strong state.

When the Nazis rose to power at the end of January 1933, Schmitt's initial reaction was of dismay at realizing Schleicher's political failure. After cautiously observing the turn of events he made his move immediately after 24 March, the day the enabling act was promulgated by the Reichstag. The next day he completed a commentary on that piece of legislation which he then sent to be published in the *Deutsche Juristen-Zeitung*. There he interpreted the enabling act as having somehow activated the notion of constituent power or *pouvoir constituant*,[9] which meant that

---

[9] The notion of constituent power is analysed by Carl Friedrich in his

the Weimar constitution had been formally superseded. This revolutionary action had cancelled the effects of the German revolution of 1918. The Nazis had attained in a few days what Schmitt had strived to defend during Weimar: a strong state. The Nazi regime acknowledged the great service Schmitt had rendered and immediately invited his collaboration. This began on 1 April, scarcely two months after Hitler's rise to power. Installed as regime's *Kronjurist*, he soon climbed to prominent positions within the government and his profession. In November 1933, for example, he was appointed Director of the Association of German National Socialist Jurists, and in June 1934, he became the editor of the *Deutsche Juristen-Zeitung*. Unforgivably, he also began to adopt the most despicable aspect of Nazi doctrine, their anti-Semitism, of which one cannot find traces in any of his earlier writings. The Nazis, however, who showed more interest in strengthening the party than in strengthening the state, soon found their *Kronjurist* was dispensable. In 1936 Schmitt lost much of what he had gained politically and his ideas were no longer seriously considered by the Nazi authorities.

After the war, the Russians detained him briefly in Berlin and the Americans then interned him for more than a year under suspicion of collaboration with the Nazi regime. In March 1947 he was transferred to the Nuremberg Tribunal. Set free without charge after weeks of interrogation, Schmitt retired to his native town of Plettenberg, which he baptized San Casciano. Since then a sanitary zone has encircled his work, particularly in the English-speaking world. Friedrich Hayek, an author of much influence in North America who read his work intently in the 1920s and 1930s, recognized him as Hitler's *Kronjurist* and the father of totalitarianism.[10] Only after his death on 7 April 1985, at the age of ninety-seven, and particularly after the fall of the Berlin Wall, has a more detached discussion of his views become possible.

Constitutional Power and Democracy in a chapter entitled 'The Constituent Power, the Amending Formula and Revolution' (Friedrich, 1950: 132–55). In the 1st edition of this book, in a footnote to his discussion of the enabling act, Friedrich refers to the article that Schmitt published in the *Deutsche Juristen-Zeitung*, 1 April 1933 (Friedrich, 1937: 522). In the 1950 edition, the reference to Schmitt is omitted (Friedrich, 1950: 616; compare with Schwab, 1990: 73).

[10] Hayek, 1967: 169.

II

For Schmitt's critics, his extensive and relentless critique of liberalism during the Weimar period was responsible for the subversion of the juridical and moral basis of the Weimar republic's liberal democracy. This critique was manifested in the decisionism which he opposed to normativism and the liberal abhorrence of leadership and authority; in his notion of sovereignty defined in opposition to the rule of law; in his concept of the political as the ability to distinguish between public friends and enemies; and in his option for strong political leadership which he opposed to the ineffective parliamentarism of the Weimar republic and paved the way for the Führer. These were the mephistophelean ingredients used in his campaign against Weimar's parliamentary democracy. Admittedly, Schmitt was able to elaborate a comprehensive and infinitely detailed exposition of the ideal conditions on which rested the legitimacy of that system. These conditions demanded a parliamentary regime defined by the principles of publicity and discussion, a legislature bound by a recognition of fundamental individual rights, an executive restricted to the use of measures in situations of emergency, a non-interventionist and neutral state guided by the rule of law and a society allowed to order its own affairs in freedom. Already one of his earliest critics cautioned against being deceived by Schmitt's prescriptions. These were mere 'ideological arguments' intended to undermine the legitimacy of the republican constitution, and deployed 'not to favour a parliamentary-democratic *Rechtsstaat*, but to show that it had become illegitimate and disfunctional and ought to be overcome' (Fijalkowski, 1958: 31). More recently, another critic has pointed out that Schmitt was not a Hobbesian rationalist who only intended to 'impose internal peace on a society that would otherwise consume itself itself in a civil war of fanatical sects' (Holmes, 1993: 42). The point is that Schmitt 'was not interested exclusively in the legal order', that his interest in the normal peaceful situation was always counterbalanced by mythical bellicism and 'by his Maistrean fascination with adrenaline-producing danger and conflict' (ibid.: 42). This, according to Holmes, is 'Mussolini, not Hobbes' (ibid.: 24).

The supporters of Schmitt's Weimar corpus acknowledge its

anti-liberal edge. But this critique, instead of undermining Germany's republican basis, is interpreted as a warning with respect to the dangers faced by the constitution. Schmitt observed that the principal danger lay in positivist interpretations like the one elaborated by Kelsen. He believed that Kelsen's relativist functionalism and value neutrality eviscerated the constitution's republican substance. Against those who interpreted article 76 in a literal fashion and recognized no limits to the Reichstag's faculties for constitutional reform, Schmitt stated that 'constitutional reform does not mean the abrogation of the constitution' (1928: 103). Against legal positivism, but also against Marxism and Nazism, he opposed his own conservative option.[11] But when Hitler rose to power on 30 January 1933, and particularly after 24 March when the Reichstag passed an enabling act which granted the government exceptional powers, Schmitt understood that his only alternative was Hobbesian obedience in exchange for political protection. This mutual relation between protection and obedience, which Hobbes saw as a calculus based on reason and not on irrationalist myths, is used by his apologists to defend him as a Hobbesian.[12]

Is there any other more plausible explanation for Schmitt's unreserved capitulation to Nazi ideology, which even led him to adopt anti-Semitic views he did not espouse before the Nazi takeover? His apologists appeal to the persecution unleashed against him by the security apparatus of the SS in 1935, which led to his marginalization from official functions the next year, is

---

[11] On 19 July 1932, Schmitt published an article in a newspaper sympathetic to Schleicher, the *Tägliche Rundschau*, in which he tried to dissuade those who intended to vote for the Nazis in the coming election of 31 July. 'Whoever provides the National Socialists with the majority on July 31, acts foolishly ... He gives this still immature ideological and political movement the possibility to change the constitution, to establish a state church, to dissolve labour unions, etc.' (Schmitt, 1932d; compare with Noack, 1993: 103; Bendersky, 1983: 153).

[12] According to Bendersky, Schmitt was neither an irrationalist nor a nihilist thinker and was not off the mark when he identified himself 'intellectually' with Hobbes (Bendersky, 1983: 59, 200). Based on this view of Schmitt as a Hobbesian, Bendersky then claims that 'Schmitt had always considered obedience to the legally constituted authority as a fundamental political precept' (ibid.: 200; compare with Schmitt, 1938: pp. x and xviii). And again as a Hobbesian, Schmitt 'firmly believed that the Enabling Act had inaugurated a new legal order' (Bendersky, 1983: 200).

unconvincing (compare with Bendersky, 1983: 219–42). It is true that on 15 December 1936 he had to resign the presidency of the Association of National Socialist German Jurists and his post as editor of the *Deutsche Juristen-Zeitung*. But he did not lose his chair at the University of Berlin and was not expelled from the party. He was able to carry on his academic duties up until the end of the war.

In order to rescue Schmitt's Weimar writings and political philosophy, his apologists have explained his later behaviour as due to a flawed moral character. According to Bendersky, for instance, 'Schmitt's Nazi career definitely revealed a personal weakness so far as moral principles are concerned'; at the same time, this collaboration with the Nazis ought not 'to overshadow all other aspects of his life and work' (1983: 282). If boundless ambition and lack of moral character alone could explain his sudden conversion in March 1933, which then led to an obsequious intellectual capitulation to the most perverse aspects of Nazism, this admission should be able to save the core of Schmitt's conservative thought from Nazi contamination. But while it is true that opportunism was an ingredient in Schmitt's intellectual adventure, and his apologists have been right in pointing this out (Gottfried, 1990: 3), this does not necessarily absolve his entire Weimar output. It is still possible to discern aspects of his conservative thought in his Weimar writings that may be said to configure and predetermine his intellectual abdication to Hitler's authoritarian figure.

These aspects of his conservative thought bore a revolutionary inflection and were developed early on by Schmitt, in the aftermath of the German revolution of 1918. The overt revolutionary connotation of the distinction, introduced in his *Die Diktatur*, between a commissarial and a sovereign dictatorship, his attempt juridically to legitimate the latter by means of the notion of constituent power, his hard decisionism, his enthusiasm for the irrational power of Mussolini's national myth, the unbounded admiration he manifested in his *Political Theology* for political Catholics like de Maistre and Donoso Cortés, these are some of the considerations that gave a revolutionary edge to his earlier conservatism. To identify and define Schmitt's early revolutionary conservatism and distinguish it from the more liberal rendition of the conservative position that he attained later, particularly in his

Verfassungslehre, is one of the aims that guides my argument in this book.

III

Most of Schmitt's liberal critics have interpreted his intellectual work during the Weimar republic as aimed at one target: the philosophical demolition of liberalism. Richard Thoma advanced this thesis in his 1925 review of Schmitt's *Parlamentarismus*, which he read in the light of Schmitt's early radical critique of liberal institutions. Schmitt wrote, at the conclusion of that work, that irrational myths, espoused by anarchists like Sorel, could bring about an authority 'based on a new feeling for order, discipline and hierarchy' (Thoma, 1925: 82). This prompted a puzzled Thoma to retort:

> I would hazard to guess, but not to assert, that behind these ultimately sinister observations there stands the unexpressed personal conviction of the author that an alliance between a nationalistic dictator and the Catholic Church could be the real solution and achieve a definitive restoration of order, discipline and hierarchy.

Thoma wrote this in spite of Schmitt's explicit claim that his intention was the reform of parliamentary rule, that his book neither called for the dismantling of liberal institutions nor contained a principled attack on liberalism. This showed how much Thoma was influenced by his reading of Schmitt's earlier writings. But who could blame him for suspecting the sincerity of Schmitt's call for the reform of parliaments? After all, Schmitt had earlier extolled the extreme views of de Maistre, Bonald and Donoso Cortés; he had, moreover, explored an interpretation of the *Reichspräsident* as the subject of constituent power and as sovereign dictator, and had berated German romantics for their incapacity for decisive action.[13]

---

[13] Schmitt's conservative readers interpreted his work in the same manner. Leo Strauss, for example, passed a similar judgement. In his review of *The Concept of the Political* he claimed that Schmitt's affirmation of the political was a thesis 'entirely dependent upon the polemic against liberalism' (1932: 92). Again Georg Dahm appeared to confirm this view: '[Schmitt's works] are, from the start,

The discussions of the 1920s and 1930s were revived in the English-speaking world during the 1980s with the publication of the translation of three of Schmitt's works – *Political Romanticism*, *Political Theology* and *The Crisis of Parliamentary Democracy* (or *Parlamentarismus* for short). In her introduction to *Parlamentarismus*, Ellen Kennedy, in agreement with George Schwab, noted that Schmitt wrote this book as a way of testing the inner consistency of the Weimar constitution. According to Kennedy, Schmitt held that 'the Weimar constitution contained two principles, one liberal and the other democratic. During these years Schmitt began to identify these two principles with the *Reichstag* and the *Reichspräsident*, respectively' (1985: p. xx). This provides the context for the distinction Schmitt drew between liberalism and democracy. In order to offset the liberal ingredients of the constitution, Schmitt began to stress its democratic aspects. Kennedy observes that Schmitt explored the possibility of enhancing direct democratic mechanisms, such as plebiscites and referendums. But more than that, 'Schmitt asserted that the essence of the Weimar constitution was the democratic principle expressed in article 1, not its liberal principles' (Kennedy, 1985: p. xxxiv). It was as a defender of the democratic nature of the constitution that the *Reichspräsident* was to be allowed 'to act as a commissarial dictator' (ibid.). Because critics, like Thoma, 'read [Schmitt's *Parlamentarismus*] together with' his earlier works, they interpreted it as an attack on democracy. Kennedy, however, maintained that Schmitt was not interested in attacking democracy but liberalism. Accordingly, she identified Kelsen's legal positivism as 'the ultimate target of his political thought' (ibid.: p. xxxv).

In a review of Kennedy's work, Habermas acknowledged the philosophical height to which Schmitt lifted the discussion concerning parliamentarism. Schmitt made it his aim to study the essence of political phenomena by means of traditional philosophical categories. But this endeavour proved in the end to make 'a mockery of parliamentary institutions' (Habermas, 1986: 1054). Habermas had a warning for left-wing intellectuals who tried 'to fill the gap left by non-existent Marxist theory of democracy with Schmitt's fascist discussion of democracy' (ibid.). In

directed at one specific aim: the unmasking and destruction of the liberal *Rechtsstaat* and the superseding of the legislative state ...' (1935: 181).

his view, Schmitt ridiculed the 'medium of discussion that is public and guided by argument' (ibid.). Openness and public discussion, which he restricted to liberal theory and practice, should be equally seen as democratic assumptions. According to Habermas, just as a democratic constitution could not be detached from 'the process of public discussion', so too liberalism presupposed a 'conception of a general formation of opinion and popular will' (ibid.). Schmitt's attempt to separate democracy and liberalism clouded and disfigured a true understanding of democracy. Habermas believed that Schmitt's intentions were transparent. By detaching democracy from the more abstract humanism espoused by liberalism, it became subservient to the attainment of a national identity under the guidance of an acclaimed dictator. Schmitt could thus draw the fundamental outline of a *Führer-demokratie*.

Kennedy and Habermas coincided in attributing capital importance to the distinction Schmitt drew between liberalism and democracy. They again implicitly agreed that Schmitt's motivation in drawing that distinction was his desire to reject liberalism, pre-eminently embodied in the parliamentary institution, and retrieve some form of classical, pre-liberal democracy. But while Kennedy was content with stressing Schmitt's call for a plebiscitary democracy, Habermas was, I believe, justified in casting a shadow on the democratic quality of that plea. He noted that democracy was enlisted by Schmitt to prop up an authoritarian cause. What Habermas failed to explain, however, was the fact that Schmitt did not propose the abolition, but merely the reform, of parliamentary politics, and that the distinction he drew between liberalism and democracy was functional to that proposal. It seems to me that Habermas suspected Schmitt's sincerity. Given that in his early work Schmitt vehemently criticizes liberalism, why would he now be satisfied with a mere reform of parliament and not its complete overhaul? Why not ascribe to him a plea for the democratic dictatorship of a Führer?

The explanation for the distinction drawn by Schmitt between liberalism and democracy lay, it seems to me, in his sincere interest in a reform of parliamentarism and not in its abolition. What may have been most sinister about him, *pace* Thoma, may after all have been this straightforwardness. Critics of Schmitt have generally read his work in the light of his early Weimar critique of liberal parliamentarism. In that light it appears inconceivable, as it did to Thoma, that he would at any point disown that criticism and succeed in the accommodation of liberalism within his system of ideas, but this is what I am prepared to argue for. The publication of his *Parlamentarismus* in 1923 revealed that Schmitt took liberalism seriously. What he now found worthy of serious consideration was the steadfast anti-political stance assumed by liberalism. This prompted his effort to distinguish it, not only from democracy, but from any political form as such. Schmitt maintained his deep reservations with respect to liberalism, but these related only to its *political* implications. Those reservations he never abandoned and they can be said to mark the continuity of his intellectual enterprise. Liberalism, as he saw it, was unable to secure the political unity of the state. In fact, the individualist and pluralist tendencies that it gave rise to promoted anti-political attitudes which, if allowed full expression, would necessarily weaken state authority. Moreover, its anti-political tendencies erased any chance of implementing policies that could counter, or at least neutralize, the democratic tide.

Contrary to what most of his critics maintain, democracy and not liberalism was, in my view, the main target of Schmitt's intellectual work during the Weimar period. My interpretation of his *Parlamentarismus* aims to prove this point. What he attempted to do here was to prevent the emergence of purely democratic politics. This he did in spite of his overt recommendation that the Weimar constitution be interpreted along the lines of a direct, plebiscitary democracy. This recommendation proposed the concentration of political power in the hands of an authoritarian figure, the *Reichspräsident*. Schmitt, like many of his generation, found himself grappling with the most striking outcome of the German revolution of 1918 – the extinction of monarchical legitimacy in Germany. He ultimately came to accept the legitimacy of Weimar's democracy when he realized that its revolutionary edge could be tamed. The distinction between liberalism and democracy introduced in *Parlamentarismus* was actually meant to moderate the democratic onslaught. Liberalism, in his view, was neither a political form nor a state form. In its anti-political stance it remained indifferent to democracy, aristocracy or monarchy. Liberalism recommended a balance of political powers and forms, a political *status mixtus*, that could moderate and neutralize the political sphere. Democratic procedures were left in place merely as a means of entrusting elected officials with representative roles.

Before drawing the distinction between liberalism and democracy in his *Parlamentarismus*, Schmitt had attacked liberalism because it seemed inextricably bound to democracy. He charged liberalism for its inability to withstand the democratic avalanche. But as a universe of ideas distinct from democracy, and interpreted as an apolitical, neutral posture, attentive only to the protection of individuals, liberalism appeared to Schmitt in 1923 as the best way to neutralize democracy. Liberalism was objectionable only when it assumed a political stance. If the pluralism that was congruent with liberalism were allowed political expression, the unity of the state would be put in jeopardy.[14] Schmitt's paramount concern was the attainment and safeguard of the unity of the state. Once he came to the view that liberalism was, at its core, *not* a political form, his reservations subsided. Nineteenth-century liberalism tried to fashion a state in its image and likeness, and aimed at exporting pluralism onto the political sphere. But if kept at a clear distance from any political form, liberalism ceased to be a threat. Schmitt was now able to aim his attack at the democratic populace, which he would attempt to disarm by means of a democratically elected sheriff.

The distinction between liberalism and democracy, which Schmitt introduced in 1923, marked the beginning of his *rapprochement* with liberalism. This accommodation allowed him to identify what he feared most: the increased pace of the democratic revolution. Schmittian scholarship has for the most part assumed a strict unity and continuity in his Weimar writings. Thus, what he wrote in *Parlamentarismus* is read in line with his earlier *Die Diktatur* and his *Political Theology*. The anti-liberal stance of this early work is then projected onto his later Weimar writings. In *Parlamentarismus*, however, he was able to extricate liberalism from popular democracy, and could henceforth aim all his efforts at taming democratic absolutism.

This *rapprochement* with liberalism was mediated by his reading of Hegel's political philosophy. In Hegel's 'relative rationalism'

---

[14] In his article 'Der Begriff des Politischen', Schmitt opposes the pluralist theory of Harold Laski for negating 'the sovereign unity of the state, i.e. political unity' (1927: 12). His plea for political monism is one of the features that remains constant in his Weimar theory of the state (compare with Schmitt, 1930: 30–3).

he found the conceptual framework that sanctioned an accommodation between a liberal civil society and a conservative political state. Hegel rejected popular sovereignty, defended the monarchical principle (compare with Ilting, 1973: 105–8) and deployed the figure of the monarch to offset revolutionary redistributive demands and thus secure the unimpeded business of civil society. The lesson drawn by Schmitt was that acquiescence with liberal pluralism need not threaten political unity, on condition that the state were placed in the hands of a strong figure like the *Reichspräsident* – his diluted rendition of the Hegelian prince. Schmitt recognized that in post-revolutionary Germany the monarchical principle had succumbed together with monarchical legitimacy. Exercising a purely 'prudential duty' (Mehring, 1988: 127), he embraced the triumphant democratic principle as a substitute for monarchical legitimacy. At the apex of the state now stood the *Reichspräsident* whom he conceived as a commissarial dictator, a democratic agent whose mandate was the preservation of the unity of the state.

IV

The argument of this book as a whole seeks to lay out the philosophical lineaments of Schmitt's theory of the state and the constitution. This is the appropriate context for an explanation of his conservative critique of Weimar liberalism and his tactical accommodation, beginning in 1923, with the democratic legitimacy that his conservative philosophy induced him to repudiate. Each chapter studies the complex reworkings and tactical adaptations of that unitary conservative strategy during the Weimar republic and the initial stages of the Nazi regime. There appear to be many shifts and turns in Schmitt's intellectual progress, but there is an underlying continuity in his endeavour (compare with Bielefeldt, 1996: 394). A conservative theory of the state and the constitution defines the line of argument that unifies his intellectual output.

Schmitt's theory of the state and the constitution postulated the existence of a meta-legal standpoint, a substantive ground on which rested the manifold of legal and constitutional phenomena. There was a metaphysical core to Schmitt's thought whose vestiges were to be found in all his works. A metaphysical community linked the distinction between the juridical (*Recht*)[15] and its realization in *Der Wert des Staates*, the distinction between the substance and the exercise of sovereignty in *Die Diktatur*, the notions of absolute constitution and constituent power in the *Verfassungslehre*, the concept of the political in *The Concept of the Political*, the concept of movement in *Staat, Bewegung und Volk*, and the meta-legal conception of a concrete order formation in *Über die drei Arten des Rechtswissenschaftlichen Denkens*. This constellation of ideas was the bulwark of his defence against legal positivism, for which legal systems were closed in themselves and not in need of objective principles that accounted for their unity and organization.

In Chapter 1, I examine six fateful months in Schmitt's life, from November 1932 to April 1933. This period was determined by the most dramatic of his tactical accommodations, when he went from defending the integrity of the Weimar constitution to proclaiming its demise, from constitutional adviser to Franz von Papen and Kurt von Schleicher in 1932–3 to his drafting of a key piece of legislation for the Nazis. During these months Schmitt published three important legal and political texts: a conference address to the *Langnamverein*, an association of German industrialists, on 23 November 1932; a brief legal commentary, published on 1 April, on the occasion of the promulgation of the enabling act on 24 March 1933; and a substantive legal commentary on the *Reichsstatthaltergesetz* promulgated by Hitler on 7 April 1933.

The first text was a conservative plea that decried party factionalism and appealed for a further strengthening of state authority. It could be read as an anticipated agenda for Schleicher's stint as Chancellor. Schmitt's strong state was not meant to interfere in any way with the affairs that properly belonged to civil society. His conservatism was combined with a liberal view that sought to leave civil society to a large extent free of state regulation and

---

[15] In this case I have translated the term *Recht* and included it in parentheses. In other cases, I refer to German terms without attempting to translate them. The difficulties in translation have been noted by Maitland. 'The task of translating into English the work of a German lawyer can never be perfectly straightforward. To take the most obvious instance, his *Recht* is never quite our *Right* or quite our *Law*' (Gierke, 1958: p. xliii).

ruled mainly by spontaneous market mechanisms. The strength of this state was dependent on its ability to remain neutral[16] and depoliticize society. This it could do by monopolizing the political and assuming the full scope of its protective function. Schmitt referred to this authoritarian state as 'qualitative total state' and compared it to the *stato totalitario* of Italian fascism. The two texts that he published shortly after Hitler rose to power showed Schmitt's enthusiastic support for a new revolutionary state whose strength was bolstered by the absence of an essential liberal ingredient, the separation of the executive and legislative powers. Schmitt was *personally* responsible for advancing an interpretation of the enabling act of 24 March, the *Instrument of Government* of Hitler's regime, as the revolutionary abrogation of the Weimar constitution. Implicit in his argument was an appeal to the notion of constituent power, an appeal that had the effect of destroying the Weimar constitution and placing in its stead the enabling act as a provisional constitution.

The foundations of his conservative theory of the state and the constitution can be discerned in the book he was writing when the German revolution of 1918–19 broke out. His reaction to this historical event is the theme of Chapter 2. *Political Romanticism*, published early in 1919, sought to settle accounts with those whom Schmitt deemed usurpers of the conservative legacy. His aim was to draw a clear line of separation between the political romanticism of Adam Müller and Friedrich Schlegel and the true conservatism of Catholic traditionalist thinkers like de Maistre and Bonald. While these, and also Burke, took an intensely partisan side against the French revolution, Adam Müller found no 'moral pathos' in the face of it. For Schmitt the occasionalism and subjectivism of the romantic spirit precluded the possibility of engaging in decisive action. In their indecision romantics were closer to liberalism than to a genuine conservative philosophy never shy to acknowledge political interests. In *Die Diktatur* and *Political Theology*, Schmitt translated the counter-revolutionary

---

[16] In his *Die Hüter der Verfassung*, written a year earlier, Schmitt had clearly defended a state that was at the same time strong and neutral: 'The majority of the projects that demand depoliticization forget a simple truth, namely that in order obtain a neutrality in the sense of an independent objectivity, exceptional strength and energy are required in order to confront the powerful interest groups' (Schmitt, 1931: 115)

aims of the Catholic traditionalists into the basic outline of a theory of the state and the constitution. Modern revolutions had been able to legitimate the generation of a new constitutional and legal order by an appeal to the *pouvoir constituant* of the people. An argument from legitimacy could appeal to no other foundation than the decision of the subject of *pouvoir constituant*. In Germany, that decision had determined not only the abrogation of the monarchy, but also the sovereign dictatorship of the Weimar constituent assembly and the novel democratic legitimacy. But the new legal order could not be seen as the ultimate order of things. Schmitt's conservative thought, nurtured by the substantivist disposition of traditional metaphysics, emphasized the issue of legitimacy and relativized legality. Legitimacy furnished the conditions for the realization of legality. Nothing could prevent the revolutionary upsurge of a new legitimacy which could in principle abrogate the existing legal order and push for the re-establishment of the monarchical principle. Schmitt's adversaries would later make him responsible for this relativization of Weimar's legally constituted order.

Schmitt's accommodation to the reality of the Weimar constitution and the liberal philosophy that sustained it is the theme of Chapter 3. His tactical acknowledgement of liberalism manifested itself in 1923. Though the aim of his *Parlamentarismus* was a critique of parliamentarism, the book advocated its reform rather than its abrogation. Parliamentarism advocated discussion, the tendency he abhorred in romanticism and liberalism. But now, by distinguishing between liberalism and democracy, he could reserve a space for the manifestation of the political. After all, the political could be embodied not only by democratic, but also by monarchic and aristocratic forms. To think that constitutions could contain only liberal rule-of-law elements was a mistake. There was enough room left for political elements. The Weimar constitution, for instance, supported a political *status mixtus* which embraced plebiscitary mechanisms side by side with a monarchical figure like the *Reichspräsident*, his role enhanced by the dictatorial powers contained in article 48. By 1926, Schmitt would acknowledge the futility of maintaining a revolutionary posture *vis-à-vis* the Weimar regime and expressed acceptance of its constitution. 'Today the revolutionary situation that lasted between November 1918 and February 1919 is over; the sovereign dictatorship of a constituent national assembly does no longer exist. For seven years now the Weimar constitution is valid in Germany' (Schmitt, 1926: 27).

The possibility of a synthesis between liberalism and a politically conservative option, facilitated by Schmitt's distinction between liberalism and democracy, bears comparison with Hegel's *rapprochement* of a liberal civil society and a conservative state, although Hegel does not open the door to dictatorship. In Chapter 4, I consider the work of Jean-François Kervégan who recognizes Schmitt's Hegelian debt, but contends that Schmitt distorted Hegel's liberalism by disregarding the dialectical intent of his political philosophy. Kervégan's aim is to keep Hegel safe from contamination with Schmittian views. It seems to me, on the contrary, that an approximation of their positions is possible on two conditions. First, Schmitt's decisionism must be defined in a way that allows a compromise or juxtaposition between political and liberal principles. His strong decisionist state need not be seen as poised to intervene illiberally in every aspect of civil society. Second, Schmitt's decisionist reading of Hegel should not be taken as a complete distortion.

In Chapters 5 and 6, I examine two central issues in Schmitt's theory of the state and the constitution – sovereignty and the *status mixtus* – as he deals with them in his *Verfassungslehre*. This work contains his most systematic interpretation of the Weimar constitution. The accommodation of liberal and conservative themes determines his view of it as a mixed constitution, a balance between the rule of law and political ingredients. 'The constitution of the modern liberal *Rechtsstaat* is always a mixed constitution' (Schmitt, 1928: 200). This represented a significant deviation from the ideal constitution envisaged by liberalism, which negated the political and sought to circumvent claims for state sovereignty. 'The tendency of the liberal rule of law is to repress the political' (ibid. 41). By contrast, Schmitt rejected as vain and fictional the attempt to expel the political. His *Verfassungslehre* boldly incorporated the political and combined it with the principles of the liberal *Rechtsstaat*. It was both a theory of the state and a theory of the constitution.

There has been no critic of Schmitt more consistent and constant than Hayek. He has presented Schmitt as the father of Nazi totalitarianism and as the most dangerous critic of liberalism. In

Chapter 7, I show that the distance Hayek seeks to establish between himself and Schmitt is greatly reduced when we observe the affinities of his position with what Schmitt maintained during the last years of the Weimar period, where he tried to reconcile liberalism with an authoritarian view of democracy. In truth, Hayek owed much to Schmitt, more than he cared to recognize.

In spite of his conservative critique of liberalism, Schmitt remained tied to liberal assumptions. And if this was so, he could not have strayed far from Hobbes. This is gist of Leo Strauss's objection to Schmitt. In Chapter 8, I examine that objection, in the context of Heinrich Meier's book on Schmitt and Strauss. My claim is that Strauss was right in affirming that Schmitt was a Hobbesian and that he was also right when he reminded Schmitt of his conservative revolutionary determination. He was wrong, though, in thinking that Schmitt could not hold fast to both views and interchange positions in response to the situation at hand. When the rule of law sufficed, he would live with the rule of law; when it did not suffice, he would summon a dictator.

Chapter 9 examines Schmitt's analysis of the total state which he first presented in his *Die Hüter der Verfassung* (1931). In it he opposed the twentieth-century total state to the absolute state of the seventeenth and eighteenth centuries and the neutral state of the nineteenth century. In both these cases, a clear separation was maintained between civil society and the state, which had the effect of preserving the latter's independence and autonomy. By contrast, the total state identified state and civil society. This meant a weakening of the authority of the state. Stepping beyond the limits that separated its interest from that of civil society, and becoming involved in what was the exclusive concern of civil society, meant that the state lost its autonomy and independence and advanced towards its own extinction. Confirming his anti-democratic stance, Schmitt blamed the rise of the total state on the emphasis on democratic identity. In his *Legalität und Legitimität* (1932), the total state was contrasted with an authoritarian state. Confirming his accommodation to liberalism, he followed Heinz O. Ziegler's views which opposed democracy to authoritarianism and liberalism to totalitarianism. This left open the possibility, exploited by Hayek, of harmonizing a liberal market society under an authoritarian state. The last time Schmitt made public reference to this notion was in his keynote address 'Strong State and Sound Economy' to a meeting of Northern Rhine and Ruhr industrialists. This time he reversed himself and extended the use of the term 'total state' to include the authoritarian state he sponsored. This was to be understood as qualitative, as opposed to the purely quantitative total state of democracy. A translation of this address appears as an appendix to this book.

1 • Crossing the Rubicon: Schmitt and the Nazi Revolution

Then came the enabling act of 24 March, 1933 . . . That was the true Rubicon.
(Schmitt in Tommissen, 1975: 105–6)

On 23 November 1932, six days after President Hindenburg accepted the resignation of Franz von Papen as German Chancellor, Carl Schmitt delivered the keynote address at a conference sponsored by the *Langnamverein*, an association of iron and steel industrialists in the Ruhr. It was later published as an article with the programmatic title 'Strong State and Sound Economy,' only days before Hitler rose to power in January 1933. This would be one of Schmitt's last public pronouncements during the Weimar republic. It deserves to be examined both as a condensed presentation of his constitutional ideas and as a summary statement of his political options. As such it should contribute to clarify the issue that continues to divide Schmitt's apologists and critics – how to interpret and evaluate his collaboration with the Nazis which began a few weeks after Hitler's rise to power. Was that collaboration, as his critics contend, prefigured and predetermined by his intellectual production during Weimar? Was there a continuous line of argument running through all of Schmitt's intellectual output, beginning shortly before the First World War and leading directly to his involvement with the Nazis?

The difficulty these critics face is how to account for the liberal trend detected by Alexander Rüstow in Schmitt's conception of a free economy supported by a strong state (Rüstow, 1932). Schmitt opposed what he took to be the totalitarian interventions of the state that sought to force civil society into conformity with democratic patterns. Schmitt's apologists, by contrast, have emphasized discontinuity in Schmitt's thought, and explained his Nazi conversion as due either to obedience or to opportunism. The former was Schmitt's own explanation. He was acting as dutiful citizen when he rendered support and obedience to the

Nazi state, for this was a legally constituted state which he saw as able to offer protection to its citizens. The latter explanation has presented Schmitt as the master tactician, who collaborated with the Nazis and came to adopt some of their most abhorrent views, only *in foro externo*, possibly as a matter of personal advancement, or in a better scenario, as a matter of personal survival. His boundless ambition, his insincerity and opportunism would require censure and his lack of moral fortitude should be condemned. His apologists are willing to sacrifice his character so as to safeguard and preserve his Weimar productions as the scholarly legacy of a serious conservative constitutional jurist. His diagnosis of the Weimar circumstances could thus be given serious consideration and used for an analysis of the present (compare with Koenen, 1995: 11).

In this chapter, I examine a critical period in Schmitt's personal chronology – from November 1932 to April 1933. This marked Schmitt's transition from his role as constitutional and political adviser for Papen and Schleicher's governments to his collaboration with the Nazi regime in the capacity of a constitutional expert. This collaboration began in the offices of the Ministry of the Interior on 1 April 1933, and his commitment to National Socialism was formalized a month later, on 1 May, the day he added his signature to the Nazi Party register. An examination of his intellectual chronology during this period is indispensable to gauge the meaning of his decision to collaborate with the new regime. Was his overall strategy, namely his defence of the state as the condition of freedom, contained in that decision or was it thereby compromised? If the latter, if his decision to collaborate with the Nazis could not be said to be predetermined by the strategic commitments made during the Weimar republic, a fundamental discontinuity would affect Schmitt's intellectual evolution.

Aside from the issue of whether or not his conversion to National Socialism constituted a discontinuity in his intellectual strategy, it was undoubtedly a fundamental shift in his tactical allegiances. During the last years of the Weimar republic, for instance, possibly the key ingredient of his constitutional theory was the separation of state and civil society, a view that accorded with classical liberal demands. His aim in doing so was to strengthen state authority by reinforcing its unity. In so far as political parties were responsible for promoting federalism and reinforcing the tendency towards policracy, Schmitt saw the need to curb the role of party politics. It was as part and parcel of this strategy that he justified his participation as legal counsel for Papen's government in its action against Prussia in June 1932 and also his public opposition to the Nazi Party. The main doctrinal point that defined this strategy was his defence of the inviolability of the constitution. In his personal diaries and later recollections one finds evidence that by late January 1933 he was growing increasingly uneasy at the prospect of Hitler's imminent rise to power. At the time of Hitler's appointment as Chancellor by President Hindenburg, Schmitt's diaries show a noticeable lapse into a mood of depression. A few weeks later, after the Reichstag promulgated an enabling act on 24 March 1933, his concerns and depression seem to have evaporated. It was at this point that he reached the determination to collaborate with the new regime. Almost immediately he began to reap the fruits of that collaboration in the form of honours and official appointments. In the coming months and years Schmitt's involvement would deepen to the point of even adopting a strident anti-Semitic stand and supporting some of Hitler's juridically most aberrant measures.

Rejecting the possibility of a link between his political conversion and his doctrinal defence of a strong state and other theoretical points developed during Weimar, some authors, though critical of his Nazi involvement, have not allowed 'this [later] phase in his writing to distort their interpretations of his earlier works' (Bendersky, 1983: 280). George Schwab and Joseph Bendersky have effectively refuted the view that Schmitt's 'Weimar works were intended to pave the way for the one-party state' (ibid.). As a conservative thinker, Schmitt's ultimate intentions were to offer an interpretation of the Weimar constitution along the lines of a strong authoritarian executive state. He understood the meaning of totalitarianism and saw in it a menace not only for a strong state but also for a free market economy. A strong state and a free economy comprised the two main ingredients of Papen's business-oriented programme, fully supported by Schmitt. But all this does not exonerate him from the charge that he prepared the way for the Hitlerian total state. When the Nazis attained power and promulgated the enabling act, he rushed to signal this as the advent of a national revolution. Mustering his prestige as a conservative jurist he declared that a new beginning had taken effect, one which could convincingly undo the democratic institutions generated by the German revolution of 1918 and issue forth new ones. Not much later, Schmitt would openly acknowledge that the Weimar constitution, whose inviolability he had stringently defended, had ceased to exist. In his view, the enabling act of 24 March was a revolutionary act that stepped beyond constitutional limits. It was not a mere reform of the constitution on the basis of its article 76. At the same time, that law could be said to conform to Weimar legality for it was enacted by the Reichstag according to constitutional procedures. By submitting to this newly established regime, whatever its merits or demerits, Schmitt could see himself doing what any loyal citizen should do – obeying the legal authority that offered protection.

I pay special attention to three key texts written by Schmitt during this crucial period. The first text is the one mentioned above: his conference at the *Langnamverein* which contained his call for a strong state and a free economy. The second text was written immediately after the promulgation of the enabling act and published on 1 April in the *Deutsche Juristen-Zeitung*. This was the first public sign of Schmitt's accommodation to the new regime. In evidence here were those ideas and options of his Weimar production that he chose to place at the disposition of the new authorities and which had to do with the conservative revolutionary aspects of his thought. Finally, the third text is the commentary he wrote for the law promulgated by Hitler on 7 April 1933, the so-called *Reichsstatthaltergesetz*.[1] Schmitt had been invited to collaborate in the formulation of this law and was later asked to write an official commentary which was published shortly afterwards (Schmitt, 1933d). It was this initial collaboration that positioned him towards his advancement as the regime's *Kronjurist*.

---

[1] The full title of this law was the following: Second Law for the Coordination of the States and the Reich. A week before, Hitler had promulgated the first Law for the Coordination of the States and the Reich, but it was seen as insufficient for the purpose of placing state governments under Nazi control. The second law that was passed for this purpose placed all provincial governments under the supervision of a lieutenant governor, a *Statthalter*.

I

The original aim of the organizers of the *Langnamverein* conference, which was scheduled to take place at Düsseldorf after the elections of 6 November 1932, was to shore up Papen's regime and the economic programme he had laid out on 28 August in his Münster address. In agreement with the desires of big business, the Münster programme emphasized wage cuts for workers and reductions in unemployment benefits. Job creation was to be promoted through tax relief for industrialists and not through government intervention. Business leaders wholeheartedly approved of this programme and pledged full support for the Chancellor.[2] By contrast, the Nazis, in a reversal of previous programmatic statements, attacked the Münster programme. They adopted a new party line, characterized by a radical socio-economic course of action which included deficit spending to finance job-creation programmes, nationalization of banking and currency, etc. This, and their collaboration with the Communists, earned them the distrust of a majority of big-business leaders.[3] During the campaign leading to the 6 November elections, the Nazis maintained their anti-capitalist rhetoric which only confirmed to business leaders that they were right to continue supporting the beleaguered Papen regime (compare with Turner, 1985: 272–90).

The election results proved to be only a temporary set-back for the Nazis. Despite losses in their parliamentary standing, the opposition held the majority in parliament. Hitler continued his relentless attack on Papen and demanded the chancellorship for himself. On 17 November, Hindenburg, persuaded by Schleicher,

---

[2] According to Henry Ashby Turner, big capital, who understood that the welfare state had crippled the economy, saw that Papen's plan was, at last, 'summoning up the wisdom and courage to dismantle both these misguided measures and the political order that had given rise to it. In Franz von Papen, the business community belatedly realized, it had found a chancellor to whom it could accord its full an enthusiastic allegiance.' (Turner, 1985: 277).

[3] One should also take into account that alongside Schmitt's sympathy for Italian fascism, he manifested an aversion for National Socialism, which he shared with the majority of big-business leaders. The Nazis not only opposed Papen's pro-business economic policies but also accused his regime of unconstitutionally violating the democratic will of the people. Schmitt's own anti-democratic stance clashed with this populist rhetoric.

acknowledged Papen's predicament and accepted his resignation. The *Langnamverein* conference, which had been convened in Düsseldorf as a show of support for Papen, met in an 'atmosphere of uncertainty and mounting pessimism' (Turner, 1985: 302). Schmitt was speaking in lieu of the cabinet representative who was to brief the membership on the content of the now failed constitutional reforms proposed by the Chancellor.[4] According to Ashby Turner, 'one observer reported afterwards that most industrialists he had talked with favoured Hitler's appointment as chancellor'. They also thought he would last only a few weeks in office (ibid.). By contrast, two of the participants – Max Schlenker (business manager of the *Langnamverein*) and Fritz Springorum (chair of the association and a Ruhr steel magnate) – exuded an air of confidence and optimism. In the preface to the volume devoted to the conference, Schlenker commended the reforms promoted by Papen (1932: 2),[5] and so did Springorum in his foreword (1932: 6), who also read a telegram from Papen regretting his absence from the conference (ibid.: 69–70). Schmitt's attitude was more guarded. Even though he generally agreed with the Chancellor's economic plans, he opposed the Papen–Gayl constitutional reforms. In this he followed Schleicher, who thought they would create political instability and lead to a civil war (compare with Bendersky, 1983: 173–4).

The fact that he was Schleicher's legal adviser and member of his clique influenced some contingent aspects of Schmitt's *Langnamverein* speech. But its overall argument marched in unison with what he had first developed in *Der Hüter .de Verfassung*, published the year before. There he sought to reinforce the authoritarian tendencies he discerned in the Weimar constitution by clearly demarcating the realms of the state and of civil society. He blamed party politics for weakening state

---

[4] The reform plans were publicly announced by Interior Minister Gayl on 11 August. By restricting voting rights and adding a conservative senate to the *Reichstag*, these reforms were meant to strengthen the government's hand by a drastic alteration of the democratic substance of the constitution.

[5] Schlenker's enthusiasm was with Papen's reforms and not necessarily with Papen himself. He could thus conclude his preface with an ominous remark: 'West German business is ready to follow any government that is brave enough to advance the recent reforms and to give business enough leeway to develop its own unfailing forces' (1932: 2; compare with Maus, 1986: 87).

authority and espoused a strong state to provide the necessary protection for the development of a free economy. In his *Langnamverein* speech, he used the formula 'qualitative total state' (as opposed to the 'quantitative total state' of totalitarianism, which he saw as a weak state) to refer to this strong state. Despite the anti-liberal resonances conjured by the notion of a state described as both strong and total, it was well-received in liberal circles, where his views were interpreted favourably. A noted neoliberal economist, Alexander Rüstow, did not hesitate to confirm the liberal ancestry of Schmitt's conception of the total state (1932: 69).

In this conference, Schmitt deployed many of the principles and essential elements of his theory of the state and the constitution. He summed it up by adopting the conference's striking motto – only a strong state[6] can preserve and enhance a free-market economy. Schmitt's address began by reviewing three epochal events in Germany's recent history: first, the establishment, on 28 March 1930, of a presidential regime, instigated by Schleicher and supported juridically and ideologically by Schmitt's interpretation of article 48 of the Weimar constitution; second, the Prussian coup of 20 June 1932; and third, the enigmatic decision handed down by the supreme court at Leipzig on 25 October of that same year which appeared to confirm the legality of the government's decision that led to the Prussian *coup*. Schmitt did not hide, first of all, his disappointment with the results shown by the presidential system since its inauguration in 1930. One could not avoid 'the general impression that the state has grown weaker and the circumstances have worsened and become more chaotic' (Appendix: p. 214). But he was still prepared to defend 'the practical usefulness and energy of article 48' in the face of a campaign to discredit and defame it. Second, he was also willing to credit that failed regime with one, in his view, crucial achievement: the Prussian *coup* of 20 July. That decision went to the core of 'the Weimar constitution's worst design defect – the dualism between the Reich and Prussia' (App.: p. 214). Third, that sole achievement had been, in turn,

---

[6] In the Papen circle, the notion of a strong state had been popularized by Walter Schotte, a conservative author. In his book *Der Neue Staat*, Schotte equated party-state and corruption, and called for 'a new state, that ought to be a strong state, free from interests, upright and independent from parties' (compare with Heller, 1933: 291; Sontheimer, 1962: 206; Bentin, 1972: 105).

compromised by another decision, the one handed down the preceding month by the supreme court at Leipzig. Schmitt noticed that when a strong state asserted itself, it sparked an immediate reaction that brought together a vast coalition of the most unlikely confederates. Despite his disappointment with that decision, Schmitt was still hopeful that a strong state would prevail in the face of a number of opposing forces.

The first one of those opposing forces was revived by the court's decision. It represented an outdated view which Schmitt associated with liberal proceduralism and which had been extensively debated in Germany between 1919 and 1924. This was the view that politics and the state ought to be eliminated and that experts expressing objective technical or economic points of view should decide all matters. Schmitt mentioned this view but did not discuss it here in any length. He had sought to dispose of it in an article entitled 'The Concept of the Political', first published in 1927 and re-edited earlier in 1932 as a book.

In the mean time, another misguided view, representing a totally opposed standpoint, had become equally pervasive. Schmitt described this view by means of a tantalizing formula, the 'total state'. That notion represented a centralized state that had expanded in every direction and politicized every domain of human existence. There was no sphere that could remain free from its interventions, so that 'not even a bowling club [could] continue to exist without maintaining a good relation with the state' (App. p. 218). Politicization was most visible in the sphere of economics. 'After years of attempting to reduce the state to economics, it now [appeared] that economics [had] become entirely politicized' (App.: p. 216). According to Schmitt, the bearers of the total state were the total parties.

> If we take a closer look, we see that we do not have a total state but a *plurality of total parties*. Each party realizes in itself the totality, totally absorbing their members, guiding individuals from the cradle to the grave, from kindergarten to burial and cremation, situating itself totally in the most diverse social groups and passing on to its membership the correct views, the correct ideology, the correct form of state, the correct economic system, and the correct sociability on account of the party. (App.: p. 219)

This conception of the total state, first adopted in his *Der Hüter der Verfassung*, matched Schmitt's long-standing critique of parliamentary democracy. Political parties were responsible for diluting the real meaning of representation.

Only a strong state could make possible the task of decentralizing economic decisions and securing the autonomy of intermediate social institutions. But decentralization was not supposed to devolve power of decision to individual entrepreneurs alone. In economic matters, the antithesis 'state versus individual' was to be rejected. According to Schmitt, it was necessary to conceive of 'an intermediate domain between the state and the singular individual' (App.: p. 224). Instead of a twofold antithesis, there was a tripartition consisting of the state, the individuals and an intermediate public though non-state sphere. First, the state could lay a claim to certain economic functions that by their very nature belonged to it. Schmitt had certain commercial entitlements in mind, like postal services, that could be legitimately claimed by the state. Second, he recognized the sphere of the individual entrepreneur, the domain of pure privacy. And thirdly, Schmitt envisaged an 'intermediate *non-state, but still public* sphere'. This was the sphere of 'economic autonomous administration (*Selbstverwaltung*)', which comprised a number of things: 'industrial and commercial chambers, non-voluntary unions of every sort, associations, ... mixed economic enterprises, ... monopolies of every kind chartered in the public interest but administered autonomously by commercial agents' (App.: p. 226). This distinction between the state and a decentralized economy could be rendered effective only if the state remained strong enough to keep politics from interfering in matters that pertained properly and exclusively to business.

> [O]nly a strong state can depoliticize, only a strong state can openly and effectively decree that certain activities, like public transit and radio, remain its privilege and as such ought to be administered by it, that other activities belong to the above mentioned sphere of self-management, and that all the rest be given to the domain of a free economy. A state that is to bring about this new order ought to be, as was said, extraordinarily strong ... At present, it is evident that the state, today only intermittently and momentarily a state, needs to gain particularly solid

authoritarian foundations by means of new arrangements and institutions (App.: p. 227).[7]

Finally, Schmitt had to contend with another viewpoint, from within his own conservative camp. He opposed the constitutional reform espoused by Chancellor Papen in conjunction with the Interior Minister Gayl. The Papen–Gayl project contemplated the introduction of a second parliamentary chamber designed along corporatist lines. The aim of the project was the depoliticization of parliament by means of the elevation of a fraction of it above partisan politics. Its members would represent special social interests and were to be nominated, not elected by universal suffrage. Springorum, the Chair of the *Langnamverein* conference, had endorsed this conservative view when he introduced Schmitt's keynote address (1932: 6).

Schmitt proposed a conservative etatist alternative to this corporatist view. Corporatism could operate only under the guidance and constraint that the state offered. Economic interests were not of themselves harmonious. Any attempt to organize them would actually make the disharmonies more acute.

> Whoever organizes interests as such, simultaneously organizes opposed interests and possibly increases, by means of the organizing, the intensity of the opposition. When these organized interests come to the table, and once serious conflicts of interest ensue ... the assembly will soon dissolve into its component parts. (App.: p. 227)

Conservative corporatist views, like the one promoted by the Catholic Church in its 1931 encyclical *Quadragessimo Anno*, adopted the medieval structure of professional intermediate associations or guilds as a model of economic regulation. Schmitt offered a poignant critique of this 'somehow idealized' conception, and suggested its anachronicity. Medieval Estates, for instance, did not have to contend with the issue of the 51 per cent

---

[7] Schmitt's interest in decentralization was again expressed in an article published on 18 March 1933, in *Deutsches Volkstum*, a review produced by Wilhelm Stapel and Albrecht Erich Günther, leaders of the revolutionary conservative movement in Germany. Schmitt wrote: 'Only a strong state can generate genuine decentralization, bring about free and autonomous domains, and guarantee the independence of the bodies of autonomous administration' (1933b: 229).

majority. Our 'conception of the 51 per cent majority, that puts the remaining 49 per cent in the shade, was certainly not available' (App.: p. 229) at that point.

The corporatist second chamber proposed by the Papen–Gayl reform plan could not help to strengthen the state and enhance its authority. By contrast, Schmitt believed that only a strong state could ensure that a second chamber maintained the independence it needed to adjudicate between conflicting interests. Only a strong state could 'bestow this second chamber the required respect and authority for its members to free themselves from professional attachments' (App.: p. 229). Only under the protection of a strong state could its members 'dare to submit to a unified collective resolution in a way that externally preserve[d] their respectability and nobility without immediately being chased away by their unsatisfied clients' (App.: p. 229). Still, Schmitt found the non-democratic features of this second chamber appealing. The lower chamber, generated by the universal suffrage 'of the essentially dispossessed masses' (App.: p. 229) was the seat of instability and revolution. In the face of this, the upper chamber would be able to 'preserve duration and continuity' (App.: p. 229). But in the present German circumstances the proposal for a second chamber was inauspicious. Attention ought to be directed, not to unpredictable constitutional experimentation, but to attaining a strong state, a state that was 'capable of acting and ready for its great tasks. Were we to have it, we would then create new arrangements, new institutions, *new constitutions*' (App.: p. 230). Schmitt opposed the reform of the constitution but seemed ready to prescribe its overhaul and the creation of a new one. That statement would prove to be premonitory. He would later interpret the enabling act of 24 March 1933 as the foundation of the new constitution he had envisioned in his *Langnamverein* speech.

II

On 3 December, a few days after the conference, President Hindenburg appointed Schleicher as Chancellor of the Reich. Schleicher's plan of action seemed hopeful but he soon found out that he had miscalculated. His idea of a multi-party agreement to form a government of national consensus failed to gain the necessary support. By the end of January 1933, Schleicher, in line with the political guidelines outlined in Schmitt's presentation before the *Langnamverein*, suggested to President Hindenburg the dissolution of parliament and the inauguration of an authoritarian regime. He thus sought to forestall Hitler's ascent to power. Hindenburg did not approve the plan.

On 26 January the Catholic prelate Ludwig Kaas, head of the Centre Party, sent a letter to Schleicher warning him not to proceed with his planned course of action. In his opinion there was manifest illegality in 'the current of thought espoused by Schmitt and his followers in that it tends to relativize constitutional law' (Noack, 1993: 163; compare with Schwab, 1970: 98). On 27 January Schmitt attended a dinner party at the house of Lieutenant Colonel Erich Marcks, Schleicher's press secretary. He wrote in his diary:

> Friday, 27.1.33 ... Alone and depressed I leave, around 8, towards Marcks's house. Duschka [Schmitt's wife] is sick in bed ... Marcks is deeply depressed. Something incredible has happened. The Hindenburg myth has come to an end. The old gentleman proved to be MacMahon. Disgusting. Schleicher will resign; either Papen or Hitler will succeed him. The old man has gone crazy. It is a terribly cold night and I return home at eleven. (Noack, 1993: 159; compare with Tommissen, 1975: 102)

The Chancellor resigned the next day. On the Sunday, the Centre Party's newspaper *Germania* published Kaas's letter to Schleicher denouncing Schmitt's project. Schmitt wrote again in his diary:

> Sunday, 29.1.33. I did not sleep well; I get up at nine thirty. *Germania* published the Kaas's letter to the government of the Reich where he warns about my interpretation of art. 48 and declares it unconstitutional. The old man is thus encouraged to name Hitler... At midday I buy the *Koelnische Volkszeitung* and go to the Friedrichstrasse station. I watch the film *Ballhaus zum goldenen Engel*. At home I receive a phone call from [Ernst] Jünger. He welcomes the collapse of halfway solutions between atheism, rationalism and Marxism. I debate whether to reply to Kaas. I call Popitz again and meditate a response... (Noack, 1993: 160)

On the morning of Monday, 30 January, possibly one of the most dramatic days of this century, Schmitt sent his vehement response to Kaas: 'I do not relativize constitutional law, but I struggle against a destructive use of the state and the Constitution, against a functionalism that stays neutral with respect to truth and values' (Noack, 1993: 163).

When a few hours later he arrived at the Cafe Kutschera a grand commotion awaited him. Hitler had just been named Chancellor. That night, while the Nazis celebrated their victory and held a torchlight parade under the Brandenburg Arch, Schmitt went back to his home in Flotow Street by the Tiergarten. He lay in bed feeling sick. Wilhelm Stapel paid him a visit.[8] In deep distress they uncorked a bottle of red wine and discussed the events of the day. 'We talked about Prussia. Stapel thinks that Hindenburg is not a true Prussian' (ibid.: 161; compare with Lokatis, 1992: 50). Next day his cold persisted and he was forced to cancel his lectures. He wrote in his diary:

> Ridiculous situation. I read the newspapers, I become anxious, I get furious. Thus goes the day. In the afternoon I receive the visit of Horst Michael who narrates the latest gossip on Schleicher's fall, on Marcks and Ott. Marcks has resigned his post as press director with immediate effect. (Noack, 1993: 161)

February marked an interlude. Hitler dissolved Parliament on Wednesday 1 February and called for elections to take place on 5 March. In a radio interview with Veit Roskopf, taped earlier and broadcast that same Wednesday, Schmitt declared: 'I am a theoretician ... a pure scientist and nothing but an intellectual' (Bendersky, 1983: 201). On 6 February he was visited by Ferdinand Hermens. Hermens kept a record of their conversation. Schmitt informed him that on the night of 30 January he had bumped into Marcks in the Tiergarten, who told him that Hitler's rise was a great disappointment for General Schleicher, and that the General and his friends would do everything necessary to stop the Nazi adventure. Schmitt must have shared the state of mind of his confederates. His intimate links with the Schleicher circle not only eliminated the possibility of obtaining political favours from the new regime but also posed a threat to his academic career. It is

---

[8] Stapel was a prominent member of the conservative revolutionary movement and editor of the journal *Deutsches Volkstum* (compare with Lokatis, 1992).

known that on 16 February he met Papen, the new Vice-Chancellor, to discuss Kaas's attack on his constitutional theory.

On Monday 27 February the Reichstag burnt down. The next day a government decree suspended basic constitutional rights. The Communist Party was accused of sabotage and at least 4,000 of its members were imprisoned. Parliamentary elections were held on 5 March. The Nazis obtained 288 seats which, added to the 52 of the Nationalists, did not amount to the two-thirds necessary to pass a special law of extraordinary powers. Nevertheless, they obtained an absolute majority that allowed them to overcome the opposition and demoralize it. A symbolic element of capital importance was a presidential decree of 12 March that eliminated the black-red-gold flag of the Weimar republican system (article 3 of the Weimar constitution) and replaced it with one which included the swastika. Schmitt would soon note how this action 'ceremoniously negated and eliminated the spirit and foundation' of the republic (Schmitt, 1933f: 5).

Communists were outlawed and expelled from parliament. This allowed the Nazis to have the Reichstag pass a law that declared a state of emergency in Germany on Thursday 23 March and enacted it the next day. (It was approved by 444 votes in favour, which included 72 from the Catholic Centre Party, and 94 against.) By means of this enabling act, whose official name was *Das Gesetz zur Behebung der Not von Volk und Reich (Act to Relieve the Distress of the People and of the Reich)*, the separation of powers succumbed and the executive acquired legislative power. Hitler's sovereign dictatorship was now formally installed (compare with Schwab, 1970: 105).

The promulgation of this law is the factor that could explain Schmitt's conversion.[9] On 25 March, the day after the enabling

---

[9] On 28 April 1947, Schmitt presented before the Nuremberg Tribunal his own very selective account of his conversion to the Nazi movement: 'It was not after January 30, 1933 but only after the announcement of the Enabling Act of March 24, 1933 that I asked myself what position I, as a constitutional jurist, should take with respect to the transformation of Germany into a one-party state. After consulting with friends – not with Nazis – I applied for membership in the party through the appropriate local group in my then residence in Cologne on May 1, 1933' (Bendersky, 1987: 125). Schmitt fails to mention his publication on April 1 of a reckless commentary on the enabling act in which he enthusiastically embraced the Nazi revolution (1933c), and his acceptance on that same day to take part in the drafting of a key piece of Nazi legislation (1933d).

act was promulgated, he hurriedly wrote a commentary for the *Deutsche Juristen-Zeitung*, the official fortnightly review of the German legal profession. It may be inferred that the article was completed and submitted to the publisher that same Saturday, for the next day he had to leave for Weimar to attend a conference, and from there Schmitt planned to proceed to Rome for a holiday.[10] In his brief commentary he defined the scope and meaning of the enabling law of 24 March. Later in the year, in his book *Staat, Bewegung und Volk*, while surveying the constitutional developments that had taken place since the Nazi takeover, Schmitt would state that, more than a mere constitutional reform, it actually meant the abrogation of the Weimar constitution and the genesis of a new one. In this early commentary he would lay the basis for that conclusion.

Schmitt was the first to observe the peculiarities of this law when compared to other enabling laws enacted during the Weimar period (compare with K. D. Bracher quoted in Morsey, 1992: 193). The commissioned empowerment of October 1923, for example, kept itself within constitutional limits. In the present case, Schmitt argued, a new legislator had been established, the cabinet. This was now empowered not only to promulgate decrees but also laws in the formal sense. The cabinet had also been granted the faculty to promulgate constitutional laws.[11] By means of the latter power, the cabinet could now, of its own accord, proceed to reform the constitution. Articles 1 and 2 of the enabling act of 24 March referred to laws without qualification, and its article 3 included

---

[10] Koenen thinks that it took Schmitt 'only a few days' (1995: 236) to complete this article, but does not take into account that on Sunday he had to leave Berlin to attend the conference at Weimar. Koenen also notes that, as a rule, an article had to be submitted ten days in advance to be published in the forthcoming issue (ibid.: 236 n. 44). The swiftness in drafting his commentary and the aplomb of his argumentation led Josef Becker to intimate that Schmitt participated as a consultant to the Ministry of the Interior officials who prepared the text of the enabling act and that, together with Georg Kaisenberg and Franz Medicus, he acted as an official commentator (Becker, 1961: 200 n. 34). Schmitt explicitly denied Becker's allegation (Koenen, 1995: 236 n. 44).

[11] In the same issue of the *Deutsche Juristen-Zeitung*, Georg Kaisenberg wrote, contrary to Schmitt's view, that the enabling act of 24 March did not include the right formally to reform the constitution (Kaisenberg, 1933: 460). In the next issue of this review, Otto Koellreutter, who by then had signed up as a member of the Nazi Party (compare with Koenen, 1995: 248), sided with Schmitt on this matter (Koellreutter, 1933: 520).

article 76 of the Weimar constitution among the articles that could not contravene the legislation enacted by the executive.[12] With article 76 out of the way, the executive had now gained the 'faculty to promulgate new laws to replace the existing ones' (Schmitt, 1933c: 456). Schmitt interpreted this as meaning that a 'portion of power to enact constitutional laws (*verfassunggesetztgebende Gewalt*)'[13] had been conferred on the executive. This was Schmitt's first step towards underscoring the revolutionary and foundational significance of the enabling act of 24 March, in spite of the fact that the letter of the new law did not declare the abrogation or destruction of the Weimar constitution. The Reichstag had not formally appealed to the *pouvoir constituant* in enacting it, but passed it as an ordinary law in virtue of its legislative power. Since the constituent power was not explicitly exercised the constitution could be said to be formally untouched. It was possible to say that it had been violated or suspended but not abrogated or destroyed.[14] That Schmitt was prepared to take that further step is clear from the continuation of his argument.

---

[12] Article 3 of the enabling act states: 'Articles 68 to 77 of the constitution cannot be applied to legislation enacted by the executive' (Friedrichs, 1939: 54).

[13] Ibid. This ambiguous formula was used here by Schmitt for the first time. In his *Verfassungslehre* (Schmitt, 1928: 98), he drew a distinction between constituent power (*verfassunggebende Gewalt*) and the constituted power to reform the constitution (*verfassungsgesetzlichen Gewalt*). As far as I can tell, this hybrid notion of a *verfassungsgesetzgebende Gewalt* was never used before by Schmitt. According to Bendersky, this act meant to Schmitt 'much more than a major constitutional amendment ... It represented instead a revolutionary change in the essence of the constitution itself, as decisive a transformation as the revolution of 1918' (Bendersky, 1983: 197). Strictly speaking, a comparison between the revolution of 1918 and the enabling act could be made by appealing to the notion of *pouvoir constituant*. Bendersky further argues that 'because the constitution had not been officially abrogated and the institutions of the Reichstag, the Reichsrat and president were immune from decrees under the Enabling Act, Schmitt continued to argue that parts of the Weimar constitution were still valid' (1983: 198).

[14] Schmitt had another possibility open to him. He could have said that the constitution had been eliminated in the sense of *Aufhebung*. He knew, as he had admitted in his *Parlamentarismus*, that 'a constitution is identical with division of power. In article 16 of the *Declaration of the Rights of Man and Citizens* of 1789 this found its most famous proclamation: "Toute société dans laquelle la garantie des droits n'est pas assurée, ni la séparation des pouvoirs déterminée, n'a pas de constitution" ... Dictatorship ... is essentially the elimination (*Aufhebung*) of the separation of powers, i.e. elimination of the constitution' (Schmitt, 1923b: 52; compare with Schmitt, 1921: 148–9. I owe this reference to Ingeborg Maus).

The next step in Schmitt's argumentation was to expose the legal foundations of the enabling act of 24 March. The law rested formally on article 76 of the constitution, the article that contained the conditions and procedures to be followed in cases of constitutional reform. But Schmitt had earlier opposed the latitudinarian view held by Anschütz, according to which the faculty to reform the constitution presented no limitations.[15] He now dismissed the issue posed by the difficulties in interpreting article 76 by invoking the notion of a *verfassungsgesetzgebende Gewalt*, a power to issue constitutional laws. Against an act based on this power, Schmitt acknowledged, no right to revision could be invoked. He had thus found a way to agree with Anschütz's interpretation by circumventing his own earlier strictures. If the power in question was not the one beckoned by article 76, and if by means of that power it was possible to promulgate constitutional laws and not merely to issue constitutional reforms, the power Schmitt was intimating was really the *verfassunggebende Gewalt*, or constituent power, which could only be activated after having stepped outside the constitutional domain, for instance during revolutionary situations.[16] A confirmation of this view was furnished by Schmitt himself when he stated that the new enabling law was 'an expression of the triumphant national revolution' (Schmitt, 1933c: 456) and then proceeded to equate the Nazi revolution with the German revolution of 1918. Such a comparison could only be drawn on the basis of the formal appeal to the notion of constituent power.[17]

---

[15] Compare with what Schmitt writes in his *Legalität und Legitimität*: 'By contrast, in Anschütz value neutrality extends from his still functionalist legal system to an absolute neutrality towards itself. It opens a legal avenue for the abrogation of legality and thus advances towards suicide by means of its own neutrality' (1932a: 50).

[16] Earlier, in his *Verfassungslehre*, Schmitt had strictly defined the limits beyond which constitutional reform would mean abrogation or destruction of a constitution. Thus, he stated that 'the reform of constitution is not the destruction of a constitution' (1928: 103). Again, in his *Der Hüter der Verfassung*, Schmitt rejected the view 'that discovers an almighty sovereign and even the subject of constituent power in article 76' (Schmitt, 1931: 16; compare with Schmitt, 1929b: 37-8).

[17] In his *Die Diktatur*, Schmitt interpreted the Convention's decision on 10 October 1793 to suspend the constitution of 24 June 1793, as having been based on an appeal to the *pouvoir constituant* (Schmitt, 1921: 148). The Convention's decision in 1793 and the enabling act of 24 March 1933 could be constructed as parallel cases.

Further confirmation of Schmitt's implicit appeal to the notion of constituent power was his reference to the famous sentence of the Reich's Supreme Court on 8 July 1920.[18] According to Schmitt, this sentence showed that the legitimacy of the Weimar constitution did not rest on the legal system defined by the former constitution, namely the constitution of 1871. This was so because the activation of the constituent power of the people meant the destruction of the constituent power of its former subject, namely the monarch. In his *Verfassungslehre*, Schmitt had maintained that a new constitution could not be subservient to the normativity of an earlier one. It would be 'a meaningless conceptual game' to apply the prescriptions of a no longer valid constitution to a new one (Schmitt, 1928: 89). By thus retrieving the circumstances of 1918 and applying them to those of 1933, Schmitt was defining Hitler's rise to power as a revolutionary event. By invoking the notion of constituent power, Schmitt was flashing a green light inviting the Nazi regime to define itself formally as a revolutionary government and proceed to act accordingly.

Still, Schmitt had to acknowledge that the enabling act of 24 March included a number of reservations that forestalled an outright revolutionary break with the constitutional status quo. The main reservation had to do with the figure of the *Reichspräsident*, whose role, according to Schmitt's own interpretation, continued to be that of protector of the constitution (compare with Schmitt, 1931). The *Reichspräsident* retained all his faculties – the faculty to enact extraordinary legislation under article 48, the supreme command of the armed forces, the right to pardon, the faculty to dissolve the Reichstag and the faculty to name and dismiss the Chancellor. Also, article 5 of the enabling act stated that 'the present government' would be the subject of its extraordinary faculties so long as it would not 'be dissolved by another one' (Schmitt, 1933c: 457). This meant that the enabling act empowered that particular cabinet and no other. This

---

[18] The Court stated: 'The new state power established by a revolution (the Councils of Workers and Soldiers) cannot be denied constitutional recognition. Its illegal foundation cannot be adduced against it, for a legal foundation is not an essential proof of state power. A state cannot exist without state power. The abrogation of the old power gives rise to a new power which occupies its place' (compare with Schmitt, 1928: 89).

prompted Schmitt to raise the issue of the identity of the present government in order to dispel any doubts concerning its revolutionary nature. He postulated that the identity of this new government was decisively defined 'by the political leadership of the Chancellor of the Reich'. And added: 'The present government is essentially determined by its Führer' (ibid.). The chance still existed that the Reich Chancellor might lose the *Reichspräsident*'s confidence and be removed from office. But then, Schmitt warned, one would be facing a *political* issue, which could not 'be solved in advance and without taking the situation into account' (ibid.: 457–8). A similar proviso contained in the enabling act of 13 October 1923 presupposed a 'a pluralist party state' dependent on ephemeral party coalitions. Now a completely new situation had emerged. 'The present government wants to be the expression of a unified national political will, which seeks to put an end to the methods of the plural party state, methods that were destructive of the state and the constitution' (ibid.: 458). The affirmation of the political now took precedence over constitutional requirements and reservations. It was natural to conclude that the new set of circumstances demanded that the Weimar constitution be superseded and that a new constitution be put in place. In fact, the changes in the cabinet (Hugenberg's resignation, for instance) that occurred soon afterwards did not cancel the validity of the enabling act (compare with Neumann, 1966: 53).

A few weeks later Schmitt would formally declare that the enabling act of 24 March was the provisional constitution, and a few months later he would not hesitate to acknowledge that the Weimar constitution had not been just reformed, but effectively abrogated.[19] An effective abrogation of the Weimar constitution could not have taken place without the activation of the *pouvoir*

---

[19] Bendersky rightly observes: 'To [Schmitt] that act was much more than a major constitutional amendment, or a temporary emergency provision similar to the Enabling Act of 1923. It represented instead a revolutionary change in the essence of the constitution itself' (1983: 197). But then he adds: 'Nevertheless, because the constitution had not been officially abrogated ... Schmitt continued to argue that parts of the Weimar constitution were still valid' (p. 198). It is true that the constitution was not officially abrogated, but it is a mistake to suggest that Schmitt argued for the validity of the Weimar constitution. On the contrary, stating that Hitler had assumed the *pouvoir constituant*, even if only a 'portion' of it, meant that the constitution had been surpassed. The provisions contained in the

constituant. (I examine Schmitt's distinction between the destruction and the abrogation of a constitution in Chapter 5.) In 1936, Schmitt did finally acknowledge the obvious, namely that the so-called enabling act of 24 March had formally *abrogated* the Weimar constitution:

> The Act to Relieve the Distress of the People and of the Reich of 24 March, 1933 gives the government the faculty to enact laws, and most certainly laws in the formal sense. With that a decisive step was taken towards eliminating the separation between the executive and the legislative. Seen through the conceptual framework of Weimar constitutional law, that was only a legislative 'enabling', a so-called constitutional reform, or more accurately, an enabling act to abrogate the constitution (*ein verfassungsbeseitigendes Ermächtigungsgesetzt*). (Schmitt, 1940: 227)

Schmitt never said that the enabling act meant the activation of the constituent power, but that was precisely what he had in mind. Even though only a 'portion' of that power to reform the constitution was said to have been conferred on the cabinet, that he made the assertion showed reckless temerity. First, Schmitt knew full well that the constituent power was indivisible. (How could it not be if it was effectively to ground the political unity of a state?) Giving away a portion of it really meant giving it away in its entirety. Second, by insinuating that the notion of constituent power was at stake, he was making use of his own distinction between commissarial and sovereign dictatorship. The distinguishing mark of the latter, as he first defined it in *Die Diktatur* (Schmitt, 1921), was the capacity to appeal to the notion of constituent power.

---

body of its material articulation could still be invoked, but its original soul, the *pouvoir constituant* of the German people, had been replaced by the sovereign will of the Führer. If that was not the case, it made little sense to acknowledge the Nazi takeover as 'our national revolution'. Schmitt was evidently well aware of the revolutionary implications of the doctrine of a *pouvoir constituant*, which coincided with what Hobbes wrote in ch. 26 of the *Leviathan*: 'If the Sovereign of one Commonwealth, subdue a people that had lived under other written Lawes, and afterwards govern them by the same Lawes, by which they were governed before; yet those Lawes are the Civill Lawes of the Victor, and not of the vanquished Commonwealth. For the Legislator is he, not by whose authority the Lawes were first made, but by whose authority they now continue to be Lawes.'

The brief commentary concluded with an announcement of the great tasks that could be accomplished with the new powers acquired by the regime. In overt revolutionary vein, Schmitt warned: 'Let us not bury the legal foundations of the new state under the sophisms of the old party state. Not only the state but also public law must be renewed and purified' (1933c: 458). This fiery rhetoric contrasts with the sombre tone of the observations he entered into his personal diary at the end of January. Schmitt may have intended to explore some form of accommodation with the new regime and was only testing the water and trying the right kind of approach. In fact, by summoning the notion of constituent power, with whose revolutionary inflection he was well acquainted, he had crossed the Rubicon, as he himself would later acknowledge (compare with Koenen, 1995: 235).

Schmitt's revolutionary appeal to the notion of constituent power bore its fruit once he got to the other shore. In his *Staat, Bewegung und Volk*, he would now write: 'the Weimar constitution is no longer valid' (Schmitt, 1933f: 5). All its essential principles and rules had been abrogated. What existed at that moment, he acknowledged, was a new constitution – the so-called enabling act of 24 March (ibid.: 7).[20] What neither his detractors nor his apologists have been able to see is the continuity that links his arguments in 1933 with the notion of sovereign dictatorship first developed in his *Die Diktatur*. Inspired by Sieyès, the function he attributed to the notion of constituent power determined the revolutionary nature of a sovereign dictatorship (ibid.).

III

Schmitt decided not to wait in Berlin for a reaction to the publication of his commentary. Next day, Sunday 26 March, he left for Weimar, accompanied by his friend Popitz,[21] to attend a

---

[20] Schmitt referred to this law passed by the *Reichstag* as the 'so-called' enabling act. He did so in order to signal that this particular law of empowerment ought not to be compared to other such laws promulgated during the duration of the Weimar republic. He read it as the closing act of the Weimar republic and simultaneously as the inaugural act of Hitler's national revolution.

[21] Schmitt recalls his friendship with Popitz: 'I met him in Berlin in 1929. We were united in our growing friendship, until his death on February 2, 1945, by

conference organized by the *Deutschen Vereiningung für Staatswissenschaftliche Fortbildung* to be held between then and 1 April (Koenen, 1995: 241–5). After the conference his plans were to proceed to Rome to attend Holy Week celebrations and stay there for a few days before taking up his duties as Constitutional Law Professor at the University of Cologne. The Weimar conference was attended by more than 700 participants eager to learn about the latest events in Berlin. These events, particularly the enabling act just promulgated, had deeply affected this audience. 'Under the immediate impression of the historical events, both speakers and audience ... bore witness to a deep need to reflect on the great conjuncture of our public life' (Löning, 1933: 675). The Weimar conference provided Schmitt with the perfect setting to publicize the revolutionary agenda he had laid out in his forthcoming article for the *Deutsche Juristen-Zeitung*.

There are two extant accounts of Schmitt's presentation at this conference: one by Georg Löning, the organizer of the conference, and another by one of its participants, a legal councillor whose last name was Brodführer (1933). According to Löning, Schmitt's presentation, entitled 'Emergency Laws in Modern Constitutional Life' ('Staatsnotrechts in modernen Verfassungs-leben'), pointed 'directly at the present rejuvenation of the state' (1933: 675). He reported that Schmitt, based on his 'earlier investigations', proceeded 'to advance' them by 'consigning the opposition between legality and illegality to the "inventory of failed antitheses"' (ibid.). One ought to understand the 'national revolution' not as the triumph of might over right but as 'the elevation of legitimacy over legality, of what already exists over what is still only apparently valid' (ibid.). According to Brodführer's report, Schmitt claimed that it was a mistake to assume that right was protected by legality. On the contrary, 'to overstep legality does not mean chaos; it may certainly prove to be wrong, but it is also plausible that legality may have lost its inner meaning' (Brodführer, 1933: 254). Schmitt had appealed to a notion of

---

common work and scientific interests, by a common neighborhood and personal trust and by the common German destiny' (1958: 8). Bentin, while noticing the close affinity of their intellectual positions, remarks how convenient it was for Schmittian apologetics to make him appear in close proximity to one who died for his participation in the conspiracy to murder Hitler (1972: 124).

'substantive justice' as the justification for overhauling legality. And, as he had done in the forthcoming article for the *Deutsche Juristen-Zeitung*, he boldly compared the Nazi national revolution to the German revolution of 1918.[22]

After some sightseeing in Weimar in the company of Popitz on the morning of 29 March (Koenen, 1995: 245), he boarded a train to Jena to visit his colleague Otto Koellreutter, who told him he had become a member of the Nazi Party. From there he continued on to Munich where he arrived on 30 March. He intended to stay there for a few days, meet old acquaintances and then proceed to Rome. The following entry is to be found in his diary:

Friday, 31. 3. 33. I slept comfortably in the Continental Hotel. I take breakfast in my room. The boycott against Jews seems to have started. I thought with sadness of Eisler. Duschka has gone to Hamburg; no letter yet. A telegram from Berlin; that I should return immediately: meeting at the State Ministry tomorrow at 5 in the afternoon. Enthusiastic and relaxed, but sad to have to interrupt this nice holiday travel ... (Noack, 1993: 170)

The telegram was signed by Papen, Vice-Chancellor and Prussia's Commissar, but the idea of inviting him had originated with Popitz (Tommissen, 1975: 107; Koenen, 1995: 329). Schmitt was informed that he had been selected, together with Popitz, to become a member of the committee studying what was to be called the *Reichsstatthaltergesetz*, which was an expansion of the first coordination law to regulate the relations between the Reich and the German states.

This extraordinary invitation to collaborate was probably due to the fact that the content of his article for the *Deutsche Juristen-Zeitung* had been well-received by the new regime. Popitz, who attended cabinet meetings regularly and was privy to ministerial discussions (Koenen, 1995: 244 n. 84) and also belonged to the

---

[22] In *Staat, Bewegung und Volk*, published by the end of that same year, Schmitt would look back at his intervention at the Weimar conference and present it as proof that he was not now belatedly endorsing the view that the enabling act was the 'provisional constitutional law of the new Germany'. He had already done so, he wrote, on 31 March 1933 (1933f: 7 n. 1). Incidentally, Schmitt is mistaken about the date. According to his diary, on Friday 31 March, he was already in Munich where he had arrived the night before.

editorial board of that journal, must have disclosed to Vice-Chancellor Papen the content of Schmitt's commentary. The Nazis had been given an important and in all likelihood unexpected contribution. Here was a jurist of great weight and prestige, Papen's former *Kronjurist*,[23] offering them a green light to overcome any remaining obstacles imposed on them by Weimar's constitutional framework. More than that, they could now advance as though they confronted a terra incognita, with great possibilities for political experimentation. After all, the enabling act of 24 March had been raised to the standing of the Weimar constitution. The Nazis may not have thought that it would be so easy to launch a revolution of that magnitude in so short a time.

In his diary, Schmitt recorded his participation in this legislative commission. On that Friday, he took the night-train back to Berlin and on Saturday 1 April he went to the Wilhelmstrasse offices to discuss the new law of coordination with Papen, Popitz and the Secretary of State Werner Naumann. (What this 'coordination' intended was to submit all state and regional administration to the rule of the party without an intervening electoral process. The two laws, once promulgated by the cabinet, abrogated the German federal system.) After the meeting, Popitz drove Schmitt home. In his diary he mentioned the concern he felt that night for the destiny of his Jewish friend Eisler, who feared the anti-Semitic wave unleashed by the Nazis.

Schmitt devoted Sunday to drafting the legal text. The committee met twice on the Monday at the Ministry of the Interior. During the morning session he noticed the hopeless situation of Vice-Chancellor Papen, 'the poor Papen' (Noack, 1993: 172). Schmitt had by now become aware of changes within the cabinet. Power had shifted from the conservatives to the Nazis. He went home for lunch and was picked up by Popitz at four o'clock. Hermann Göring attended the afternoon meeting. Schmitt described him as 'impetuous; he solved problems in a couple of minutes ... Göring had something Wilhelminian about him, possibly the type of person needed for these times' (ibid.: 173). The discussion continued on Tuesday afternoon at the Ministry with Papen, Popitz

---

[23] In 1932, Schmitt, as an adviser to Papen, defended the government's decision to intervene in Prussia.

and two Nazi officials, Werner Naumann and Friedrich Landfried. Papen informed him that he would be invited to a reception hosted by Hitler. This produced in him great curiosity and tension. On Thursday morning, he received an invitation from Georg Kaisenberg to write an official commentary on the law that was being drafted. The reception took place that evening:

> At nine thirty, Kaisenberg called, obtrusively; wanted a brochure on the new *Reichsstatthaltergesetz*, impertinently, for the series he and [Franz] Medicus publish. I dragged the matter but did not say no ... At about seven I phoned Steinhard and rented a stiff collar. At a quarter to eight I go to Popitz's house by taxi; from there to the press reception offered by Hitler and Goebbels. I could see them perfectly. There is great excitement. Hitler like a bull in the ring. Excited by this show. Papen was friendly, but had obviously nothing to say (Noack, 1993: 175; compare with Tommissen, 1975: 188).

Next day, 7 April, the *Reichsstatthaltergesetz* or second Coordination Law was signed by Hitler.[24] Schmitt must have seen this law as the fulfilment of the task that he had envisaged during the Prussian *coup* of June 1932. This was indeed 'a sort of second Prussian coup' (Koenen, 1995: 332), which would finally dissolve the separation between the central government of the Reich and the state governments, and dissolve the parliamentary system in the states.

On Saturday 8 April he spent the whole day dictating his commentary at the Carl Heymanns Verlag, the publishing house which would bring it out. On the Sunday, he worked all morning and afternoon on the manuscript. Later he visited Popitz and discussed the matter at hand. By Monday the manuscript would be finished and ready to go to press. In his diary he observed: 'dreadful work' (Noack, 1993: 176). A few weeks later, Schmitt

---

[24] The same day Hitler also promulgated the so-called Law for the Restoration of the Civil Service. With this Hitler obtained the legal weapons to purge the enemies of the regime from public institutions: 11 per cent of university professors were sacked; law faculties lost 210 professors, mostly Jews. This opened the way for the promotion and hiring of faculty staff sympathetic to the regime.

[25] The copy of Schmitt's *Reichsstatthaltergesetz* that I used is from the Philipps-Universitäts Marburg. It bears an ink stamp with the date of acquisition, 5 May 1933.

published his commentary to this second Coordination Law.²⁵ It appeared in a series entitled 'The Law (*Recht*) of the National Revolution' officially edited by the Reich's Interior Ministry and thus bearing its official seal of approval. The commentary's short preface betrays the zeal of a convert.

> The German revolution has, in a few days, enacted a reform of the Reich that overcomes centuries of internal conflict within the state. What was not achieved in the year 1871 after a victorious war, the failure to make the German Reich a German state, is now a political reality. What was neglected by the Weimar constitution, after the November 1918 collapse, and was further corrupted by the weakness of the federal party state nested in that constitution, has now been healed and may recover ... Nowadays, the German revolution's constitutional law has already laid new foundations for the construction of the Reich. The promulgation of the *Reichsstatthaltergesetzt* on 7 April 1933 meant the greatest and most decisive step towards a new state order of Reich and provinces. (Schmitt, 1933d: 3)

It is plain that, by now, Schmitt had unambiguously embraced the revolutionary elan unleashed by the Nazis. Here he was, at the very centre of things, fully aware that he had gained a chance effectively to intervene and change the course of German history. Federalism had been, for many centuries, the main obstacle encountered by conservatives in their effort to secure a strong sovereign German state. But now the Führer had promulgated a law, drafted under Schmitt's own expert supervision, that abrogated the federal system. Schmitt referred to what the Nazis had accomplished in the span of a few weeks as the 'German revolution' (ibid.). But this was a conservative revolution whose aim was not so much the continued self-assertion of civil society, but the affirmation of the authority and unity of a strong state.²⁶

This new law signified a profound alteration in the design of the German state. In 1972 Schmitt would admit that this law was 'a structure that one ought to consider in order to understand

---

²⁶ Surely the Nazi revolution meant the liquidation of the bourgeoisie's political existence. But, as Ingeborg Maus notes, the bourgeoisie allowed this to happen in order to save its social existence and continue to assert its own interests undisturbed under the protection of a strong state (1986: 105).

subsequent developments' (Tommissen, 1975: 107). The legal justification for the new configuration, formally equivalent to a reform of the constitution, rested on the enabling act of 24 March. In a bold move, Schmitt now proclaimed that this enabling act had become 'the provisional constitution of German revolution' (1933d: 8). The relations between the state and the different states (*Länder*) rested on this 'new constitutional foundation' (ibid.: 9). As I have already indicated, a few months later Schmitt would draw out what was implied in his daring interpretation of this enabling act – the Weimar constitution had ceased to exist. This explains why Schmitt was so eager to set the enabling act of 24 March apart from other historical instances of this kind of legislation. What was involved in this case was the notion of constituent power. It is true that the body of the Weimar constitution, the corpus of legal and constitutional prescriptions, was still standing, but it was now animated by a different spirit, by a new subject of constituent power.

Below, I examine Schmitt's elaborate account of the destruction of the constitution of 1871 during the German revolution of 1918–19. Then, a new subject of *pouvoir constituant*, the people, brought about the demise of monarchical legitimacy and the monarchical principle. Now, in a reversal of fortunes, democratic legitimacy had been superseded and constituent power was now in the hands of figures with monarchical standing. In fact, the *Führerprinzip* would shortly function as the monarchical principle had done previously. For the moment, Schmitt thought that the revolutionary role of the Führer could be balanced by the conservative functions of the President.

> According to the present new order, the power of the Reich is born by the President and the Chancellor of the Reich. The President bears it as protector of the historical continuity and as an authority based on tradition; the Chancellor bears it as the Führer of the German movement, who has been able to launch the German revolution and the state's new formation. (ibid.: 10)

The conservative revolutionary aspect that would so clearly determine Schmitt's work during the first year of Nazi rule, was balanced by the manifestation of views that expressed a more liberal persuasion. Here again one could see a continuity with themes developed during the Weimar period. Schmitt stated that the *Reichstattshaltergesetz* balanced two opposed points of view. It gave 'unchallenged precedence' (ibid.) to the political leadership of the state, but at the same time the autonomy of the states (*Länder*) and their many historical, economic and social idiosyncrasies was acknowledged. Political leadership was now the monopoly of the Chancellor of the Reich. It would be a mistake to see in his eminence a 'danger for the reasonable autonomy of the states' (ibid.). It would be a mistake to read this law as 'unitarian' or 'anti-federalist'. Schmitt added: 'Venerable truth and experience teach that only a very strong state may institute and defend a free economy, so too only a very strong and unified state power may institute and defend the reasonable freedom and independence of the states or *Länder*' (ibid.). This is not different from the ideal qualitative total state he defined in his 1932 *Langnamverein* address. In Schmitt's view, the national revolution brought forth by the Nazis fulfilled the authoritarian liberal position he had outlined on that occasion.

Having completed his first commission, Schmitt left Berlin on Monday 10 April. He would take with him the proofs of his commentary and revise them on the way. He spent two days with his colleague Carl Bilfinger at Halle, where they discussed his commentary and talked about joining the Party. On Holy Thursday, he was able to send the definitive text back to Berlin and went to join his wife and daughter in Cologne, where he was to start his new duties as professor at the university. A student of his, Gunther Krauss, relates an encounter he had with him in Cologne: 'In spring I had a chance meeting with him in the street, in Cologne if I am not mistaken. His recommendation to join the Party was so emphatic that I took it as an order' (Krauss, 1990: 59). On 1 May, exactly three months after the rise of the Nazis to power, the highly respected conservative jurist joined a large queue of citizens in front of the headquarters of the National Socialist Party in Cologne, and awaited his turn to sign up as a member. His party number was 2,098,860 (Tommissen, 1975: 106). Thus began what he would later describe as his intellectual adventure.

2 • Political Romanticism and the Catholic Counter-Revolution

Cuando la legalidad basta, la legalidad; cuando no basta, la dictadura

(Donoso, 1970: 306)

I

Unlike Burke or de Maistre, Schmitt seems to have anticipated the German revolution of 1918-19. His book *Politische Romantik* (*Political Romanticism*), which he began in 1917 and published in early 1919, must be read as a counter-revolutionary treatise (Schmitt, 1919; 1925a; 1925b). In it Schmitt examined two strands within the tradition of European conservative thought: political romanticism and the Catholic counter-revolution. His aim was to draw a clear line between the conservatism of Catholic thinkers like de Maistre and Bonald and the stance assumed by the political romantics. According to Schmitt, one should not unqualifiedly classify Catholic counter-revolutionary thinkers and romantic figures like Adam Müller and Friedrich Schlegel under 'the same category of political intellectuality' (Schmitt, 1919: 18 and 110; 1925a: 49; 1925b: 33). The passion Schmitt evinced in his criticism of political romantics betrayed a political intention.[1] His study explored the metaphysical and ethical roots of the romantic as such but it is undeniable that he expected that study to yield a political bonus. He wanted to deny political romanticism genuine conservative credentials, and to discern a liberal trait in its lack of political commitment. His ultimate aim was to strengthen the political effectiveness of the conservative

---

[1] In 1925 Schmitt re-edited the book, revised its argument and added a preface (Schmitt, 1925a). The extensive changes he introduces in the new edition may be in order to shift the focus of attention from a purely political interpretation of the book. The new preface contains this warning: 'a way of thinking that is interested only in politics (*eine nur politisch interessierte Betrachtung*) will never understand political romanticism correctly' (1925b: 10; 1925a: 14).

option he favoured, Catholic counter-revolutionary conservatism. It was essential, if this radical position was to have any chance of prevailing as a political alternative, to keep it quite separate from political romanticism.

The occasion chosen by Schmitt for his confrontation with political romanticism was the claim that identified Friedrich von Gentz, Metternich's aide, as a political romantic figure indistinguishable from Müller and Schlegel. The generation of liberals that came to life in Germany after 1815 persuasively associated the Restoration and the feudal reaction that ensued with the spirit of romanticism. Thus in 1840, Arnold Ruge could still identify Gentz, together with Schlegel, as a leader of the romantic movement. Schmitt disagreed. Gentz may have befriended romantic intellectuals and may have even shared some of their aims, but on the whole he was not a romantic.[2] Like de Maistre, he should be recognized as someone 'completely rooted in the classical character of the eighteenth century' (Schmitt, 1925b: 23).[3] What set him apart from romanticism was 'the rational clarity of his thought, his reasonable, matter-of-fact attitude,[4] his sense of the limits of the efficacy of the state, his instinctive animus against people like the Schlegels and his hatred of Fichte' (ibid.). Moreover, during the Restoration era, 'in spite of all his pliancy toward Metternich', he demonstrated the best appreciation of the 'liberal demands' of the period 'as soon as he could only free himself from the fear of a revolution' (ibid.). This remarkable statement anticipated Schmitt's own ambivalent

---

[2] Compare with Treitschke's account of the rift between Gentz and political romantics in his *History of Germany in the Nineteenth Century*: 'The soberminded Gentz felt utterly alien from this dream-world of theological politics (*theologisierende Politik*), and declared to his friend Müller that everything characteristic of science – clearness, method, and consistency – was conspicuous by its absence' (1916: ii, 364 [modified translation]; 1886; II, 114). Schmitt shared with Treitschke an antipathy towards Müller. Schmitt noted: 'Treitschke's judgement of Müller is well-known; whatever antipathy it may be based on, it remains substantively correct' (1919: 108).

[3] Schmitt looked at Gentz through Treitschke's eyes: 'Gentz, although in the centre of his being he always remained a Kantian, declared that de Maistre's writing was the leading book of the century, and exclaimed in delight, "This is the man for me!"' (Treitschke, 1916: iii, 453).

[4] In 1925, he added another trait to this portrait of Gentz's character: 'capacity for legal argument' (1925a: 32–3; 1925b: 23).

attitude towards liberalism.[5] It is as if all the characteristics he ascribed to the Catholic conservatives formed part of his own perceived conservative animus and should serve as an appropriate description of his personal political aspirations.

Political Romanticism aimed to distinguish between a thinker like Gentz, whose conservatism Schmitt appreciated and sought to emulate, and the erratic and irrational romantics he exposed. Extricating conservatism from romanticism meant disentangling it from Fichtean subjectivism and allowing it to sink its roots in the reality of substance. Conservatism found its true ground in substantive realities, the transcendent God of traditional metaphysics or the new modern deities – community and history. A substantive conservatism could then support a strong state capable of decisive action. No romantic reservations could favour particular groups or special interests when stringent measures needed to be taken, for instance, during revolutionary situations. Subjectivities were accidental encumbrances that could not stand in the way of substance. But a substantive conservatism did not need to be envious of individual initiative. A state that was strong and disposed of the necessary means to secure its autarchy could adopt a genuine liberal attitude and seriously take subjective demands into account.

By tracing the philosophical roots of the theoretical and moral aspects of romanticism, Schmitt attained a better understanding of its idiosyncrasy and its difference from Catholic conservatism. He blamed the Cartesian *cogito* for initiating the process that led to the demise of the 'old ontological thought', and the corresponding destruction of the 'most elevated and stable reality of the old metaphysics, a transcendent God' (1919: 48–9; 1925b: 58). Henceforth, the philosophical task would be determined by the search for the new reality that would replace God as the supreme dogma of metaphysics. Even before the epistemological question initiated by Descartes could be settled by German idealism, two contestants defined the terms of a new ontology: community and history. First, the French revolution produced community as a revolutionary demiurge. But this was not the community envisaged

---

[5] This ambivalence towards liberalism was heightened in the 2nd edition. There he added the following trait to this description of Gentz: 'He had a sense for just "balancing"' (1925a: 33; 1925b: 23). This statement matched his own new appreciation of parliamentarism and the *status mixtus*.

by Rousseau. The individualist temper of the general will was abrogated when the social contract was translated into concrete practical terms by the Jacobins. In the revolutionary collectivity they envisaged, individuals who dissented and refused conformity to the will of the people found themselves in the position of 'atheists' who had rebelled against 'the one supreme sovereign' (1919: 49; 1925b: 59).

Second, the communitarian view was assumed by conservatives like Bonald and de Maistre. But the traditionalist community they espoused was stripped of its revolutionary propensity by the infusion of history. This second demiurge, the 'conservative God', restored what the other deity had revolutionized (1919: 53; 1925b: 62). History was able to refashion 'the universal human community into a historically concrete nation' (1919: 53; 1925b: 62). It thus reinstated the capacity to produce particular legal systems and particular languages as 'expressions of the individual *Nationalgeist*' (1919: 53; 1925b: 62).

The conservative point of view presented history as destiny. Bonald and de Maistre denied what Rousseau and the Jacobins had postulated: the sovereignty of the people. 'The unrestrained fanaticism of the Jacobins was "unhistorical" thought; the quietism of the Restoration could justify itself with the claim that everything that happens is good because it is a historical event' (1919: 53; 1925b: 62). This substantive conservatism also stressed historical duration as opposed as the isolation of particular historical moments or turning-points. 'The appeal to duration is the given conservative and traditionalist argument' (1919: 54; 1925b: 62). *Longum tempus* (long time) was the ultimate justification; *tempus docebit* (time will tell), the ultimate lesson. Herein lay the service that religion and 'noble families' rendered to the state (1919: 54; 1925b: 62). De Maistre, Bonald and Burke appealed to history as the creative power that formed nations and maintained their identity. These thinkers did not come up with the idea of the *Volkgeist*, but what was new was their turning of the historical development responsible for the *Volkgeist* 'into a superhuman creator' (1919: 56; 1925b: 63).

By setting out the synthesis of the two ultimate realities, Hegel confirmed the dethronement of the 'God of the old metaphysics' (1919: 56; 1925b: 64). The people as *Volkgeist* became an instrument of the dialectical development of history, the *Weltgeist*. But there was enough indeterminacy left for the *Volkgeist* to move either towards revolution or reaction, towards liberalism or conservatism.[6] In spite of the use of Christian terminology and a prevalence in his thought of conservative elements, Hegel did not lead back to the 'old God of Christian metaphysics' (1919: 57; 1925b: 64). Stahl proved his superiority by denouncing Hegelianism as anti-Christian and retrieving the notion of a personal God acknowledged by Schelling in 1809. Schmitt paid him further tribute by admitting: 'Stahl war kein Romantiker' (1919: 57; 1925b: 64)

Unlike Stahl, the romantics did not advance towards the recognition of a personal God and remained undecided in the battle between community and history. Retreating to subjectivity, they identified with Fichte's absolute ego and its creative disposition. A recognition of the reality of community, history or a personal God would mean the dethronement of 'the self as creator of the world' (1919: 57; 1925b: 64). The romantic *recherche de la réalité*, the longing for reality, demanded fulfilment. But 'reality itself was not to be gained in a subjectivistic fashion' (1919: 68; 1925b: 73). Schmitt modelled his attack on romanticism on Schelling's objections to Fichtean subjectivism. Without recourse to substance, the romantic subject made itself master of the universe by deconstructing reality and reducing the sum total of things to points.

> The reproach that Schelling made against Fichte – that he annihilated nature – became a true frenzy of destruction among the romantics ... Everything is reduced to the point. Definition, which the romantic rejected so completely because it comprises a limitation and a restriction, becomes a punctuation without substance. (1919: 71; 1925b: 75)

Having nullified substantive reality, 'romantic anarchy' could henceforth ensue without hindrances:

> The world dissolves into figures; the purpose is 'the manipulation of the universe'. Substanceless forms can be related to any content; in the romantic anarchy everybody can form his own world and

---

[6] In *The Concept of the Political*, Schmitt reiterates this bifurcation in Hegel's political thought (1932b: 61).

make of each word a vessel of infinite possibilities. (1919: 72–3; 1925b: 76)

When this universal dissolution overstepped the bounds of imagination and intermixed in arbitrary fashion with ordinary reality, the result was a 'universal exchange and confusion of concepts, an enormous promiscuity of words' (1919: 73; 1925b: 77). This was no longer a world, a universe, but a muddled pluriversum of dispersed points and disjointed moments. Instead of grasping the world as cosmic order and preserving its substantive unity, the romantics attained a 'subjectivized *ludus globi*' (1919: 74; 1925b: 78). Their 'will to reality' yielded only subjective impressions and appearances. No ontological conception could take root here. The possibility of agreeing on any substantive nomological order evaporated when subjective freedom expanded without attainable bounds. 'Neither the cosmos, nor the state, nor the people, nor historical development has any intrinsic interest for [them]. Everything can be made into an easily managed figuration of the subject that is occupied with itself' (1919: 71; 1925b: 75).

Returning empty-handed from their *recherche de la réalité*, the romantics soon found out what this meant: giving up on any course of rational action. Reality would still flaunt its daily *de facto* power but all they could do was to retreat to their intimate domains where they would enjoy sovereign possession of themselves. In ordinary life, the absence of the objective signposts provided by the old metaphysics of substance made individuals feel helpless in the hand of a power they could not control and which in fact played games with them. Their *recherche de la réalité* had to end at this point, which was also where their quietism and moral passivity began.

After examining the theoretical aspects of romanticism, Schmitt sought to articulate the philosophical roots of its moral attitude. In accordance with humanitarian liberalism, the romantics negated substance in order to affirm the freedom of the subject. But in the end, in spite of this emphasis on subjective autarchy, they came to the realization of their own powerlessness. They lapsed into a state of passivity and withdrew from the world of politics. 'We are helpless in the hand of a power that plays with us' (1919: 74; 1925b: 78). The feeling of being an instrument of community or history was a common feature of post-Kantian philosophy. From Schelling to Marx, from Schopenhauer to Freud and Adler, individuals were seen as mere tools of a superior, uncontrollable power, but this 'need not lead to a fatalistic or quietistic suspension of human activity' (1919: 77; 1925b: 81). For a Catholic conservative like de Maistre, who engaged in immediate political action, the conception of individuals as tools in the hand of God was not just abstract theory but deep-seated conviction. With him 'the feeling of dependence on God is connected with the feeling of dependence on the national community and its historical development' (ibid.). Engaging in political activity, however, had nothing to do with social constructivism. Burke, de Maistre and Bonald abhorred '"artifice" in political affairs, artificial constitutions based on the calculations of a clever individual, and the fabricators of political constitutions and geometricians' (1919: 78; 1925b: 81; compare with de Maistre, 1980: 129). Again, this rejection of artificial construction had nothing to do with the Adam Müller's 'unmanly passivity' (Schmitt, 1919: 112; 1925b: 128). Romantic passivity, which relinquished all causality to community and history, which they took to be the 'true causes', introduced the problem of occasionalism.[7]

'The problem of the true cause is the problem of occasionalism' (1919: 78; 1925b: 85). Schmitt added: 'The problem of occasionalism is not merely metaphysical; it is just as much an ethical problem' (1919: 87; 1925b: 94). He raised this issue to strike at the philosophical foundations of romantic passivity. 'The essence of romanticism: passivity' (1919: p. v). Passivity was also the essence of occasionalism. It was appropriate, then, that Schmitt, when he traced the origins of the romantic spirit, turned his attention towards Descartes. He noticed the difficulty that entrapped Descartes when he tried to coordinate the interactions of body and mind and his inability to solve it in a satisfactory fashion. Malebranche, faced with the same difficulty, came up with better results. He postulated God as the 'true cause' of each and every physical and corresponding psychical event. God was the only true cause; everything else was just an occasion that invited God's

---

[7] In the 2nd edition Schmitt noted that on closer examination neither community nor history were the true causes that took everything as occasion, but rather the romantic subject itself (1925a: 119; 1925b: 82).

action. 'In fact, it is not the human being who acts, but rather God; his intervention is in every single case the real efficacy' (1919: 79; 1925b: 86). Occasionalism did not explain the mind–body interaction; it simply made this interaction illusory by postulating an encompassing third entity, the true reality. '[T]he path from Malebranche leads directly to the unconditional passivism that destroys all activity' (1919: 161; 1925b: 116).

Avoidance of decision by means of an occasionalist sublation of opposition into a higher third was similar to the romantic thought-process. It was an easy way to dispose of oppositions and refuse to dissolve them by engaging in appropriate action. The romantic as a subjective occasionalist would reduce activity to a purely 'spiritual movement' (1919: 87; 1925b: 94). Faced with 'alien activity', i.e. with actions over which one could not claim ownership, all that remained to be done in order to act morally was to add approval or disapproval. 'Freedom is only *consentement* ... God creates and produces. The human being follows the event with his feeling' (1919: 87; 1925b: 97). Occasionalism allowed romantics to avoid taking responsibility for their actions. By contrast, 'the good Christian and patriot de Maistre',[8] who espoused an objective occasionalist view, took himself to be an 'instrument' in the hand of God and 'did not exclude activity and a consciousness of responsibility' (1919: 87–8; 1925b: 94).

When romantics converted to Catholicism, they were still motivated by their unfinished *recherche de la réalité*. At first, they believed they could retain God, community and history without giving up their subjectivity. When they realized that a decision was unavoidable and that subjectivism had to dissolve, 'the romantic situation comes to an end' (1919: 58; 1925b: 65).

According to Schmitt, 'where political activity begins, political romanticism ends' (1919: 162; 1925b: 160). The response of the romantics when confronted by a political event had been to take refuge within the confines of their absolute selves. From that isolation they could passively contemplate how events unfolded without being drawn into them. Their eager discussions of political affairs invariably turned into endless idle chatter. Unlike the

---

[8] In the 2nd edition, Schmitt omits de Maistre and refers to Malebranche (1925a: 135; 1925b: 94).

deliberation that precedes action, romantic discussion was only a substitute for decisive action. 'Romantic activity is a contradiction in terms' (Schmitt, 1925b: 160). It was a common mistake to associate political romanticism with actual political movements, whether reactionary or revolutionary. 'Romanticism not only lacks [a] specific connection with the restoration ... it has no necessary relationship to revolution either. The isolated and absolute ego is elevated above both and uses both as an ocassion' (ibid.). Schmitt also warned against any attempt to assimilate Catholicism to romantic attitudes. Romantic enthusiasm for the Church had nothing to do with the Church itself. This was most apparent in the case of Adam Müller, Schmitt's political romantic *par excellence*.

> [I]t is a mistake to call him a romantic on the grounds that he was a Catholic. This popular conception is to be explained only as a consequence of that dilettante's conflation of romanticism with the romanticized object. Catholicism is not something that is romantic (ibid.: 49–50).

Romantic apoliticism avoided the forks in the road. It could not suffer to burden the autonomous self with decisions that might lead to objective commitments and entanglements. Only aesthetically conservative, the romantic affirmation of the superiority of the subject could flourish within the private spaces available in the liberal society.

Catholic conservatives like de Maistre, Bonald and Donoso Cortés, and not the romantics, were, in Schmitt's view, the true adversaries of humanitarian liberalism. What separated these Catholic traditionalists from the romantics was their ability to decide politically, to confront the either–or head on.

> In the romantic, the 'organic' conception of the state rests on this inability to make a normative evaluation. This conception repudiates the 'juridical' as narrow and mechanical and it searches for the state that is above right and wrong ... The root of romantic sublimity is the inability to decide, the 'higher third' factor they are always talking about, which is not a higher factor but a different third factor: in other words, it is always a way out of the either–or. (ibid.: 117)

By contrast,

> all the founders of the counterrevolutionary theory ... Burke, de Maistre, and Bonald, were active politicians, each with his own responsibility. For years they maintained a tenacious and energetic opposition against their governments. They were always filled with the sense that they were not elevated above the political struggle, but were instead obligated to decide in favour of what they regarded as right. (ibid.: 116)

By thrusting the notion of decision to the fore, these conservatives were able to assume a political standpoint. Burke, Bonald, de Maistre and Gentz sided actively against the French revolution. But 'Adam Müller finds no immediate moral pathos' in the face of it (ibid.: 122). Only an understanding of the concept of the political allowed for a clear understanding of the real meaning of notion of the state, and a host of other political notions. Engaging in endless discussion and conversation could not enhance the ability to decide between right and wrong. In the real world of politics, political activity involved making decisions, facing risks and responsibilities, and putting an end to the discussion.

> Where political activity begins, political romanticism ends, and it is no contradiction and no accident that the successors of Bonald and de Maistre, the politically active royalists of the Third Republic, derided the revolutionary ideology of the liberal bourgeoisie as romanticism with the same determination that the liberal German bourgeois – when he made the attempt to become politically active – discovered the romantic in his monarchical reactionary opponent. (Schmitt, 1919: 162; 1925b: 160)

Thus concluded the 1919 edition of *Political Romanticism*. In the 1925 edition, Schmitt appeared to be more emphatic when he associated romantic passivity with humanitarian liberalism and its negation of the political. He noted, in 1919, how Adam Müller used discussion and conversation as the model of human interaction and projected it onto the cosmic order. 'The entire world, the universe, is a conversation' (1919: 130). In 1925, he added: 'This manifests the romanticizing of liberal "discussion" and "balance", and, at the same time, the liberal origins of romanticism' (1925b:

139). Schmitt now realized that the logic of liberal parliamentarism was defined by romantic discussion and conversation (compare with Schmitt, 1923c: 36).

II

The intellectual task attempted by Schmitt immediately after the publication of *Political Romanticism* and prior to 1923, was a bid to reassert the juridical validity of notions such as sovereignty, authority and dictatorship. These non-romantic notions were needed to strengthen the state and keep it from drowning in the vortex of civil society. The rise of liberalism had depoliticized public discourse to such an extent that the real nature of the state had been obfuscated. Schmitt took the view that it was futile simply to repress political life and attempt to cover it up with the language of abstract legality. Hence, to read the Weimar constitution as a purely formal juridical document missed its true meaning. Schmitt treated the constitution as a distinguished patient invited to lie on his couch and confess to its repressed political intentions. Then its impeccable liberal façade would crumble and the real proportions of its article 48 would come to light (compare with Schwab, 1970: 37–43). This is what he achieved in the last pages of his *Die Diktatur* (Schmitt, 1921: 201–3).

According to Schmitt, the latitude of article 48 was open to interpretation, for there was the possibility of reading into it either a commissarial or an absolute dictatorial role for the *Reichspräsident*. Section 2 of article 48 bestowed unlimited powers on the *Reichspräsident* in cases when the security and order of the German state were at risk. It granted him an unlimited commission, which he could use to suspend all individual rights for an indefinite period. Eugen Schiffer, the Minister of Justice, actually admitted in the Reichstag session of 3 March 1920, that the *Reichspräsident*, by virtue of that unlimited delegation of power, could decide to spray German cities and towns with poison gas (ibid.: 201). No limitations were posited in the pursuit of any predetermined aim. Still, an unlimited empowerment to action did not entail the transfer of legislative power to the executive. That would have meant the dissolution of the entire constitutional framework. This is what Schiffer had realized when he was reminded of the views expressed by Delbruck and Count Dohna on 5 July 1919, during the forty-seventh session of the Constituent National Assembly. He had then retracted the conclusion that the unlimited empowerment of the *Reichspräsident* included the capacity to legislate and administer justice, and not just the faculty to dictate *de facto* measures. An unlimited entitlement to legislate and administer justice would configure the sovereign or revolutionary, and not merely commissarial, dictatorship of the *Reichspräsident*.[9] Schiffer's prudent reassessment of what that unlimited commission implied aimed at salvaging the intentions of the framers of the constitution.[10] But, as Schmitt was quick to note, one could also understand the Reichstag, and even the *Reichspräsident*, as 'bearers of a *pouvoir constituant*' (1921: 202). This would mean that an absolute dictatorship could be fitted within constitutional bounds. The constitution itself would become a 'precarious provisional arrangement', as was the case of the French 1814 *Charte* when its article 14 was interpreted according to the directives of the monarchical principle (ibid.). According to Schmitt, this and other contradictions within Weimar's constitutional design were not at all unexpected. They were part of an attempt to accommodate a 'combination of a sovereign and a commissarial dictatorship' (ibid.: 203).

Schmitt explained this uneasy accommodation as the confluence of two distinct elements. On the one hand, a liberal, apolitical element stressed the protection of individuals. Individuals were assured a sanctuary for their immunities and privileges. From this perspective the state ought to be seen as an intruder whose actions required close supervision. On the other

---

[9] A historical account of the distinction between sovereign or revolutionary dictatorship and commissarial dictatorship is given by Georg Schwab (1970: 30–7).

[10] Joseph Bendersky believes that here one finds proof that Schmitt displayed his fidelity to the Weimar constitution by restricting the role of the *Reichspräsident*, during situations of emergency, to a commissarial dictatorship (1983: 34–5). But the 'prudent statement' he attributes to Schmitt was only Schmitt's account of Schiffer's own prudent retraction, when reminded of the opinions of Dohna and Delbruck. By stating Schiffer's views Schmitt exposed the contradictory nature of the constitution itself, which combined inconsistent ingredients: absolute and commissarial dictatorial powers (compare with Estévez Araujo, 1989: 197–200).

hand, a political form, resting on the *pouvoir constituant* of the people, allowed for an interventionist political state. A democratic *volonté générale*, Schmitt recognized, could override and render superfluous the inalienable human rights (1921: 140), hence the need to distinguish between liberalism and the political. The existence of the state, particularly if it responded to those unlimited political demands, contradicted the spirit of liberalism, which saw in those demands a permanent threat to the freedom of individuals. The tensions and contradictions within the Weimar constitution were powerful arguments aimed by Schmitt against humanitarian liberalism. The mere existence of a state proved that the attempt to dispense with notions such as sovereignty, dictatorship and politics was futile.

Historically, the transition from feudalism to the modern state was mediated, according to Schmitt, by the concept of the papal *plenitudo potestatis* (fullness of power). The rise of this notion during the thirteenth century was a 'legitimate revolution' (ibid.: 43). Papal sovereignty within the domain of the Church overcame the characteristics of the feudal state and anticipated modern notions of sovereignty. The fourteenth-century conciliarist reaction, with John of Paris and Marsilius of Padua, contested the monarchical omnipotence claimed by the popes and defended the sovereignty of the ecclesiastical community. This view was confirmed by writers like d'Ailly and Gerson, but was also tempered by them. Gerson acknowledged the *plenitudo potestatis* of the popes and their monarchical rule, but distinguished between the substance and the exercise of juridical omnipotence (ibid.: 44).[11] In his *De Potestate Ecclesiae*, for instance, Gerson wrote that the *plenitudo potestatis*, which resided with both the Pope and the Council, was exercised by the Pope, but was substantially vested in the Council that could regulate its exercise (ibid.; compare with Gierke, 1958: 52-3, 156-7). According to Schmitt, this same distinction was made by the nineteenth-century constitutional theory of the state. Article 14 of the French *Charte* of 4 June 1914 assumed that the exercise of sovereignty was limited but that the substance of

---

[11] Schmitt relied on Johann Baptist Schwab's account of this distinction. Schwab's terminology differed slightly: 'Gerson distinguished between power in itself and power in its bearers and in relation to its exercise' (1858: 738).

state sovereignty was in principle unlimited and always in a state of latency (Schmitt, 1921: 193).[12]

The emergence of the modern sovereign state was thus the result of the triumph of the *thèse royaliste*, the assertion of absolute monarchical sovereignty over feudal seigneurial claims. The transition from monarchical absolutism to liberal constitutionalism and the rule of law presupposed that the challenge to the sovereign unity of the state posed by the aristocratic Frondes (*thèse nobiliaire*) had been met. If henceforth an individual or a group of individuals conspired to alter the public order, this was to be seen as a perfectly normal event, calculated and regulated in advance.[13] The unity of the state could not thereby be placed in jeopardy. Classical liberalism acknowledged that the juridical value of absolutism lay in having definitely secured the unity of the state that had been menaced by the Frondes. Once that unity was attained, it became necessary to limit what liberals then interpreted as royalist excesses and arbitrary rule. The notion of sovereignty could be safely dissolved or, even better, transferred from the monarch to each individual citizen. Liberalism presupposed the elimination of all social groupings, all intermediate

---

[12] Schmitt paid special attention to article 14 of the French *Charte* of 4 June 1814: 'Le Roi est le chef suprême de l'état, il commande les forces de terre et mer, déclare la guerre ... et fait les règlements et ordonnances nécessaires pour l'exécution des lois et la sûrete de l'état' (Schmitt, 1921: 193). In the light of the monarchical principle, this article was read by monarchists as an expression of the monarch's 'autorité préexistante ... supérieur et antérieur à l'acte constitutionnel' (Kaufmann, 1906: 80). In accordance with Jean Gerson's distinction between the substance and exercise of sovereignty (Schmitt, 1921: 44), Schmitt maintained that the constitutional regulations contained in the *Charte* could be said to regulate, i.e. control and limit, the exercise of the sovereign's *plenitudo potestatis* but not its substance which remained intact. Ordinarily, the power of the monarch manifested itself in a limited fashion through fixed and determined legal rules. In extraordinary circumstances, however, it could manifest itself substantively and thus move outside the normal legal channels. According to Schmitt, a recognition of the substance of the monarch's *plenitudo potestatis* rested on the distinction between law (*Recht*) and the conditions of its realization (*Rechtsverwirklichung*) (1921: 194). Certain factual conditions ought to be present for the rule of law to function as such. The sovereign decides when those conditions are present. 'The question of who decides on the juridically non-regulated case becomes the question of sovereignty' (ibid.; compare with Heller, 1927: 66).

[13] According to Schmitt, the notion of state of siege was introduced in the nineteenth century to impose legal regulation on the management of states of emergency.

associations, and the isolation of individuals. Condorcet was able to justify, according to Schmitt, switching his allegiance from monarchy to republicanism, in the following terms:

> the time is past when there existed within the state powerful groups and classes. The *associations puissantes* have vanished. While they existed, *un despotisme armé* was required to contain them. Now individuals confront a unified totality. Thus, *il faut bien peu de force pour forcer les individus a l'obeissance*. (1921: 204)[14]

Europe in 1848, Russia in 1917 and Germany in 1918 proved Condorcet to be wrong. Within the state there arose new powerful associations whose 'antagonist force' created exceptional situations. These required the development of totally new frameworks of reference. In particular, the Marxist notion of a dictatorship of the proletariat went beyond the notion of commissarial dictatorship, which could still be placed within traditional parameters. It represented an absolute dictatorship grounded on a revolutionary *pouvoir constituant*, very much the same power that was claimed by the National Convention in 1793, and which Schmitt presented as an example of absolute dictatorship. Schmitt concluded his *Die Diktatur* with the thought that the Weimar republic, like the situation of Marx and Engels as described in their address to the Communist League in 1850, had retrogressed to the state of affairs of France in 1793 and was thus compelled to employ the same measures (1921: 205).[15]

---

[14] Compare with the section in *Die Diktatur* (Schmitt, 1921: 102–12), where Schmitt distinguishes between Montesquieu's defence of the role of intermediary associations, a pluralist position for which Schmitt shows no sympathy, and Voltaire's plea for centralization. The background of this section, and the one which discusses Condorcet, lies in the dispute between two eighteenth-century French schools of historical thought, one defending *thèse nobiliaire* sustained by Fénelon and Boulainvilliers and the other the *thèse royaliste* supported by Dubos (compare with Mathiez, 1930: 99–100; Kondylis, 1986: 80–102).

[15] In their *Address to the Central Committee of the Communist League*, Marx and Engels wrote: 'As in France in 1793 so today in Germany it is the task of the really revolutionary party to carry through the strictest centralization' (Marx and Engels, 1978: 509–10). Schmitt admits that Catholic political thinkers, like Bonald and Donoso Cortés, coincide here with Marx and Engels. The revolutionary centralization of power proposed by the latter must be countered by an extreme centralization of reactionary power (compare with Schmitt, 1921: 147).

Schmitt's self-imposed task was to bring to light what lay beneath Weimar's liberal façade. It was one thing to recognize the sovereign rights of individuals and quite another to attribute broad unlimited powers to the executive authority, powers that could even configure an absolute dictatorship. If conceived as an outlet for the *pouvoir constituant*, the *Reichspräsident* would be empowered to go beyond the limits set by the constitution itself. Schmitt sought to bring out this repressed aspect of the constitution, its revolutionary stance, in order to graft onto it his own counter-revolutionary programme, a programme he thought he shared with de Maistre, Bonald and Donoso Cortés.[16] Novalis's observation that Burke wrote a revolutionary book against the revolution could be extended to the work of these thinkers. It seems to me that it should be also extended to Schmitt's *Die Diktatur*. Indeed it was by revolutionary means that Schmitt intended to contest the revolutionary claims of the proletariat. The dictatorship envisaged by Marx was an extension of the enlightened rationalist dictatorship. The conservative reaction contested the expulsion of the will from the constitutional empire of reason. For the Enlightenment there could only be an administration of things which left no room for ultimate decisions. The enlightened despot was a rational edifying dictator, who centralized control and administered the state according to plan. To Burke, de Maistre and Bonald this appeared repugnant. Schmitt notes their aversion to a priori constitutions, 'to "artifice" in political affairs, artificial constitutions based on the calculations of a clever individual, and the fabricators of constitutions and political geometricians' (1925b: 95). Only a decisionist, non-constructivist way of thinking such as theirs could fully restore and bring to life the political eminence of the *Reichspräsident*. He alone would then decide on the living exception.

---

[16] By adopting the notion of *pouvoir constituant*, Schmitt assumed a genuinely revolutionary standpoint and appears to have gone beyond the purposes envisaged by the Catholic counter-revolutionaries. According to Zweig, for example, de Maistre rejected written constitutions because he saw in them expressions of the revolutionary doctrine of the *pouvoir constituant* (1909: 5). His repudiation of anything revolutionary meant that the counter-revolution he espoused was to be understood as a non-revolutionary event. In his *Considérations sur la France*, de Maistre wrote: 'On s'est accoutumé à donner le nom de *contre-révolution* au mouvement quelconque qui doit tuer la Révolution; et parce que ce mouvement sera contraire à l'autre, on en conclut qu'il sera du même genre: il faudroit conclure tout le contraire' (1980: 159).

The notion of sovereign dictatorship developed by Schmitt in his *Die Diktatur* manifested his desire to keep alive what he saw as the foundation of the now disintegrated German monarchy, namely the monarchical principle. The French *Charte* of 4 June 1814 constituted its paradigm. The monarchical principle allowed the monarch, in virtue of his *pouvoir constituant*, to stand above the constitution, so that from the monarch's point of view the constitution appeared as something precarious and provisional. According to Schmitt, article 14 of the *Charte* meant an express manifestation of sovereignty, and not just a commissarial empowerment to deal with emergencies. The monarch was not a dictator, commissarial or sovereign. Like the sovereign dictator Schmitt modelled after him, the French monarch 'did not consider it anticonstitutional to issue decrees that violated existing laws and even the constitution itself, when he alone judged it necessary for the security of the existing order' (1921: 193). While the function of a commissarial dictator was the preservation of the constitutional order, the aim of a sovereign dictator was the elimination of 'the whole existing order' and the generation of a new constitution, the only true constitution. According to Schmitt, in such circumstances an appeal was made to the constitution that would be enacted, not to the one that actually existed (ibid.: 137). This abrogation of the existing order was to translate into the adoption of a revolutionary stance whereby a sovereign dictator could place himself above the constitution. This could be seen prima facie as a purely political move, as something completely 'devoid of juridical value' (ibid.). But what abided above and beyond a constitutional system was not purely a *Machtfrage*. A sovereign dictator appealed to a power that, though not constituted, was definitely the 'foundation' of a constitution. Here resided, according to Schmitt, 'the meaning of the *pouvoir constituant*' (ibid.). It allowed one to transcend the limits of a legal system without trespassing the limits of the juridical (*Recht*). Schmitt's sovereign dictator fell within the bounds of legitimacy and could thus borrow the juridical status that was bestowed on traditional commissarial dictators.[17]

---

[17] John McCormick claims that the primary aim of *Die Diktatur* was to present 'temporary dictatorship ... as an appropriate use of functional rationality' (1995: 12). But, in agreement with Volker Neumann, I believe that Schmitt here

In sum, Schmitt formulated the notion of sovereign dictatorship and adopted the related doctrine of the *pouvoir constituant* to highlight the perceived disharmonies within the make-up of the Weimar constitution. The framers of the constitution had attempted to accommodate a 'combination of a sovereign and a commissarial dictatorship' (ibid.: 203). By enhancing the role of the *Reichspräsident* as a bearer of *pouvoir constituant* and potential sovereign dictator, Schmitt looked to exploit those perceived disharmonies in favour of a strong state. In view of the uncertainties of the new democratic course chartered by the Weimar constitution, Schmitt's ultimate aim was to strengthen the state by reinforcing its unity. Later, in his *Verfassungslehre*, when circumstances proved more auspicious for the state, the role of the *Reichspräsident* would be de-emphasized. Even though Schmitt still recognized analogies between *Reichspräsident* and Kaiser, the former could not be presented as the Kaiser's heir 'because the juridical foundation was not the same' (1928: 292). The *Reichspräsident* was a plebiscitary figure, resting on the sovereignty of the people; the legitimacy of the Kaiser was based on the monarchical principle. If the monarchs of the Restoration period had recognized the Estates 'as representatives of the *whole* politically unified people' (1928: 52), this would constitute a contradiction. They would have surrendered the key element of their legitimacy – the monarchical principle. Equally contradictory would now be the attribution of constituent power to the *Reichspräsident* as heir to the Kaiser. The juridical foundation of the Weimar republic was not a monarchical but a democratic legitimacy.

III

In his *Political Theology*, which was published shortly after *Die Diktatur*, Schmitt explored the notion of sovereignty, so maligned

---

promoted the notions of sovereignty and sovereign dictatorship by upholding their juridical value. 'The theory of sovereignty is the theory of the successful coup d'état. Had the Kapp-putsch been successful, Kapp would have proven himself to be sovereign. In spite of this, Schmitt is nonetheless persuaded that the emanations of the will of the subject of sovereignty that stands above the Weimar constitution have a juridical character' (Neumann, 1980: 61).

by liberal thinkers and rescued from oblivion by the Catholic conservatives.

De Maistre spoke with particular fondness of sovereignty, which essentially meant decision. To him the relevance of the state rested on the fact that it provided a decision, the relevance of the Church on its rendering of the last decision that could not be appealed. Infallibility was for him the essence of the decision that cannot be appealed. (1922b: 55)

For Schmitt this meant that the foundations of a legal order rested on a transcendent source: a subject who had the will to decide politically. The capacity and willingness to make political decisions defined sovereignty. Sovereignty in turn secured the unity of the state, and the state was henceforth in the position to generate a system of law. Liberal constitutional theories, like the one developed by Kelsen, reversed this order of generation. A supreme underived basic norm, Kelsen's *Grundnorm*, grounded a legal order whose central point was the sovereign state. There was no transcendent subject of *pouvoir constituant*, no *natura naturans*, no eminent legislator to which the state's highest authority could be traced. 'The basis for the validity of a norm is only a norm' (ibid.: 19). According to Schmitt, 'Kelsen solved the problem of sovereignty by negating it ... This [was] in fact the old liberal negation of the state vis-à-vis law (*Recht*) and the disregard of the independent problem of the realization of law (*Recht*)' (1922b: 21; compare with Schmitt 1921: 194). Kelsen drew no distinction between state and law (*Recht*) and identified the state with the legal order (*Rechtsordnung*) (Schmitt, 1922c: 27).[18] He thereby eliminated authority merely at the level of definitions. It was easy for Schmitt to prove that

---

[18] A 'fear of arbitrariness' and the wish to banish exceptions fuelled Kelsen's demand for legal determinacy (Schmitt, 1922b: 41). According to Schmitt, Kelsen's belief that the Humean and Kantian critique of the notion of substance could be transferred to the theory of the state, prevented him from understanding the medieval distinction between the substance and exercise of sovereignty. In his view, the conciliarist positions defended by Gerson and Cardinal d'Ailly did not disavow the Pope's *plenitudo potestatis*. While the exercise of the *plenitudo potestatis* belonged to the Pope, its substance was vested in the Council, who regulated its *applicationem et usum* and could thus prevent arbitrariness (Schmitt, 1921: 44).

this was simply a cover-up. The living authority of the state, put to sleep by liberal enchantments, would of necessity wake up at the slightest invocation.

Schmitt recalled the year 1848, when the notion of authority was invoked by Donoso Cortés, 'one of the foremost representatives of decisionist thinking and a Catholic philosopher of the state' (1922b: 51), to justify his call for a 'dictatorship of the sword' to offset the 'dictatorship of the dagger' (Donoso Cortés, 1970: 323). Donoso realized that by then the monarchical principle had perished, that the absolutist forces, after defeating the revolt of the feudal Frondes, were incapable of resisting the challenge of an adversary who made similar absolutist demands. The *pouvoir constituant* that the kings received from God was now reclaimed by democrats, seen by Schmitt as atheists who paid their respects to a secular demiurge, the people. Royalists and democrats had fought over matters of sovereignty. At the moment of victory, democrats unfurled a banner inscribed with the sovereignty of the people. In 1848, Donoso observed how liberalism had tried to intervene, as a third party, in this battle between political theists and political atheists. 'According to Donoso Cortés, it is characteristic of bourgeois liberalism not to decide in this battle but instead to begin a discussion. He straightforwardly defines the bourgeoisie as a "discussing class", *una clase discutidora*' (Schmitt, 1922b: 59). Liberals evaded a decision and fixed their attention on endless parliamentary discussions and debates in the press. The liberal bourgeois wanted 'neither the sovereignty of the king nor that of the people' (ibid.: 60). He oscillated between the two. 'The hatred of monarchy and aristocracy drove the liberal bourgeois leftward; the fear of being dispossessed of his property, which was threatened by radical democracy and socialism, drove him in turn toward the right, to a powerful monarch whose military could protect him' (ibid.: 61). Lorenz von Stein saw this contradiction but did not attempt to resolve it. He interpreted it as the mutual interpenetration of opposites, a true *complexio oppositorum*, which could be compared to the organic complexity of life. Schmitt quoted from Stein: 'Pulsating life consists in the continuous penetration of opposite forces, and in actuality they are really opposites only when cut away from life' (ibid.: 61).

The counter-revolutionary Donoso, by contrast, was incapable of this kind of organic thinking and could not conceive of a metaphysical compromise of the sort attained by Stein. Since authority, in the traditional sense, no longer seemed effective, Donoso proposed dictatorship as an alternative. 'Dictatorship is the opposite of discussion' (Schmitt, 1922b: 63). If one agrees that the role of government is to decide, it follows that there ought to be a dictatorial moment lodged somewhere in every government. The power to decide is 'inherent in the mere existence of a governmental authority' (ibid.: 55). Schmitt, too, thought that it was a matter of indifference how political decisions were arrived at and what their content might be. What really mattered was that decisions were made without delay and without appeal. To evade decisions was to miss the essence of the political. But by remaining indifferent towards content, Schmitt turned his back on the question of legitimacy. This is what marked the revolutionary nature of his conservatism, a conservatism with intimations of existentialism. Like Donoso, he reduced 'the state to the moment of decision, to a pure decision not based on reason and discussion and not justifying itself, that is, to an absolute decision created out of nothingness' (Schmitt 1922b: 66; compare with Zweig, 1909: 2). This hard decisionism, a trait of his revolutionary conservatism, would later yield to a softer view, which would manifest his accommodation to liberalism.[19]

If Schmitt's critique of liberalism put him within the conser-

---

[19] Jean-François Kervégan fails to observe that Schmitt's early Weimar period was marked by a hard version of decisionism. He thinks that during the whole Weimar period Schmitt espoused soft decisionism. Soft decisionism, according to Kervégan, maintains that the exceptional conditions underlying the validity of a system of norms should be understood as purely circumstantial and impermanent. He believes that Schmitt's position did not harden until 1934, when he realized the 'permanence' of the exception, so that only a 'revolutionary situation' could be interpreted along the lines of this hard decisionism (1992: 45–6). As evidence, Kervégan quotes the following passage: 'the sovereign decision is an absolute beginning ... [It] arises from a normative void and a concrete disorder' (Schmitt, 1934b: 28). I agree with Kervégan that this hard decisionism cannot refer to Schmitt's late Weimar position. But it is surely strange to suggest that Schmitt's conception of decisionism would harden only after he had abandoned it in favour of institutionalism. It seems obvious to me that in this quoted text Schmitt is referring to the revolutionary position he held during his early Weimar period. After the revolutionary events of 1933, Schmitt perceived the futility, and possibly also the danger, of maintaining a hard decisionist posture. His distancing from this

vative camp, the existentialist tone of this hard decisionism was more akin to a conservative revolutionary outlook. Other conservative revolutionaries, like Spengler, also gave up any claim to legitimacy, monarchical or democratic. They saw that the preservation of traditional ways of life and past institutions was illusory. Their pessimism led them to think that their present was beyond redemption, that history had passed its verdict: Western culture was exhausted, its soul had perished. Traditional conservatives thought that the past retained its vivifying force; revolutionary conservatives, on the contrary, stoically gave up any efforts to revitalize tradition. When the cultural soul of a nation died nothing could revive it. National integrity, in the absence of spiritual forces to sustain it, ought to be affirmed by the decisive will of one single individual.

IV

The plea for a strong state was the one theme that stood out in Schmitt's early Weimar production. The theme linked this early production with his work later in Weimar and the Nazi period, and marked the conceptual ground that confirmed the continuity of his theoretical and practical interests. If the state was to maintain its strength and survive, one ought to affirm its sovereignty, authority and unity. The state could not yield to the factitious temperament of civil society. This was the site of pluralism and the dissolution of state unity.[20] In *Römische Katholizismus and Politische Form* (*Roman Catholicism and Political Form*), published in 1923, three facets articulated Schmitt's plea for a strong state. First, Schmitt attributed the modern state's difficulty in protecting its unity and authority to a complex set of attitudes

---

radical posture is confirmed by the republication, in 1933, of his *Politische Theologie*. In the preface he explicitly took a distance from the clearly hard decisionist position defended in that book. Had Kervégan incorporated into his account of Schmitt's thought a more thorough examination of the historical circumstances determining its evolution, he would have realized that in his mature Weimar production Schmitt's foremost concern was not, as he maintains, 'the refutation of liberalism in all its forms' (1992: 109), but an attempt to come to terms with its classical version, prior to its radicalization by democratic and pluralist positions (pp. 110 and 112).

[20] Schmitt adopts Treitschke's view that 'political romantics' weakened the

and ideas espoused by contemporary liberalism, and also assumed by democrats and socialists, which he designated as 'the economic point of view'. In essence, the economic point of view sought to minimize the role of the state and dissolve its separation from civil society. By eliminating the state's autonomy and diluting its authority, civil society was given a free rein spontaneously to put its own affairs in order. Second, in opposition to the economic point of view Schmitt affirmed the viewpoint of the political. The affirmation of the political secured the ultimate foundation on which rests the state's claim to authority. Third, Schmitt observed that the Catholic Church had preserved intact an awareness of the political and had kept faith in the true meaning of authority. Only the Church was in the position and had the will to affirm the political and frustrate the prevalence of pure economic thought. The Church did so by endorsing a form of rationalism opposed to the rationality of economics and technology. The Church was not the seat of irrationalism but it embodied a form of rationality, akin to juridical thinking, that was foreign to the culture that issued from the Enlightenment.

Schmitt introduced his discussion of the economic point of view by noting how 'scientific-technical methods' had become pervasive in modern thought (1923a: 18). This modern methodology had, for instance, altered our politico-theological conceptions. Traditional thought understood God's rule of the world as the personal rule of a king over the state. But nowadays God was understood impersonally as the engine that drove the cosmic machine. For the mechanical and mathematical mythology the world had turned into a 'colossal dynamo' (ibid.). Again, traditional thought was hierarchical and conceived of society as an order of ranks. But the world-view of the modern industrial entrepreneur and the industrial proletarian contained no class

---

state by their emphasis on medieval conceptions of social pluralism and communal autonomy. 'Thus everything which German political science had secured during the last century and a half, since Pufendorf had delivered our political thinkers from the yoke of the theologians, was once more put into question, and political doctrine was degraded anew to the theocratic conceptions of the Middle Ages ... "Corporation, not association" was the catchword of the political romantics, most of whom associated with the term no more than the indefinite conception of a weak state authority, limited by the power of the guilds, diets of nobles, and self-governing communes, and in spiritual matters subjected to the control of the church' (Treitschke, 1916: ii, 363–4 [modified translation]; 1886: ii, 114).

hierarchy. 'American financiers and Russian bolchevists are united in their struggle in favour of economic thought, namely the struggle against politicians and jurists' (1923a: 19). Their common concern was technology.

The economic point of view claimed to be the bearer of objective, honest and rational thought. But, according to Schmitt, its rationalism was of a limited range and was reduced 'to prescribing rules for the manipulation of matter' (ibid.: 20). Economic thought assumed, without any questions, the content of human needs, whatever they were. Effective demand was the ultimate standard of value: 'In modern economies, highly rationalized production is matched by completely irrational consumption. A wonderful rational mechanism satisfies any and every demand, always with the same earnestness and precision, whether it be demand for silk blouses or poison gas . . . ' (ibid.).

Second, in *Römischer Katholizismus* Schmitt advanced the notion of the political without defining it. This he would do later, in an article entitled 'The Concept of the Political' (1927). Now he referred to the political by contrasting it with the economic point of view. The political was linked up to juridical thought and related to ideas like representation, authority, hierarchy. Schmitt disassociated it from Machiavellian uses of power. Machiavelli reduced the political to politics, to the sphere of technical control and management of power which obeyed its own set of rules. But this kind of manœuvring was an isolated factor of political life and did not concern the political as a whole (Schmitt, 1923b: 23).

In order to counter the prevalence of economic thought, the political appeals to categories other than production and consumption. It claims 'to be more than economics' (ibid.: 24) and stakes a domain of its own, separate and independent from other spheres of culture. Certain power-wielding groups like capitalists and proletarians that have embraced economic thought could interpret that claim as hubris. Economics is an autonomous domain, separate from political, moral and any other concerns. The laws that regulate the market ought not to be tampered with by political or other non-economic considerations. What those economic groups do not realize is that their objective apolitical standpoint has a recognizable aim in view: 'getting state power into their own hands' (ibid.). This places them at the heart of a political struggle, which uses a new avenue, an economic avenue, for the acquisition of political power and authority. The political, according to Schmitt, is 'the demand for recognition and authority' (ibid.). When capitalists claim to be the original producers of wealth and claim it as their rightful possession, and when workers challenge that claim, this is not 'a struggle over production and consumption, it does not relate to mere economics, but arises from a distinct pathos of moral or juridical conviction' (ibid.: 24–5). The economic point of view does not have the indispensable moral weight to declare who really is the 'master of modern wealth' (ibid.: 25).

Schmitt had a warning for capitalists. The anonymity fostered by the economic point of view and joint-stock companies could expedite the dissolution of private property as a chance souvenir. There was some hope for them, however, as long as they recognized the need to make room for the juridical and the political. For the economic point of view they adopted incorporated 'certain juridical notions like possession and contract' (ibid.: 38). Only when the economic point of view allied itself to technological thought did it attain a radical disposition.

Third, for centuries, from Cromwell to Dostoevsky's Grand Inquisitor, the political disposition of the Catholic Church had provoked distrust and fear. 'An anti-Roman prejudice ... fed the battle against popery, jesuitry and clericalism' (ibid.: 1). In this century, however, the reproach that survived was directed most often against the Church's opportunism and elasticity, her willingness to make pacts with the devil and ally herself with a whole array of conflicting currents and groups. But this was the result, explained Schmitt, of her having 'a strong weltanschauung'. Inner strength allowed her, 'in accordance with the tactics of political struggle, to join the most diverse groupings' (ibid.: 8). The comparison that came closest to his mind was imperial universalism by which Rome, for example, could simultaneously embrace opposed standpoints: tradition and progress, conservatism and liberalism (ibid.: 9). The Church inherited this Roman *complexio oppositorum* and also adopted Polybius and the idea of a *status mixtus*. The government of the Church thus embraced without contradicting itself all state-forms, namely monarchy, aristocracy and democracy.

The essence of this *complexio oppositorum* consisted in its capacity to remove itself from the material conditions of life. This is the capacity that is bestowed on the Church by its adherence to the principle of representation and which confirms its superiority to the points of view of economics and technology. The Church, according to Schmitt, did not possess economic or military power but retained intact the pathos of authority. The essence of authority consisted in concrete personal representation. The Church represented the concrete personality of Christ and through Christ could claim to represent humankind. Representation made sense only in the realm of the juridical and the political and could not be considered as an economic category. According to Schmitt, the Church required the existence of a state, because without it there was nothing 'that could correspond to its representative disposition' (ibid.: 34). Were the economic point of view to succeed in its attempt 'thoroughly to depoliticize the state' and attain its utopian ideal of an apolitical society, the Church would still be the bearer of the political. This is the reason why only the Church could be in the position to affirm the political and frustrate the prevalence of pure economic thought. The Church did so by endorsing a form of rationalism opposed to the rationality of economics and technology. The Church was not the seat of irrationalism but embodied a form of rationality, akin to juridical thinking, that was foreign to the culture that issued from the Enlightenment.

3 • Freedom and Authority: *Complexio Oppositorum*

I

In 1923, Schmitt published *Die geistesgeschichtliche Lage des heutigen Parlamentarismus* (1923b), translated as *The Crisis of Parliamentary Democracy* (1923c). In this book (*Parlamentarismus* for short), he showed that contemporary parliamentarism had strayed away from its ideals as defined by nineteenth-century liberals like Bentham, Guizot, de Tocqueville and John Stuart Mill. As practised in the Weimar republic since 1919, parliamentarism had, according to Schmitt, 'lost its moral and intellectual foundation and only remains standing through sheer mechanical perseverance as an empty apparatus' (1923c: 21). The catalogue of ills that Schmitt collected from everyday experience included familiar themes:

> the dominance of parties, their unprofessional politics of personalities, 'the government of amateurs', continual governmental crises, the purposelessness and banality of parliamentary debate, the declining standard of parliamentary customs, the destructive method of parliamentary obstruction, the misuse of parliamentary immunities and privileges by a radical opposition which is contemptuous of parliamentarism itself, the undignified daily order of business, the poor attendance in the House (ibid.: 19).

What is surprising is that he could join the chorus of those who sought the reform of parliamentary practice, rather than the one calling for its demise. The latter was clearly audible in Germany at that point. Those familiar with *Political Romanticism* or *Political Theology* may have expected an attack on parliamentarism as a system of government. An urgent call for dictatorship and an end to fruitless discussion summarized Schmitt's revolutionary conservative programme. What one found in the preface to *Parlamentarismus* was something quite different. Schmitt now appeared to promote a reform of parliamentary life and for this he proposed an inquiry into the philosophical principles, the *ultimum sapientiae* of parliamentarism. This must have sounded suspicious to a critic of Schmitt like Richard Thoma. How could anyone believe this to be a liberal appeal to reform, coming as it did from one who had engaged until recently in an inquiry into the *ultimum sapientiae* of dictatorship and counter-revolutionary politics?

Schmitt's reform proposal assumed that contemporary parliamentarism was facing a crisis due to a betrayal of its original ideals. The institution devised by classical liberals had been defiled by the prevalence of democratic ideals. The segregation and inflection of parliament's liberal essence was mandatory. As a genuinely liberal institution, parliament ought to limit and control democracy's overwhelming leverage. By opening the door to democracy, the Weimar constitution had introduced an ambiguity which now eroded parliamentary practices and weakened the state. First, the Reichstag, like other contemporary parliaments, had ceased to be a place of rational discussion. According to Schmitt, individual deputies no longer complied with the liberal requirements of the Weimar constitution as stipulated by article 21. They could not be said to be 'bound only to their conscience' and to be free from the instructions of the particular electoral group they represented. Instead of being the 'representatives of the whole people' and 'bound by no instructions', deputies were acting as popular agents and commissaries, in accordance with well-established democratic demands. Second, the Reichstag had ceased to be, if it ever was, open to public investigation and scrutiny. Article 29 of the constitution required that its deliberations be public, but its discussions were surrounded by secrecy and only the results yielded by voting were publicly announced. Furthermore, the parliamentary commission had become a place for secret party deals whose content the public ignored. The *arcana imperii* of absolutist times were fully revived (compare with Schmitt, 1928: 318–19).

Schmitt's aim was to separate the parliamentary institution from its democratic ties. Parliaments, if allowed to function in a genuinely representative manner, should not have to yield to democratic pressures. On the contrary, much like the Catholic Church, parliamentarism could not be said to constitute a specific political form or a specific form of state (compare with Schmitt,

1923a: 10). Indifference to the political as such allowed parliamentarism to remain open to different political forms (compare with Schmitt, 1928: 305). The historical development of parliamentarism had successfully incorporated monarchical, aristocratic and democratic elements, without identifying itself with any of them. Precisely because parliaments could not be said to constitute specific political forms, they functioned as open systems that used and mixed diverse political forms. According to Schmitt, parliamentarism owed its current problems to the ascendancy of democracy. By displacing the competing monarchical and aristocratic elements, democracy acquired a disproportionate influence, disrupting the delicate balance presupposed by the parliamentary system. In his earlier works, Schmitt thoroughly identified liberal parliamentarism and democratic legitimacy. Since 1848, democratic legitimacy had supplanted the monarchical principle, which until then had secured the unity of the state. The nineteenth-century liberal-democratic *rapprochement* was interpreted by Schmitt as an irreversible pluralist trend which inevitably led to the demise of the state. The identification of liberalism and democracy precluded any possibility of securing a role for the state as guarantor of political unity. It was therefore natural that Schmitt would rely, in *Die Diktatur* and *Politische Theologie*, on a counter-revolutionary dictatorship as the only means to guard the political unity of a nation and sustain the dual onslaught arising from humanitarian liberalism and atheist democracy.

Schmitt's critics have not regarded his *Parlamentarismus* as expressing a different view from the one he defended in his earlier Weimar works. It seems to me, however, that *Parlamentarismus* marked a turning-point in the development of his thought. It was here that Schmitt came to realize the genuinely apolitical nature of liberalism. He also now understood that its pluralist demands need not be conjoined with the democratic ideals. Liberalism was not a *political* imperative and so its pluralist demands could be confined to the *social* sphere. This allowed for the configuration of a liberal civil society which shunned political activity, and at the same time the formation of a state that monopolized the political and bore its different forms. In his *Parlamentarismus*, parliaments appeared to Schmitt as the vehicle that could sustain a balanced combination of the three political forms he distinguished. He saw here an opportunity to bolster the receding monarchical and aristocratic forms, and balance them against the rising democratic form.

When Schmitt adopted his early radical stance, his immediate concern was the need to counter the challenge of revolutionary Marxism. Europe faced 1848 all over again. Against the dictatorship of the dagger feared by Donoso Cortés, he espoused a dictatorship of the sword (compare with Beneyto, 1993: 80). Since the monarchical legitimacy that supported the German Reich had ceased to exist, and Schmitt had not yet come to terms with democratic legitimacy, there was only room for an authoritarian dictatorship. Schmitt's paramount concern was the preservation of the unity of the state, most clearly upheld by those who adhered to the monarchical principle. The monarchomachists, in attacking that principle, became the forerunners of liberalism, the rule of law and parliamentarism. The very existence of the state had been compromised by this Fronde-like attack on its unity. After the German revolution of 1918–19, the monarchical principle could no longer be revived. A dictatorial regime that suspended or eliminated constitutionalism and the separation of powers seemed to Schmitt, at that time, to be the only way to subdue liberalism and democracy.

In his *Parlamentarismus*, accommodation with liberalism became possible only after Schmitt came to realize that it was not a political form. This meant that liberalism ought not to be identified with democracy, and by extension with neither monarchy nor aristocracy, the other state forms envisaged by Schmitt. Liberalism's only interest was the limitation of the political in whatever shape or form. Schmitt saw here the possibility of using liberalism as a foil for democracy. This was precisely the virtue that classical liberalism had seen in parliamentarism. By allowing the balanced manifestation of all three political forms, parliamentarism relativized and harmonized their discordant claims. Parliamentarism had been an effective tool against absolute monarchy. It should now also serve to discipline absolute democracy. According to Schmitt, the experience of Weimar parliamentarism operated under the assumption that liberalism was identical with democracy. This one-sided influence of democracy on parliamentarism was to blame for its current problems. What were now required were ways to restore parliamentarism to its classical form, which did not exclude what was politically necessary to preserve the unity of the state. Schmitt acknowledged that discussion was the heart of parliamentarism, and that discussion rested on two fundamental principles: openness and balance of powers. His discussion of parliamentarism focuses on the notion of balance of powers, for in it he saw an open path leading to a discussion of the political.

It should come as no surprise that the most interesting arguments advanced by Schmitt concern the notion of balance of state activities and institutions. The recognition of such a balance meant that in a true parliamentary regime parliament proper was reduced to legislative functions and could not assume executive functions.

> That parliament assumes the role of the legislative in the division of powers and is limited to that role makes the rationalism which is at the heart of the theory of a balance of powers rather *relative* and, as will now be shown, it distinguished this system from the *absolute* rationalism of the Enlightenment. (Schmitt, 1923c: 39; my emphasis)

This relative or moderate rationalism mentioned by Schmitt is essential to the notion of balance of powers. It implies that parliament is only 'a part of the state's functions, one part that is set against the others (executive and courts)' (ibid.: 40). The first theories of division and balance of power were developed in England and were later adopted on continental Europe. The notion that a 'constitution is identical with division of power' was a key element of that legacy; it implied that parliament was an essentially legislative and not executive organ. According to Schmitt, this was a notion 'scarcely understood' in his own days (ibid.: 41). Though he refers to dictatorship as the institution that suspends the divisions of powers, one may surmise that it was democracy that he blamed for this.

The relative rationalism of the balance theory sought to moderate the claims of reason. Prior to it, monarchomachists like Beza and the *Vindiciae* of Junius Brutus espoused a radical version of rationalism and replaced 'the concrete person of the king with an impersonal authority and a universal reason' (ibid.: 42). Reason, and not the will, constituted for them the essence of law. Absolute rationalism permitted no compromise between the rational and the irrational aspects of governance. As forerunners of liberalism and the rationalism of the French Enlightenment, monarchomachists employed the notion of rule of law (or *Rechtsstaat*) to supersede the rule of monarchs who issue concrete commands.

> The whole theory of the *Rechtsstaat* rests on the contrast between law that is general and already promulgated, universally binding without exception, and valid in principle for all times, and a personal order which varies from case to case according to particular concrete circumstances. (Schmitt, 1923c: 42)

The American tradition adhered to this view. Schmitt quotes the well-known statement by John Marshall: 'the government of the United States of America can be designated with particular emphasis as a government of laws in contrast to a government of men' (ibid.). A similar view was expressed by Montesquieu, who, in an effort to eliminate judicial discretion, declared that the judge can only be 'la bouche qui prononce les paroles de la loi' (Hayek, 1960: 167). Condorcet took absolute rationalism a step further and applied it to the executive. No state activity should escape the rule of law. Executive functions were to be assimilated without residue by the legislative functions. His radicalism objected to the American system of checks and balances which enforced legislation and 'where one must sacrifice "rational legislation" to the prejudices and stupidity of individual peoples' (ibid.: 46).

An absolutist like Hobbes, Schmitt also conceived laws as 'addressed to all the Subjects in general' (ibid.: 43; compare with Hobbes, 1968: 312). But for him law was command not counsel. We obey a law due to the will of the lawgiver and not for any other reason. His dictum *autoritas, non veritas facit legem*[1]

---

[1] Hobbes's spelling and punctuation differ slightly. He writes: '*authoritas, non veritas, facit legem*' (Hobbes, 1841: 202). The whole sentence reads: 'Doctrinae quidem verae esse possunt; sed authoritas, non veritas, facit legem.' The passage in the original English version of the *Leviathan* reads as follows: 'The Authority of writers, without the Authority of the Common-wealth, maketh not their opinions Law, be they never so true. That which I have written in this Treatise, concerning the Morall Vertues, and of their necessity, for the procuring, and maintaining peace, though it bee evident Truth, is not therefore presently Law ...' (Hobbes, 1968: 322–3).

manifested an extreme voluntarism. A division between the legislative and executive functions of the state was to be rejected (compare with Schmitt, 1928: 140). All legislative functions collapsed into the executive; legislation became immediate execution.

Between monarchomachists and absolute rationalists like Condorcet, and the authoritarian absolutism of Hobbes, Schmitt found a middle ground in the balance theory of thinkers like Bolingbroke. Bolingbroke distinguished between 'government by constitution' and 'government by will' (Schmitt, 1923c: 43), and also between the notions of constitution and government. The constitution embodied the rational aspects of the state and all that falls under the general and abstract rule of law. This was balanced by a recognition that government oversaw concrete political issues that 'change with time and circumstances' (ibid.: 44). The same 'balance between the rational and the irrational' was expressed by Alexander Hamilton in *The Federalist No. 70*:

> legislation is deliberation and therefore must be made by a large assembly, while decision making and protection of state secrets belong to the executive ... Different opinions are useful and necessary in the legislative but not in the executive, where especially in times of war and disturbance action must be energetic; to this belongs a unity of decision. (ibid.: 45)

Schmitt, then, appeared to be willing to consider a balance of powers within the state. His discussion of the 'relative rationalism' of classical liberal proposals was consistent with his demand for the preservation and enhancement of the unity of the state. There are two indications that this was so. First, he saw that the 'relative rationalism' of the balance theory opened channels for the manifestation of the irrational, for the possibility of decisive action. The legislative power could carry out its business in accordance with liberal normativism and the rule of law, but the executive power, an embodiment of 'relative rationalism', was now able at any time to adopt a decisionist style of action and assume the task of deciding what needed to be done. Secondly, the tradition of liberalism in Germany had devised an organic solution to this marriage of convenience, by wrapping 'relative rationalism' with historical thought. Schmitt thus pointed in

Hegel's direction. With a few exceptions, Schmittian scholars have yet fully to consider the impact of Hegel's political thought on Schmitt. The Hegelian system incorporated a form of parliamentarism which did not weaken the unity of the state. The apex of the Hegel's state was occupied by a prince who retained a fully representative role. In virtue of that role he was able to secure the unity of the state, without encroaching on civil society and endangering its pluralist demands. I have argued elsewhere in favour of interpreting Hegel as a conservative liberal thinker (Cristi, 1984 and 1989). Here I wish to argue that Schmitt advocated a conservative revolutionary outlook in his early works, but in 1923 he began to accommodate his conservative posture, which remained essentially unchanged, to the liberal disposition of the Weimar constitution.

For Schmitt the perfect realization of the idea of constitutional parliamentarism took effect in nineteenth-century France during the reign of Louis-Philippe. For a while, his constitutional monarchy, standing at the midpoint between absolute monarchy and absolute democracy, proved perfectly suited to protect the historical interests of the bourgeoisie. Parliamentary discussion relativized the opposed social interests of its adversaries – monarchists and democrats – and set the stage for political compromises. But Schmitt was also ready to acknowledge the limits of constitutional parliamentarism. He noted how the revolutions of 1848 marked the end of Louis-Philippe's parliamentary experiment. Faced with that failure, the response of both monarchical and democratic adversaries of parliamentary discussion was to look to dictatorship. 'Both adversaries responded with an elimination of balance, with immediacy and apodeictic certainty, i.e. with dictatorship' (Schmitt, 1923c: 52).

According to Schmitt, the apodeictic certainty of dictatorship could be of two kinds: rational or irrational. The tradition of rational dictatorship could be traced back to the Enlightenment's educational dictatorship, which he saw embodied by 'philosophical Jacobinism' (ibid.). This tradition came to an end with Napoleon's defeat but was revitalized by Marxist socialism. Socialism may have evolved away from utopianism and declared itself to be a scientific doctrine, but this did not mean that it had renounced dictatorship. Schmitt observed how, since the end of the First World War, radical socialists and anarchists had retrieved utopian aspirations 'so that socialism [could] regain its courage for dictatorship' (ibid.). This did not mean that only utopian socialism had dictatorial possibilities open to it. Dictatorship, according to Schmitt, was also available to scientific socialism.

The dictatorial possibilities of scientific socialism lay in the Hegelian construction of history adopted by Marx. According to Schmitt, 'in order to define the core of Marx's argument and its specific concept of dictatorship, one must begin [by establishing a connection with] Hegel's dialectic of history' (ibid.: 55). Before this could be done one difficulty had to be cleared away. Dictatorship appeared to be a constrained undialectical interruption of an organic historical evolution: 'development and dictatorship seem to be mutually exclusive' (ibid.: 56). By eliminating the moment of decision, development robbed dictatorship of its essential characteristic. Hegelian dialectics encompassed everything, leaving no room for the unexpected and the exceptional.

> The either/or of moral decision, the decisive and deciding disjunction, has no place in this system. Even the *diktat* of a dictator becomes a moment in the discussion and in the undisturbed development as it moves further. Just as everything else, the *diktat* too will be assimilated by the peristalsis of the world spirit. (Ibid.)

In contrast to Fichte's voluntarism, Hegel maintained a contemplative stance. The Hegelian self was not a Fichtean demiurge giving meaning and value to a God-forsaken world. Still, individuals as such could only be defined by their conscious human actions, by which they removed themselves from their natural finitude and rose to a higher sphere of self-consciousness. By this sort of awareness, individuals avoided being entrapped 'in the accidents and obstinations of the empirical' and left behind by the impetus of history. Schmitt acknowledged that the contemplative side of Hegel's philosophy left no room for dictatorship. But there was another side to it, one whose 'practical consequence [could] lead to a rational dictatorship' (ibid.: 58). This happened whenever Hegel's philosophy was 'taken seriously by active people' (ibid.: 57). In the concrete circumstances of political life, there would always be individuals who evinced a 'higher consciousness' and who, acting as bearers of that historical impetus, would shrug off the resistance of narrow-mindedness (ibid.). Echoing a Rousseauan theme, Schmitt admitted that the task of an avant-garde of higher individuals was to enforce freedom. This is what Schmitt meant by the notion of educational dictatorship, which he imputed to Hegel. In Schmitt's view, 'the Weltgeist only manifests itself in a few minds at any stage of its development' (ibid.: 58). An avant-garde that claimed a right to action on the basis of its superior rational knowledge was unavoidable: 'The world-historical personality – Theseus, Caesar, Napoleon – is an instrument of the *Weltgeist*; his *diktat* rests upon his position in the historical moment. The world soul that Hegel saw riding in Jena in 1806 was a soldier, not a Hegelian' (ibid.).

The dictatorial tendencies present in scientific socialism were not adventitious but had deep roots in Hegel's philosophy. On this depended the possibility of interpreting Marx's dictatorship of the proletariat as an educational, rationalist dictatorship. But Schmitt's interpretation of Marxism moved far beyond this view. According to Schmitt, the core of Marxism was to be found not in a scientific conception of history but in a peculiar view of history as the history of class struggle. The *Communist Manifesto* contained the true novelty of Marx's conception, 'the systematic concentration of class struggle into a single, final struggle of human history' (ibid.: 59). A single and final contradiction simplified the conflict and at the same time intensified it. In this conflict the bourgeois was 'not to be educated, but eliminated' (ibid.: 64). This was a concrete struggle, with concrete actors, and only a 'philosophy of concrete life' could furnish the needed weapons. Not a rationalist, but an irrationalist impulse now became the driving force behind socialism. Its standard-bearer was no longer the democrat Kautsky, but Lenin and Trotsky. This new concrete philosophy of life, the 'theory of the direct use of force' or 'theory of immediate action', stood 'in opposition to the absolute rationalism of an educational dictatorship and to the relative rationalism of the division of powers'. Schmitt concludes: 'As Trotsky justly reminded the democrat Kautsky, the awareness of relative truths never gives one the courage to use force and to spill blood' (ibid.).

Schmitt reiterated his view that Marxism still retained 'the possibility of a rationalist dictatorship' (ibid.: 65), but in adopting a theory of direct action it did so on the basis of an irrationalist philosophy. Marxism was only one of the tendencies that constituted the argumentative capital of Bolshevism. Its irrationalist motive for the use of force stemmed from its anarcho-syndicalist tendency. To explore the sense of this irrationalist philosophy, Schmitt discussed Georges Sorel's *Réflexions sur la violence* (1906). Sorel's irrationalism could be traced back to the anarchism of Proudhon and Bakunin. Their struggle against God and the authority of the central state took (in Bakunin) the form of a struggle against reason and scientific education. Intellectual knowledge grasped only generalities and abstractions and 'sacrifices individual fullness on the altar of its abstraction' (Schmitt, 1923c: 67). Sorel's theory of myth brought together Bakunin's anti-intellectualism and Bergson's philosophy of life. As a theory of direct action, it was opposed to absolute rationalism and particularly to the relative rationalism of parliamentarism. 'From the perspective of this philosophy, the bourgeois ideal of peaceful agreement, which all find profitable and which generates good business, becomes a monstrosity of cowardly intellectualism' (ibid.: 69). Sorel prompted Schmitt to recall the year 1848, when parliamentarism and its principles were assailed by two intransigent and extreme political adversaries that employed the same decisionist arguments: Donoso Cortés on the conservative side, Proudhon on the anarcho-syndicalist side. 'Both demanded a decision' and both announced the great last battle (ibid.). Neither accepted the possibility of mediation and both refused to relativize their antitheses. Like Donoso and Proudhon, Sorel too saw a greater danger in 'professional politics and participation in parliamentary business' (ibid.: 71).

After siding with de Maistre and Donoso Cortés and advocating their conservative revolutionary outlook, Schmitt began, in his *Parlamentarismus,* to accommodate his conservative posture to the liberal disposition of the Weimar constitution. I have argued in favour of this view in this chapter, but accommodation does not imply that he ever intended to give up his early revolutionary stance. This comes across conclusively in the last chapter of *Parlamentarismus* when Schmitt referred to the irrationalist theories of the direct use of force. Donoso Cortés had said in

1849: 'Cuando la legalidad basta, la legalidad; cuando no basta, la dictadura' (1970: 306). Schmitt appeared to be saying something similar in 1923 – when parliamentarism suffices, parliamentarism; when it does not suffice, dictatorship (1923c: 76). The theories of the direct use of force were other alternatives, and one of them, the dictatorship of the proletariat, appeared to him to be the most fearsome. Schmitt had learnt from Donoso to identify and look resolutely at his enemy. 'In order to gain a free line of fire, with a sweep of the hand, they [Donoso and Schmitt] wave[d] aside ... the neutral who linger[ed] in the middle, interrupting the view of the enemy' (Strauss, 1932: 106). This 'neutral' was parliamentarism.

II

How did Schmitt manage to liberalize a conservative posture that in many respects remained substantially unaltered? What facilitated his new, more pliant understanding of liberalism? It seems to me that the answer to these questions lies in his transformed view of Catholicism. Schmitt realized, at one point, that the universalism that the Church inherited from Roman imperialism allowed it to accommodate its solemn course through history in the face of continually changing circumstances. Retaining its own constitution unaltered, it adapted to various state and government forms. In his essay, *Römischer Katholizismus und politische Form*, the rigidity and uncompromising attitude of the counter-revolutionary Catholics gave way to a more nuanced position. Schmitt appeared no longer concerned with the Church's infallibility or its authoritarian inflexibility. On the contrary, he deflected the charge made by those who accused the Church of 'unlimited opportunism' and celebrated its 'marvellous elasticity' (1923a: 6). Adopting a quasi-romantic attitude, he praised a millennial institution allied to the most diverse governments, absolutist as well as anti-monarchist.[2] The Church supported, and in turn denounced, liberals and democrats, republicans and

---

[2] As a *complexio oppositorum*, the Church has exhibited, in the course of its history, 'astonishing adaptation' and 'stiff intransigence', and the capacity for 'manly resistance' and 'feminine flexibility' (Schmitt, 1923a: 10).

legitimists, and even socialists. Tocqueville, a liberal who showed a sympathy for democracy, and Donoso Cortés, a 'rigorous philosopher of authoritarian dictatorship' (Schmitt, 1923a: 10), were both devout Catholics. 'With every change in the political situation, all principles would seem to change, except one, that of the power of Catholicism' (ibid.: 7). All political forms are mere forms which the power of Catholicism could turn to its own purposes and advantages. The Church inherited Rome's 'political universalism' (ibid.: 8). This all-embracing attitude responded to the requirements of an imperial stance. 'Every imperialism that is something more than mere chauvinism, embraces contradictions: conservatism and liberalism, tradition and progress, and even militarism and pacifism' (ibid.: 9). This was not an accommodation demanded by inner weakness. The Church's universalism offended many national sensibilities. An Irishman, his patriotism bitterly hurt, complained: Ireland is but 'a pinch of snuff in the Roman snuff-box'. Or preferably, as Schmitt was quick to add, 'a chicken the prelate would drop into the cauldron which he was boiling for the cosmopolitan restaurant' (ibid.).

This prompted Schmitt to assert that the Church ought to be defined as a *complexio oppositorum*. The Church boasted that it 'comprises every form of state and government' (ibid.: 10). Its theology was not restrictively either–or in nature, but dialectical (ibid.: 11). Breaking with Donoso's political theology, which espoused the absolute corruption of human nature, Schmitt now admitted that the Council of Trent spoke only of 'a wounding, a weakening or clouding of human nature, and thus admits a practical application which allows for some qualification and accommodation' (ibid.; compare with 1922b: 57). The Church's *complexio oppositorum* thus incorporated a boundless adaptability and 'a most precise dogmatism and a will to decide, as the doctrine of pontifical infallibility clearly demonstrated' (ibid.: 12). The Church was thus a model of balance and moderation. It could allow the widest and most varied expression of ideas and forms, since it was assured of an absolute unity at its apex. Precisely because it conservatively maintained the political unity of a state, it could tolerate a plurality of forms of government.

Before he reconciled himself with liberalism in his *Parlamentarismus*, Schmitt first gently steered Catholicism in the same direction. In doing so he disclosed his political motivations. Being a juridically minded intellectual, he was always more predisposed to think in polemical rather than dogmatic terms. This manner of thinking determined his train of thought in this case. At the conclusion of *Römischer Katholizismus* Schmitt identified the main object of his polemic. Western civilization has endured, since the nineteenth century, the menace of two barbaric forces: the Marxist proletariat and the Russian people. It could be said that there was more of Christianity 'in the Russian hate for Western-European culture than in liberalism or in German Marxism' (Schmitt, 1923a: 52). One might argue that 'great Catholics saw liberalism as a far worse enemy' (ibid.). One could even maintain that the Church, as a *complexio oppositorum*, was not required to decide this question, that 'she will be the *complexio* of all that survives' (ibid.). Still, Schmitt urged the Church to make a decision, to take a stand in favour of Western European culture. Just as it sided with the counter-revolution in the nineteenth century and 'was more akin to Mazzini than to the atheistic socialism of Bakunin' (ibid.: 53), it should now support liberalism in the name of West European civilization. Just as the all-encompassing universalism of Catholicism was embodied in concrete historical allegiances, so too the abstract humanitarianism of liberalism may be held as the emblem of a particular tradition. Schmitt's accommodation with liberalism was thus brokered by his perception of the Church's flexible conservatism.

III

Evidence for Schmitt's explicit endorsement of the Weimar constitutional regime is to be found in a presentation he made at the first conference of the Association of German Constitutional Lawyers held at Jena on 14–15 April 1924 (Schmitt, 1924; compare with Bendersky, 1983: 74). The title of his presentation was 'Die Diktatur des Reichspräsidenten nach Artikel 48 der Weimarer Verfassung' ('The Dictatorship of the *Reichspräsident* according to Article 48 of the Weimar Constitution'). Here Schmitt clearly disassociated the *Reichspräsident*, as defined by the Weimar constitution, from the sovereign prince of the monarchical principle. It was characteristic of a regime defined by the monarchical principle that 'even when a constitution limited state functions and competences, still at a certain point there was at least the possibility to allow the full undivided power of the state to come forth' (1924: 236). Alongside the constitutional division of powers, the monarchical principle determined that there would always be an exceptional power latent in the state, a power that could 'never be encompassed without residue by the constitutional rules' (ibid.).³ The Prussian monarchical constitution acknowledged the *plenitudo potestatis* of the monarchs, by means of which they could modify by decree not only ordinary laws but also the constitution. This is what defined them as a sovereigns.⁴ According to Schmitt, the *Reichspräsident*, by contrast, could not be understood as a sovereign in the sense required by the monarchical principle. His dictatorship was necessarily commissarial 'by the mere circumstance that the constitution had come into effect' (ibid.: 241). This was in accordance with what he had maintained a few pages earlier, namely that constitution and sovereign dictatorship were incompatible notions.⁵

Schmitt's conception of the *Reichspräsident* undoubtedly retained a decisionist temper. The fact that he no longer invested the *Reichspräsident* with *pouvoir constituant*, by means of which the existing constitution could be legitimately abrogated and a new one promulgated, did not prevent a presidential decision to suspend it and rule by decree. On the contrary, Schmitt would devote much of his intellectual energies to enhancing and exploiting the possibilities that article 48 opened for dictatorial rule. But

---

³ As an example of a constitutional recognition of the monarch's power to set aside the whole constitution, as something 'provisional and precarious', when the security of the state is at risk, Schmitt mentions the French *Charte* of 4 June 1814 (compare with Schmitt, 1922: 202).

⁴ In the last analysis, this meant that the notions of sovereign dictatorship and constitution were incompatible. According to Schmitt, if the notion of sovereign dictatorship were given constitutional recognition, it would turn the constitution into something wholly 'provisional' and 'precarious' (1924: 238).

⁵ But then Schmitt added: 'as a matter of fact, and not in accordance with its juridical basis, [the dictatorship of the *Reichspräsident*] operates as a remnant of the National Assembly's sovereign dictatorship' (1924: 241). This last observation, which clashed with what he had maintained earlier (ibid.: 238; compare with Heller, 1927: 68 n. 1), reinforces the continuity thesis. The many shifts and accommodations suffered by his thought during the Weimar years and beyond, must be placed against a unified backdrop: his metaphysical conception of substance (compare with chapter 6 below).

side by side with this stress on a softer version of decisionism, Schmitt would also acknowledge the role of the rule of law. In Chapter 6, I will examine how his *Verfassungslehre* of 1928 threads these decisionist and normativist strands into a coherent system. This would mark the height of his *rapprochement* to liberalism. In 1934, in a retrospective on the development of modern juridical thought, Schmitt would provide the rudiments of an explanation of his coming to terms with the liberal *Rechtsstaat*. He viewed changes in juridical conceptions as dependent on evolving historical conditions. Just as Hobbes's decisionism was tied to the rise of the absolute state in the seventeenth century, and normativism reflected the rationalism of the eighteenth century, the intertwining of decisionism and normativism was connected to a specific condition – 'the dualist relation between state and civil society' peculiar to the nineteenth century (Schmitt, 1934b: 66). This historical condition determined 'a political unity that alternated between legality and states of exception' (ibid.). His *Verfassungslehre* systematically reproduced that alternation.

This conservative accommodation to the liberal institutions and the ruling constitutional parliamentarism of the Weimar republic had affinities with Hegel's conservative liberalism.[6] Like Hegel, Schmitt bolstered the authority of a conservative state, which maintained a monopoly of politics, while attempting to preserve the autonomy of civil society. The freedom of individuals, exercised in the context of an unalloyed market economy, demanded a strong, autonomous state. This reconciliation of freedom and authority, this *complexio oppositorum*, was not a Hegelian characteristic. It can be viewed as a persistent German trademark, one that 'has been traced back to Luther and up to Hitler' (Krieger, 1957: p. ix). In any case, Schmitt's *rapprochement* to the Weimar system was not without caveats. So long as the possibility of a socialist dictatorship of the proletariat remained open, and Schmitt saw this as intrinsic to Marxism, he

---

[6] For a characterization of Hegel's political philosophy as conservative liberal, compare with Cristi, 1989. Johann Baptist Müller uses this description to refer to a number of thinkers, like Burke and Tocqueville, whose work synthesizes liberal and conservative political principles (Müller, 1982). Similarly, Hannes Gissurarson uses it to describe Hayek's economic and political philosophy (Gissurarson, 1987).

would retain his option for an opposing dictatorship. With this insurance policy in his back pocket, as a frank warning to his adversaries, he felt encouraged to affirm an intellectual allegiance to Weimar's constitutional system. In 1926, he would express this attitude of acceptance in no uncertain terms. 'Today the revolutionary situation that lasted between November 1918 and February 1919 is over; the sovereign dictatorship of a constituent national assembly no longer exists. For seven years now the Weimar constitution has been valid in Germany' (Schmitt, 1926: 27). Like Gentz, as we saw in the previous chapter, he, too, could assume a more liberal attitude as long as he could free himself from the fear of revolution.

4 • Hegel contra Schmitt

In his struggle against Weimar, Geneva and Versailles, Carl Schmitt enlisted a number of political thinkers as confederates – Machiavelli, Hobbes, de Maistre, Bonald, Donoso Cortés, Constant and Hegel. The legitimacy of this claim has gone unchallenged except in the case of Hegel. Many have felt that his liberal credentials, most clearly manifested in his conception of civil society and his allegiance to the reformist policies espoused in Prussia by Stein, Hardemberg and Humboldt, were compromised by Schmitt, who appears to have opposed liberalism and contributed to the demise of the Weimar republic. Schmitt's attempt to tie Hegel's views to the political outlook of Hobbes and de Maistre also discredited his speculative stance. Jean-François Kervégan, for example, seeks to extricate Hegel from this troubling association and attempts both to defend Hegel's liberalism and confirm the philosophical nature of his argument (1992). Without diminishing Schmitt's Hegelian debt he attempts to show that Schmitt distorted Hegel's liberalism by disregarding the dialectical intent of his philosophy. In the process, Kervégan aims to preserve the Hegelian legacy from any contamination that might accrue to it from association with Schmitt.[1]

According to Kervégan, Schmitt's thought was unified by a single aim: the refutation of liberalism in all its manifestations. Decisionism was Schmitt's preferred weapon for this task. It would be a mistake to see this simply as a juridical response to the

---

[1] A cursory way to dismiss Schmitt's debt to Hegel consists in pointing out a reference in *Staat, Bewegung und Volk*. Schmitt there states, in connection with Hitler's rise to the Chancellorship on 30 January 1933: 'Accordingly one can say that on this day Hegel died' (1933f: 32). Marcuse, for instance, stops here and does not read any further (1967: 275 n. 79; compare with Ottmann, 1977: 222 n. 451). But the continuation of the text speaks for itself: 'This does not mean that the great work of this German political philosopher has lost its significance and that the idea of a political leadership that transcends the egoism of social interests should be abandoned. What is truly German and perennial of the powerful spiritual construction erected by Hegel, continues to be valuable for the new formation' (Schmitt, 1933f: 32).

legal positivism that dominated German jurisprudence at the time. Decisionism defined the limits of a purely juridical standpoint by positively affirming metaphysics and politics as the substantive core of legality. Questions related to legality were to be responded to in terms of their legitimacy, which in turn opened the way to meta-juridical concerns.

Kervégan sees decisionism as a leitmotif in Schmitt's thought. Schmitt opposed decisionism to normativism, which emphasized the rule of generality and pure rationality, and postulated the autonomy of legal systems. Normativism, as a manifestation of the liberal outlook, resulted from the historical struggles engaged in by the bourgeoisie against the arbitrariness and unpredictability of absolutist rule. Clear rules, known in advance by all members of society, set limits to the state and contained its political expansion. Kervégan quotes this definition of decisionism by Schmitt: 'Sovereign decision is an absolute beginning, and the beginning (in the sense of ἀρχή) is no other thing than sovereign decision. It arises from a normative void and a concrete disorder' (1934b: 28; compare with Kervégan, 1992: 44). The political and metaphysical resonances of this text are clearly audible. Whereas the expression 'sovereign decision' pointed in the direction of the political, the expressions 'absolute beginning' and 'ἀρχή' had metaphysical ancestries. Schmitt called this form of decisionism 'pure and genuine decisionism' (1934b: 28). Kervégan argues that Schmitt never really espoused this form of pure decisionism and shied away, during the Weimar period particularly, from its revolutionary implications (1992: 45). In his view, Schmitt adopted a softer view that could be combined with the principles of the liberal *Rechtsstaat* (ibid.: 40 and 58).

The problem with normativism, according to Schmitt, was its one-sidedness. By bracketing the transcendental assumptions of legitimacy on which it rested, normativism separated the formal aspect of laws from their content and moved into positivism. What Schmitt found most troublesome was the downplaying of politics and the emphasis given to formalist rule of law or *Rechtsstaat*. Kervégan notes the distinction Schmitt drew between the political and the state, a distinction which ensued from the obliteration of the state's autonomy. The infiltration of civil society's pluralism within the ambit of the state weakened its unity and its monopoly over the political. As a result, the *Rechtsstaat*, initially conceived as a form of abstract generality and aimed at imposing strict limits on state prerogative, evolved into a democratic *Gesetzesstaat* or legislative state, which covered all four corners of society with its comprehensive legislation. Unavoidably, politics spilled over into civil society instead of being contained within the state. The unintended consequence of normativism and parliamentary government was the rise of the total state. According to Kervégan, the notion of the total state referred to a complex reality: it signified simultaneously the surpassing of traditional forms of the state and the omnilateral politicization of human existence; it was both a weak state and a strong state (ibid.: 85). While Schmitt rejected a *quantitatively* total state that capitulated to the welfare demands of civil society and politicized all social affairs, he espoused a *qualitatively* total state. This implied an authoritarian reinforcement of the state by means of plebiscites instead of classical electoral methods, and the elimination of parliamentary government (ibid.: 87–8).

An understanding of the principle of decisionism is mediated by an understanding of the nature of liberalism (ibid.: 127). In agreement with Strauss and Löwith, Kervégan thinks that Schmitt's decisionism is determined by what it negates. Decisionism was merely liberalism reversed and could claim neither substantive weight of its own nor a positive foundation, whether metaphysical, ethical or theological. It was conceptually dependent on liberalism, and could only attain a determinate profile as its negation. Schmitt could have avoided this objection by defining decisionism in a radically nihilist manner. This was precisely what he did in 1934, when he declared that a sovereign decision had an 'absolute beginning' and arose from a 'normative void and a concrete disorder' (ibid.: 128). Kervégan agrees that this involves a radically nihilist posture, but he sees at the same time that this was not Schmitt's definite stand, that Schmitt hesitated: his nihilism 'remains confined within certain limits' (ibid.: 129). Schmitt was torn between forsaking all foundations or merely those of a normativist kind. This softer view of decisionism surfaces when Kervégan examines it apart from any comparison. But when he contrasts Schmitt with Hegel that nuanced view dissipates. Kervégan sees no hesitation in Schmitt, who is now said to have espoused a pure or hard decisionism that radically excluded any positive foundation and was made to spring from a normative void. He has cleared the way to bring Schmitt's unflinching commitment to immediate action closer to Hobbes and further from Hegel, who can stay undecided, caught in a tangle of dialectical mediations.

Schmitt saw himself implicitly as Hegel's contemporary heir, assuming a legacy vastly transformed by historical circumstances – Hegel's state as an *imperium rationis* was the total state that Schmitt espoused. Still, the 'foundational impulse' of his thought continued to be Hegelian philosophy which Schmitt sought both to 'prolong and replace' (Kervégan, 1992: 143). Kervégan believes that Schmitt perceived Hegel's political philosophy as sundered by 'unsurmountable ambiguities' (ibid.: 188), attempting to pass both as an apolitical liberal and a politically active conservative, as a revolutionary and as 'a conservative, a *catechonte*' (ibid.: 153). Hegel favoured a strong political state, but was much 'concerned about preventing any interference that might coerce or upset the domain of individual freedom and the sphere of social and economic interactions' (ibid.: 144).

If Schmitt's main objective was to radicalize the either–or and promote the politics of the excluded middle, why would he consider embracing an ambiguous, two-faced Hegel as his decisionist partner? Why would Schmitt care to inherit the legacy of such an unsurmountably ambiguous thinker? And how would Hegel's patronage allow him to advance his own decisionist ethics of the state? Kervégan solves this difficulty by implicitly retracting Schmitt's references to Hegel's double-facedness. He ascribes to Schmitt a political interpretation of Hegel that can match a hard decisionist posture: Hegel's ambiguities appeared to have been only a surface show; at the core he was unequivocally political, and not a liberal thinker (ibid.: 189). His political aims were discernible, for example, when he asserted the subordination of civil society to the higher aims of the state. He was a foe of normativism, which could only bring about the emasculation of the authority monopolized by the state. Given a choice between Althusius and Hobbes, Schmitt saw Hegel well-installed within the Hobbesian camp.

Having steered Schmitt along a radical decisionist path, Kervégan allows Schmitt to drag Hegel along that same path. This prompts an animated deliverance that seeks to tip the balance in favour of a non-decisionist, liberal reading of Hegel. Even if Hegel shared Hobbes's emphatic view of the state as the locus of decision, he missed no opportunity to 'multiply the concessions to liberal indecision' (Kervégan, 1992: 156). Kervégan endeavours to offer a new liberal reading of Hegel, one which should 'show the limitations and the distortions implied in Schmitt's interpretation' (ibid.: 227). The core of Schmitt's misinterpretation was a reading of the distinction between civil society and the state as an unmediated antagonism (ibid.: 234). Kervégan objects to this rigidly dualist view by underscoring the reciprocal mediations that bridge the separation between civil society and the state. The argument that he unfolds for this purpose has two parts. First, he examines Hegel's notion of civil society and dispels any attempt to approximate it to a state of nature devoid of any trace of ethical content. Schmitt's 'intransigent philosophical dualism' (ibid.: 225) is blamed for an abstract and one-sidedly political reading of Hegel that hardens the antagonism between social disorder and political order. Second, Kervégan points out that Hegel's notion of the state was structurally open and responsive to the demands that arose from civil society. The rejection of popular sovereignty, which tends to be read as an illiberal statement, did not mean that a delegate representation from civil society had no role to play within the state.

The analogy drawn by Schmitt between the Hobbesian state of nature and Hegel's civil society demonstrated, according to Kervégan, Schmitt's impatience with the role played by dialectical mediation. Civil society is not a riot of pure particularity which needs to be pacified externally by the offices of a Hobbesian sovereign. Hegelian civil society constituted the synthesis of particular and universal aims, with particularity its prevailing principle, so that only an unconscious formal universality (ibid.: 220) could arise within it, a spontaneous market order that fed on the selfish pursuits of individuals. What distinguished civil society from the state was not the absence or presence of universality but the modality of its presence. Hegel was not unaware of the dysfunctional nature of that spontaneous order, which bred the 'calculating selfishness of economic atoms' (ibid.: 302), yet it was on this unconstrained order that he based the higher forms of universality which rose from within civil society. The abstract function of a judicial system that operated within the rule of law was envisaged initially more fully. With the *Polizei*, and especially with the corporations, the substantial universality of the state sank its ethical roots within civil society even more firmly. According to Kervégan, civil society can only be conceived of as internally related to the state. Particularity is its proper principle, but it can only be actualized by means of a superior principle. This is why Hegel allowed for an active presence of the state to surface at the higher levels of civil society, so that it included a complex relation between political rationality and social irrationality. The latter was not a hindrance for the former. Hegel's notion of civil society was vastly richer and more complex than Schmitt's (ibid.: 259).

This more complex conception of civil society, the outcome of its partial politicization, anticipated Hegel's next move, namely the partial socialization of the state. The key to the extension of social concerns beyond their proper sphere lay, according to Kervégan, in the function Hegel assigned to representation. His peculiar view of representation again distanced him from Schmitt.

We can better understand Kervégan's argument in the context of a brief historical excursus that clarifies the notions of representation and sovereignty. Representation and sovereignty are the twin notions which he portrays as the mainstays of the modern conception of the state. After the collapse of traditional justifications of state authority, those notions were paraded by absolutism in its bid to secure political unity. Kervégan notes that in defining the sovereign as a *persona repraesentativa*, Hobbes identified sovereignty with representation. In his political philosophy, the sovereign was deemed able to carve a people out of a disaggregated multitude by assuming its representation (sovereign representation or *Repräsentation*). The state of nature was marked by the lack of popular identity; the people could only attain its identity when represented by the sovereign. Sovereignty could not be instituted by the people as such, but it was the sovereign who brought a people into existence through its representative capacity. By contrast, a monarchomachist like Althusius espoused a view of representation *qua* delegation (delegate representation or *Vertretung*). Sovereignty was delegated or mandated by a people whose identity and communal existence was assumed from the beginning. Already constituted, the people conspired to set up an authority that represented it as its mandated agent. Kervégan observes how these two opposed views of representation were combined in Sieyès's theory of sovereignty (ibid.: 264). The sovereignty of the people was to be delegated to their elected representatives, but these did not act as commissars or agents of the people. Rejection of an imperative mandate allowed the assembled representatives to assume, with autonomy and independence, what Sieyès considered to be the ultimate expression of sovereignty, namely the exercise of *pouvoir constituant*. Sovereignty and representation were again fused together, in Hobbesian fashion, but with a difference. The people, acknowledged Sieyès, never leaves the state of nature. The delegation of sovereignty was only temporary and could legitimately be reclaimed at any time.

Hegel, who was concerned with securing both the unity of the political order and an unmitigated social pluralism, was not unsympathetic to a similar compromise. What he was not ready to concede was Sieyès's adherence to popular sovereignty. This abstraction would surely undo that compromise, for the logic of democracy demanded identity and rejected representation. Hegel's own compromise between sovereign and delegate representation, found, on the one hand, a place for Hobbesian absolutism. Hegel was ready to ascribe sovereign representation to the prince. In no case did his liberal stand present any sort of obstacle for his embrace of the monarchical principle.[2] Delegate representation, on the other hand, was taken into consideration in the case of the Assembly of Estates. Hegel, in accordance with the Prussian reformers, rejected the idea of a representative Assembly generated entirely by universal suffrage. Delegate representation should only represent communal interests, channelled organically through the traditional estates, and not through the abstract will of atomized individuals. This alone could preserve intact the sovereign representation of the monarch. According to Kervégan, Hegel's proposal matched the requisites of constitutional monarchy, which favoured a delegate representation of

---

[2] The monarchical principle was promulgated by the German Federation in the Vienna Concluding Act of 15 May 1820. According to Karl-Heinz Ilting, Hegel supported this principle (Ilting, 1973: 105–8).

interests, 'for this allows it to maintain the monopoly of sovereign representation (*Repräsentation*) which a National Assembly would be in a position to contest' (ibid.: 310).

This interpretation of Hegel's state, which synthesizes opposed conservative and liberal views on representation, appears to match Schmitt's description of his philosophy as duplicitous and two-faced. For Kervégan, however, Hegel did not intend a mere 'conciliation' of opposed viewpoints, but their 'reconciliation', by which the terms in opposition were brought together as internally related moments (ibid.: 297). By sticking to the dualism of the either–or and the externality of the exceptional, Schmitt thoroughly missed Hegel's emphasis on mediation. The opposition Schmitt established between a disorganized multitude and a unified people, the either–or he postulated between chaos and order, was typical of Hobbes's pure decisionism.[3] By contrast, Hegel intended to place the exceptional under an institutional umbrella and to desegregate chaos and order. Hegel's view of representation as the mediation of identity allowed him to be more tolerant of extreme pluralism and diversity in civil society. According to Kervégan, pluralism was incompatible with Schmitt's hard decisionism. Whereas Hegel emphasized the constitutive role of representation in the formation of the public sphere, Schmitt showed that identity was required for the existence of a state. Representation was a necessary but not sufficient condition of political unity. For Hegel, by contrast, natural or cultural identity was superfluous.

For Kervégan's argument to work, two conditions would have to be fulfilled. First, Schmitt's decisionism would have to be defined in a way that allowed no compromise or juxtaposition between political and liberal principles. From a political point of view, a decisionist state was poised to intervene illiberally in every

[3] Schmitt recognizes decisionist features in the doctrine of papal infallibility, in Calvin's absolutist conception of God and in Bodin's theory of sovereignty. In all these cases decisionism does not appear in its purity, but within the context of an already given institutional order of things. It is Hobbes who for the first time espouses pure or hard decisionism (Schmitt, 1934b: 27–8). Hobbes's sovereign does not operate within a given institutional order, but creates a juridical order out of a concrete disorder and a normative void, 'the anarchic insecurity of the state of nature' (ibid.: 29). The sovereign's decision, therefore, does not constitute a commissarial, but a sovereign dictatorship 'that creates law and order' (ibid.).

aspect of civil society. Correspondingly, civil society must surrender its claim to autonomy and expose itself to dictatorial interventions imposed by the state. If Schmittian decisionism led to totalitarianism, as Kervégan maintains, there could be no truce with the liberal *Rechtsstaat*. Second, a decisionist reading of Hegel would have to be seen as a complete distortion.[4] It is obvious to Kervégan that Schmitt's radical anti-liberalism could only yield a totalitarian interpretation. This one-sidedness was due to Schmitt's lack of a proper sensitivity to the movements of dialectical reason. Schmitt saw duplicity and two-facedness where Hegel brought about mediation and reconciliation. If a few decisionist traces and political *aperçus* were to be detected in Hegel, they dissolved into a higher dialectical synthesis which shunned radical decisions. Schmitt's undialectical reading of Hegel was to blame for the distortion. Dialectic and decisionism do not mix.

It seems to me that Kervégan's exposition fulfils neither of these conditions. First, he fails to observe that Schmitt, during the early years of the Weimar republic, espoused a pure or hard version of decisionism that appealed to the notion of *pouvoir constituant* and wielded the monarchical principle as its paradigm. After 1923 he retreated to a softer version, which saw the exceptional conditions underlying the validity of a system of norms as circumstantial and impermanent. Kervégan believes that Schmitt's conception did not harden until 1934, when he came to conceive of the 'permanence of the exception'. A 'revolutionary situation' could now be understood along the lines of that hard decisionism (Kervégan, 1992: 45). As evidence, Kervégan produces the already quoted passage from Schmitt's *Über die drei Arten des rechtswissensschaftlichen Denkens*: 'the sovereign decision is an absolute beginning ... [It] arises from a normative void and a concrete disorder.' But this kind of decisionism does not describe Schmitt's late Weimar position, though it certainly matched his early Weimar proposals, and it is strange to suggest that Schmitt's decisionism hardened only after he abandoned it in favour of

---

[4] Dieter Henrich maintains that Hegel's constitutionalism, unlike the British model, allowed the prince to transcend the instituted decision-making processes and decide for himself (1983: 23). Arguing on the basis of Schmitt's notion of the state of exception, Ilting points out that Henrich's view amounts to acknowledging that the prince had the right to abrogate the constitution and decree its non-existence (ibid.: 199).

institutionalism. Kervégan's allegation that throughout his Weimar production Schmitt's foremost concern was 'the refutation of liberalism in all its forms' (1992: 109) must be qualified. There are forms of liberalism that are compatible with a softer view of decisionism. A respect for procedure and the rule of law has not prevented governments that espouse liberal principles from making and implementing political decisions (compare with Holmes, 1993). Only the substitution of the 'classical liberalism of Constant, Guizot and Mill' (and I should add Hegel) by its more radically humanitarian successors (Kervégan, 1992: 112), disallows any synthesis of liberal and decisionist principles.

Second, Schmitt's decisionist reading of Hegel cannot be a distortion, as Kervégan claims. In fact, much of his own argument rests on what he believes to be Schmitt's undistorted account of the Hegelian dialectic. 'What Schmitt finds profoundly objectionable in Hegel's thought is the idea of dialectic itself' (ibid.: 328). As defined by Schmitt, Hegel's dialectic concealed and erased the either–or faced by genuine decisions. Kervégan quotes from *Parlamentarismus*: 'The either/or of moral decision, the decisive and deciding disjunction, has no place in [Hegel's] system' (Schmitt, 1923b: 68). Even the decisions of a dictator were to be assimilated by the world-spirit in the course of its development. Dialectical thought offered no grounds for the possibility of an 'absolute separation between good and evil' (ibid.: 69). By contrast, Kervégan thinks that Schmitt's decisionism resisted assimilation to rational argument and discussion. Choices made by us set an absolute separation between the positive and its negation. There was no middle ground where things could be discussed.

All this rests on a serious misunderstanding. Kervégan reads *Parlamentarismus* as a decisionist call for dictatorial rule. There is no alternative to Schmitt's perception of the theoretical and practical failure of contemporary parliamentarism. This is not a new indictment though. Richard Thoma, a contemporary of Schmitt, excoriated his book for the same reason and cast doubts on the sincerity of its author. A reading of this important text from a politically conservative liberal perspective exposes a different storyline. It makes more sense to interpret it as Schmitt's attempted accommodation with liberalism, an accommodation that did not shun authoritarian politics. Schmitt here embraced

Hegel as a convenient partner, for he believed that he and other German liberals were able to invoke the genuine features of parliamentarism, namely discussion and publicity. Ideally, parliaments were instances where enlightened discussion should take place, transparently and in full view of public opinion. At the same time, parliaments should not be charged with executive or governing functions, which required deliberation, decision and confidentiality. Schmitt praised early German liberalism for adopting the idea of a balance of powers and its 'mediating elasticity' (1923b: 58). Nineteenth-century liberals, Hegel included, developed the Enlightenment's mechanical view of balance into a 'doctrine of organic mediation, and thus retain the possibility of validating the prince as a pre-eminent person and representative of the unity of the State' (ibid.: 58). In Hegel's scheme of things, the prince decided in the ultimate instance, the executive deliberated and governed, and the Assembly of Estates openly discussed all public concerns. Later, when other German liberals came up with the idea of a parliamentary government, discussion and publicity were thrown overboard in favour of the confidential deliberation of parliamentary committees. It is obvious that Schmitt, at this point, was reconciled to the idea of parliaments, but parliaments that did not govern and limited themselves to legislative functions.

In *Parlamentarismus*, Schmitt discussed in detail the parliamentary role assigned by Hegel to the Assembly of Estates. In contrast with the eternal conversation of romanticism, discussion here was a 'dialectic-dynamic process' (p. 60), adequate to legislative, but not to executive functions. He also noted that the Assembly officiated as a 'mediating organ' (p. 59) between the government and the people. Schmitt referred to paragraph 314 of the *Philosophy of Right*, where Hegel described the role of the *Stände* as 'purely accessory', In that same paragraph Hegel stated that through the openness of their proceedings 'the moment of universal knowledge attains its extension' (Schmitt, 1923b: 59). This was what allowed the public to form opinions that were informed and truthful. Schmitt quoted with approval what Hegel said about the publicity of parliamentary proceedings in the addition to paragraph 315: 'The openness of the proceedings of the assembly is a great spectacle of great educational value to the citizens, and the people learn from this above all the true nature of their interests' (Schmitt, 1923b: 59). Hegel's parliamentarian conception was the kind of which Schmitt approved. It left governing to other state bodies and was perfectly compatible with the concentration of decisive authority in the hands of a prince. While Hegel's rejection of popular sovereignty reinforced the authority of the prince, Schmitt found himself in a completely different historical context. In 1919, the *pouvoir constituant* of the German people abolished the monarchical principle and entrenched a liberal-democratic constitution. This explained the difference in their approaches. Schmitt, but not Hegel, was forced to deal with and confront democratic institutions.

On the one hand, Kervégan maintains that Schmitt distorted Hegel's thought because the dualism implied by pure or hard decisionism was incompatible with dialectical mediation. On the other hand, he has to acknowledge that pure or hard decisionism was never really espoused by Schmitt. (His formulation of this view appeared in 1934, at the precise moment when he relinquished decisionism *in totum* in favour of institutionalism.) Taken together, these two points render Kervégan's interpretation extremely problematic. If Schmitt never espoused pure decisionism, the distance that he wishes to interject between Schmitt and Hegel is considerably reduced. In fact, the moderate decisionism of his *Verfassungslehre*, where Schmitt 'juxtaposed' liberal and political elements, had considerable affinities with Hegel's mediating compromise between parliamentarian liberalism and the decisionist temper of his conservative prince.

5 • Sovereignty and Constituent Power

Schmitt's *Verfassungslehre* stands as perhaps the most systematic and least occasional of his works. While his production was marked, on the whole, by an extraordinary sensitivity to his own concrete situation, leading at one point to an unbounded and shameless opportunism, this particular work seemed to rise above the political fray, reflecting possibly the mood of 1928, which marked the halcyon days of the Weimar republic. Recently, Ernst-Wolfgang Böckenförde has tried to shake the *Verfassungslehre* from its academic bearing by relating its argument to the polemical friend/enemy theory developed by Schmitt in his 'Der Begriff des Politischen' (1927) and his characterization of the state as the political unity of a nation. Beyond this, he has connected it to the eminently partisan notion of sovereignty put forward by Schmitt in his *Politische Theologie* (1922a), where he flaunted his allegiance to the Catholic counter-revolution.

One of the arguments presented by Böckenförde in support of his thesis discusses Schmitt's definition of sovereignty and the state as its locus. According to Schmitt's *Politische Theologie*, the state had 'the monopoly of the ultimate decision' (1922a: 20). This meant that the essence of sovereignty, which he defined 'not as the monopoly of domination or coercion, but as the monopoly of decision' (ibid.; compare with Böckenförde, 1988: 287), was the ability to lift its subject above the legally constituted order. The decision Schmitt had in mind was an absolute decision, 'created out of nothingness' (1922a: 83; compare with Schmitt, 1921: 23). The whole system of legality was thus relativized by a power that stood outside and above it.

I do not wish to dispute Böckenförde's contention that sovereignty is the key notion of Schmitt's conception of public law. My concern is that an important shift marked Schmitt's work during these years, a shift that determined a difference between the conception of sovereignty he held in 1922 and the one he held in 1928, when he published *Verfassungslehre*. In Chapter 3, I have examined Schmitt's accommodation to liberalism following his realization of the non-identity of liberalism and democracy. In this chapter, I would like to examine the effect of that shift on Schmitt's understanding of the notion of sovereignty.

Section I of this chapter examines the uninhibited view of sovereignty Schmitt developed in his *Politische Theologie*, a view which approximated it to the monarchical principle (compare with Kaufmann, 1906). In section II, I compare this radical view with the apparently more balanced conception offered in his *Verfassungslehre*. Sovereignty was there redefined by superseding its identification with the monarchical principle. As a result, both monarchy and democracy could be interpreted as political forms that conveyed constituent activity. Schmitt, however, did not directly discuss the issue of sovereignty in this context. He tried to circumvent it because the constitutional theory of liberalism, the theory that defined the Weimar constitution, avoided the issue of the political in general and of sovereignty in particular. 'It is characteristic of liberal constitutionalism to ignore the sovereign, whether this sovereign be the monarch or the people' (Schmitt, 1928: 244). The ideal liberal constitution was defined exclusively in terms of the rule of law. Therefore sovereignty, an essentially political notion, should not be given any recognition in a liberal constitution. In this section I show how Schmitt surmounted this liberal view by invoking the notion of constituent power or *pouvoir constituant*. Section III discusses Schmitt's employment of constituent power as a surrogate for sovereignty. Sovereignty only attained visibility in exceptional situations. According to Schmitt, the destruction of the German imperial constitution in 1918 and the genesis of the Weimar constitution in 1919 – events where the *pouvoir constituant* of the people was determinant – exposed the notion of sovereignty. Finally, section IV examines both the subject and the activity of constituent power to confirm its conceptual kinship with sovereignty. By refusing to develop a political theological interpretation of democracy and adopting a view on representation similar to that of Sieyès, Schmitt intended to take away from the *pouvoir constituant* of the people the fruits of sovereignty.

I

In his *Politische Theologie*, Schmitt attempted to define the notion of sovereignty. He observed that it no longer played a role in the discussion of jurists and legal philosophers. A thick veil covered it, a veil that he was determined to pierce through to expose its presence in political and legal affairs and documents. According to rule-of-law liberalism, power resided in the legal system itself and not in any personal authority representing the state. Schmitt opposed this view from the very start.

When Schmitt reviewed the currently held opinions on sovereignty he observed that its commonly accepted definition – 'sovereignty is the highest underived power of domination' (1922a: 12) – was valid but too abstract. This formulation left out the crucial issue of its concrete application, namely *who* decides in cases of extreme conflict, when public order and security (*le salut public*) are in jeopardy. The all-important question concerning the subject of sovereignty was put on one side by liberalism. By raising this issue, Schmitt was betraying his adherence to the personalist concept of the state demanded by the monarchical principle.[1] This principle states that there is always the possibility for the emergence of the power of a sovereign, even when a constitution limits the powers of the state by separating them. Accordingly, the sovereign 'stands outside the normally valid juridical order and yet belongs to it, for he is competent to decide whether the constitution has to be suspended in toto' (ibid.: 13).

For some interpreters the definition cited above appeared to have a certain affinity with Bodin's definition – 'la souveraineté est la puissance absolue et perpétuelle d'une République' (ibid.: 13). This view, according to Schmitt, was incorrect for it ignored the context of Bodin's definition. His views were determined by the struggle for supremacy between the prince and the estates. Should the prince's promises to the estates or the people abrogate his sovereignty? There is a natural obligation to keep one's promises, but that duty expires 'si la nécessité est urgente'

---

[1] The personalist concept of the state demanded by the monarchical principle was defined by Stahl in opposition to Hegel and the Enlightenment's idea of natural rights (compare with Kaufmann, 1906: 85).

(Schmitt, 1922a: 14). In such cases everything reverts to the decision of the prince. According to Schmitt, the novelty of Bodin's view consisted in his ability 'to incorporate the decision into the concept of sovereignty' (ibid.). And that decision could only be left in the hands of the one person who could effectively ensure the unity of the state, the monarch.

After Bodin, the natural-law theorists of the seventeenth century, particularly Hobbes and Pufendorf, also understood sovereignty in terms of the political agent who decides on the state of exception (ibid.: 15).[2] The question about sovereignty comes down to the question about its subject, about *who* decides. 'Who is competent when there is no clear provision of competence?' (ibid.: 17).[3] In other words, who decides the extreme case? Two related illustrations offered by Schmitt prove most revealing. First he considered the monarchical principle. The context that led to the original formulation of this principle in 1814 had to do with the question of who was competent to decide in cases when the juridical order did not settle the matter of competence. Schmitt then examined article 48 of the Weimar constitution, which bestowed on the *Reichspräsident* the faculty to decide on the exception. In granting the *Reichspräsident* this 'unlimited absolute power' (ibid.: 18), the content of this article addressed the question of sovereignty precisely as Schmitt wanted to define it. Sovereignty fell into the hands of the *Reichspräsident* for he it was who had to decide on the exception.[4] In fact, Schmitt explicitly associated article 48 with article 14 of the French *Charte* of 4 June 1814,[5] the document that instituted the

---

[2] Schmitt referred this issue to what he had written earlier on the state of exception (compare with Schmitt, 1921: 22–4).

[3] In his *Die Diktatur*, Schmitt took Hobbes and Pufendorf to be supporters of 'scientific natural law (*wissenschaftliche Naturrecht*)' and opponents of the 'natural law of justice (*Gerechtigkeitsnaturrecht*)' tradition. For them the issue was not the content of a decision, but only that a decision be effectively made; the real question was *who* adjudicates, *who* had the power to decide. (Compare with Schmitt, 1921: 21–4.)

[4] Hermann Heller, a social-democrat political philosopher and jurist, accepted Schmitt's definition of sovereignty as the faculty to decide on the state of exception, but attributed that faculty to the people and not to the *Reichspräsident* (1927: 105). By contrast, Kelsen was proud to acknowledge that the Austrian constitution of 1920, which he authored, eliminated any possibility of imposing a state of exception (ibid.: 109).

monarchical principle during the Restoration period and brought the true notion of sovereignty back to life.[6]

Schmitt also noticed that, during the sixteenth and seventeenth centuries, a theology that embraced the philosophical conception of God as the sole architect of the universe determined the notion of sovereignty. This is what he referred to as 'political theology'. The modern prince was a transposition of the Cartesian God to the political world. Schmitt quoted from one of Descartes' letters to Mersenne: 'c'est Dieu qui a établi ces lois en nature ainsi qu'un roi établit les lois en son royaume' (1922a: 61). Hobbes, despite his nominalism and his attachment to science and a mechanistic view of nature, revealed the same politico-theological conception. His political views were still tied to a decisionist and personalist view of politics. The Leviathan is the 'colossal person' postulated as the 'ultimate concrete deciding instance' (ibid.).

Schmitt's conceptual and historical analyses, which tied sovereignty to the exception and brought out its decisionist and personalist elements, led conclusively to one result: only an absolute monarch could be the proper subject of sovereignty. When Rousseau entered the scene, things changed substantially. According to Schmitt, his identification of the will of the sovereign with the general will meant that 'the decisionist and personalist element in the hitherto existing concept of sovereignty' was lost (ibid.: 62). Henceforth, the unity displayed by the people eluded 'this decisionist character' (ibid.), and no democratic arrangement would be able to claim genuine sovereignty. The 'political metaphysics' of democracy could not claim political theological status. In a democratic setting 'the theistic and the deistic idea of God is unintelligible' (ibid.: 62-3). Democracy in America, as Tocqueville saw it, still maintained that the voice of the people was the voice of God. But in contemporary Germany a political philosopher like Kelsen could only 'conceive of democracy as the expression of a relativist and impersonal scientism'

---

[5] In his *Politische Theologie*, Schmitt referred to 'the *Charte* of 1815' (Schmitt, 1922a: 18). This was obviously a misprint. In *Die Diktatur*, he correctly identified it as the *Charte* of 1814 and transcribed its article 14 (1921: 193).

[6] Erich Kaufmann maintained that the monarchical principle, defined as 'l'autorité préexistant du roi, supérieur et antérieur à l'acte constitutionnel', was first introduced by the *Charte* of 1814 (1906: 38).

(Schmitt, 1922a: 63). Political theology had become unthinkable within a democratic context.

In 1922, with the revolutionary events in Germany still fresh in the memory, Schmitt evoked the counter-revolutionary thought of Juan Donoso Cortés. Donoso realized in 1848 that 'the epoch of royalism is over. There is no royalism any more, because there are no more kings' (ibid.: 65–6). In view of this exhaustion and extinction of legitimacy, Donoso advocated dictatorship. Hobbes arrived at a similar result from similar decisionist premisses: *auctoritas, non veritas, facit legem*. Laws are essentially commands. They are based on a decision concerning the interest of the state and the state's foremost interest is that a decision be made. In *Die Diktatur*, Schmitt wrote: 'the decision on which a law is based is, normativately speaking, created out of nothingness' (1921: 23). But Hobbes did not go this far. Caught within a rationalist outlook, he understood the power of the sovereign to rest on a more or less tacit agreement of the people. Only de Maistre was able to shake off that rationalist residue and radically negate the sovereignty of the people (ibid.).

Schmitt agreed with de Maistre and Donoso Cortés that monarchs were the proper subjects of sovereignty. Both in *Die Diktatur* and in *Politische Theologie* he dismissed the people as a legitimate and fitting subject of sovereignty. He did not fully perceive that democracy and the notion that sustained it, namely popular sovereignty, diverged substantially from liberalism, the slayer of sovereignty. Like his Catholic counter-revolutionary mentors, Schmitt saw no possible compromise with liberalism. Inspired by their counter-revolutionary conservatism, Schmitt contemplated but one alternative in 1922, a sovereign dictatorship as an effective surrogate for the monarchical principle.

II

Schmitt's *Verfassungslehre* did not directly discuss the notion of sovereignty, even though its thoroughly systematic argument presupposed it. The reason why Schmitt needed to circumvent it was set out in the preface to that work, dated December 1927. In it he distinguished between the political element of a constitution and its properly liberal element, i.e. the principle of the rule of law. The constitutional theory of liberalism, the theory that determined the spirit of the Weimar constitution and absorbed Schmitt's attention in this work, tried to avoid the political element as such. The ideal liberal constitution was defined exclusively in terms of the rule of law; its aim was strictly to confine the political prerogatives claimed by the state. As Schmitt admitted, the whole object of a liberal constitution aimed at marking off a sanctuary for individual freedom and disavowing the political disposition of the state. Therefore sovereignty, an essentially political notion, ought not to be given any recognition in a liberal constitution.

Despite the overtly liberal framework of the Weimar constitution, Schmitt's political sensors had no difficulty in finding the traces of sovereignty in its make-up. The constitution did not descend from heaven ready-made, but owed its existence to a decision of the German people. The genesis of a constitution was the locus where sovereignty manifested itself with greater clarity. Weimar liberalism was not self-sufficient and self-generated, but presupposed a political decision in its favour. Sovereignty could not be ascribed to a legal system in itself. In 1919, a sovereign people had decided to confirm its national unity and define the mode of its political existence by means of a constitution. This was the absolute decision on which stood a now relativized positive constitution. Schmitt saw here an opening to reintroduce the theme of sovereignty. The idea of absolute monarchy, as the sole subject of sovereignty, had perished in 1918, but absolute democracy, supported by the sovereign *pouvoir constituant* of the people, had replaced it.

In his *Verfassungslehre*, Schmitt appears to have modified his initial views on liberalism and democracy. In the first place, it was easy to expose the view held by liberals that politics and sovereignty had been decisively expelled from human affairs. In fact, a compromise had been struck between the ideals sponsored by liberals and the political decisions needed to make those ideals effective. The Weimar constitution was a case in point. Schmitt, in his *Verfassungslehre*, wanted to prove that Weimar liberalism was in fact an instance of such a compromise. In the second place, Schmitt saw the need to modify the personalist and hard decisionist conception of sovereignty he had held in *Politische Theologie*. Influenced by the views of the Catholic counter-revolution, he had envisaged monarchy as the only possible embodiment of sovereignty. In 1923, with the publication of his *Parlamentarismus*, he came to realize that democracy was a political form of government that could also serve as a vehicle for sovereignty. The notion of democracy did not include liberal relativism and the liberal distaste for the political. This meant a shift in his conception of sovereignty and a weakening of its personalist and hard decisionist aspects.[7]

These two considerations eased the way for a political reading of the Weimar constitution. Alongside its liberal elements Schmitt was now able to incorporate a political dimension. It was this rearticulation of liberal and political elements that determined the argumentative structure of the *Verfassungslehre*. An expanded view of sovereignty permitted the concurrent adoption of the liberal rule of law. Schmitt shifted from an intransigent adherence to the conservative revolutionary themes he shared with de Maistre and Donoso Cortés to a more flexible position. He saw the need to adopt an entente with liberalism, moving towards acceptance of a conservative or authoritarian reading of liberalism, a reading that did not reject sovereignty out of hand, expressed either monarchically or democratically.

The mistake of rule-of-law liberalism lay in its outright denial of sovereignty. But sovereignty, never fully repressed, could always let itself be seen.

> What has suffered the most under this fiction and this method of avoidance is the concept of sovereignty. In practice, apocryphal acts of sovereignty are exercised, which are characteristically performed by non-sovereign state officials or bodies who, occasionally and with tacit tolerance, make sovereign decisions. (Schmitt, 1928: p. xii)

The exercise of apocryphal acts of sovereignty described by Schmitt took place at the margins of normal constitutional life. It manifested the marginal presence assigned to the notion of sovereignty in the *Verfassungslehre*. As he himself acknowledged, a

---

[7] Schmitt's enduring preference for a strong state was not challenged by this acceptance of both monarchy *and* democracy as legitimate forms of government. In his *Verfassungslehre*, he recognized that democracy could be stronger and more decisive than monarchy (1928: 236).

detailed discussion of sovereignty belonged formally to the 'theory of sovereignty' (*Lehre von der Souveränität*) or a 'general theory of the state' (1928: p. xiv), and not to constitutional theory. In spite of this methodological demarcation which excluded a consideration of sovereignty from constitutional theory, Schmitt found a way to reintroduce it at the very core of the *Verfassungslehre*. Without explicit acknowledgement, he employed the notion of constituent power (*pouvoir constituant* or *verfassunggebende Gewalt*) as its surrogate.

Constituent power could function as a legal notion and fell within the range of interest of public law. It did not immediately bring the political to mind, but it adequately supplanted the notion of sovereignty. As Schmitt's exposition unfolded, it became clear that constituent power was indeed a political notion. Sovereignty *qua* constituent power appeared most clearly at the moment when a constitution was generated. According to Schmitt, a constitution did not just fall from heaven ready-made. Its existence was dependent on concrete historical circumstances. Most importantly, it was subservient to the contingent political decisions which brought it to life. The notion of constituent power represented sovereignty as a concrete manifestation of the will. It was the best way to bring monarchy and democracy under one generic notion. But, as was indicated above, the condition for Schmitt's employment of the notion of constituent power as a surrogate for sovereignty, was a shift in his conception of the latter. Hard decisionism and personalism meant that only monarchs could be genuine subjects of sovereignty. It is inconceivable to think that Schmitt would grant allegiance to the views of de Maistre, Bonald and Donoso Cortés and, at the same time, favour the sovereignty of the people. But this is precisely what he did in his *Verfassungslehre*, which marked his shift away from hard decisionism and personalism and towards a new conception of sovereignty.

III

In what follows I will direct my attention to what Schmitt had to say about the notion of constituent power in his *Verfassungslehre*. My aim is to demonstrate that the acceptance of this notion certified the presence of sovereignty in that treatise. According to Schmitt, sovereignty became visible only during exceptional circumstances, when a constitution was destroyed and another was born. In these circumstances, sovereignty showed up under the guise of constituent power. A central portion of his *Verfassungslehre*, therefore, explored the formation of the Weimar constitution. Its aim was to develop the notion of sovereignty.

The genesis of the German constitution of 11 August 1919, the so-called Weimar constitution, was the political and existential key to Schmitt's constitutional theory. He observed how the destruction of the German constitution of 1871 was attended by the abrogation of the *pouvoir constituant* that sustained it, that is, the constituent power of the monarch. According to Schmitt, this coincided with the revolutionary genesis of the new constitution, now animated by the constituent power of the German people. Schmitt's account of this constitutional genesis was guided by a basic principle: 'within each political unity there can be only one subject of constituent power' (1928: 53). In his historical study of Germany's constitutional development, Schmitt brought to light and identified this truly unique political subject. He thus distanced himself from liberal constitutionalism which relegated the subject of constituent power to the sidelines together with the question of sovereignty, postponing an unavoidable decision. During the German revolution of 1918–19, and situations of similar conflictual and critical nature, this question resurfaced, overturning the dilatory compromises that had veiled it. According to Schmitt, a constitution 'is based either on the monarchical or on the democratic principle' (ibid.: 54). Any attempt to avoid this political alternative by means of normativist fictions – the 'sovereignty of the constitution', for instance – would miss 'the fundamental political question concerning constituent power' (ibid.).

During the revolutionary events of 1918–19, the German people assumed, according to Schmitt, the exercise of constituent power. This was manifested by the democratic election of a National Assembly commissioned to write a new constitution. This action by the German people implied the destruction of the German constitution of 1871 and the abrogation of the *pouvoir constituant* of the monarch. It was this transition from monarchical to democratic legitimacy and the reconstruction of this fundamental event that fed and determined in large measure the historical matrix of Schmitt's political and juridical thought. In what follows I will examine Schmitt's account of the genesis of the Weimar constitution. I will then analyse certain aspects of the notion of constituent power that show its kinship with sovereignty.

The genesis of the Weimar constitution has to be understood in the context of Germany's constitutional monarchy and the revolution that abrogated it in November 1918. Schmitt differed from jurists like Laband, Jellinek and Kelsen, who emphasized the constitutional aspects of Germany's monarchy, and relativized its political, in this case monarchical, aspects. They denied the possibility of identifying and designating a subject of state sovereignty. In accordance with normativist view they considered that sovereignty rested abstractly on the constitution itself. Schmitt noted how the monarchical principle was being watered down by constitutionalist thinking. Monarchs were not perceived as subjects of their own will. The will of the state dissolved into mere parliamentary chatter. But in monarchical Germany, and here Schmitt followed Friedrich Julius Stahl's interpretation, 'the constitutional monarch still retained real power, his personal will was still meaningful and could not be traced back to Parliament' (Schmitt, 1928: 289).[8] Under the influence of functionalist liberalism it was possible theoretically to avoid the issue of sovereignty and constituent power. But in practice, Schmitt wrote, 'it was possible to observe, in cases of conflict, who was the subject of state power and the representative of political unity able to decide: the monarch' (ibid.: 56). According to Schmitt, the German constitutional monarchy that survived until 1918 left constituent power in the hands of the monarch.

After defeat in the First World War and the Kaiser's abdication, the social democrats proclaimed the Republic and on 10 November 1918 they formed a provisional government, exercised by a Council of the People's Commissars. This Council summoned an Assembly of Representatives, representing the councils of workers and soldiers, which decided to convoke a

---

[8] According to Kaufmann, the monarchical principle was the pivotal concept of Friedrich Julius Stahl's political philosophy (1906: 80).

Constituent National Assembly, elected democratically on 6 February 1919. Those councils constituted only a provisional government. As Schmitt notes, 'in every revolution a [provisional] government is formed until a new decision concerning the subject of constituent power is reached' (1928: 58). Subsequently, the councils of workers and soldiers transferred their power to the Constituent Assembly which assumed the exercise of constituent power. Germany then adopted for the first time, observed Schmitt, the democratic doctrine of the constituent power of the people (compare with Schmitt, 1924: 237). He also noted how pre-war liberal constitutionalism, 'seen as a method of formalist evasion of the constituent power of the monarch' (1928: 57), was incapable of registering this fact.

The National Constituent Assembly, which first met in Weimar on 6 February 1919, formulated the content of the political decision of the German people by means of constitutional proposals which would define its exercise. It was not, according to Schmitt, the subject of constituent power but merely its agent. While it exercised its commission, it held a *plenitudo potestatis*, and thus no legal or constitutional limitations (Schmitt, 1924: 238). This was the mark of a dictatorship: 'The special circumstances of a Constituent Assembly which meets after the previous constitutional laws have been abolished may be more properly designated as a sovereign dictatorship' (Schmitt, 1928: 59; compare with Pasquino, 1988: 379). No limitations could determine it other than those that it imposed on itself. It did not have competencies or a limited range of attributions, and therefore could be interpreted as a commissarial dictatorship limited by pre-existing legislation. Such an assembly was a sovereign dictatorship, but *qua* dictatorship it conducted its business only by mandate. It was not sovereign as were the monarchs who ruled according to the monarchical principle (compare with Schmitt, 1924: 238). On the contrary, it always acted in the name of the people, 'which at any moment may cancel the authority of its commissars by means of a political act' (1928: 60). The promulgation of the Weimar constitution on 19 August 1919 ended the sovereign dictatorship of the German Constituent Assembly. 'A sovereign dictatorship is incompatible with a constitutional rule of law' (Schmitt, 1924: 238).

The task embraced by Schmitt was to bring to light the

political element beneath the thick normativist veil spread over the Weimar constitution by liberalism. Schmitt knew that cases of conflict and constitutional emergencies would force the recognition of the real subject of state power, the real representative of political unity. In such situations the notion of constituent power would expose the fundamental political dilemma: democratic or monarchical sovereignty.

This is the historical context of Schmitt's decision to employ the notion of constituent power. Schmitt defined it as 'the political will whose power or authority is capable of adopting the concrete global decision on the mode and form of political existence' (1928: 75). This definition reveals Schmitt's rejection of juridical normativism, taken to formalist extremes by neo-Kantians like Kelsen. The foundations of a constitution were existential. A constitution could only rest on a concrete sovereign will and not on an abstract norm. In no way was the constituent will exhausted within the positive constitution itself. The sovereign constituent will, configured juridically as constituent power, continued to exist outside and above the constitution. A unified and indivisible existential dimension, external to the constitution, grounded the constituted powers of the state and could not be assimilated by or coordinated with them. The monarchical principle and the will of the people (the democratic principle) were understood by Schmitt as manifestations of *pouvoir constituant* and therefore necessarily fell outside the constitution.

IV

The discussion in the *Verfassungslehre* on the subject of *pouvoir constituant* and its activity confirmed its close conceptual kinship with sovereignty. Whether its subject be the monarch, the people or a strong group or association within the state,[9] constituent

---

[9] Schmitt conceived of a third possible subject of constituent power, different from the monarch and the people. A minority could also be subject of constituent power, and a state where this happened had 'an aristocratic or oligarchic form of government' (1928: 81). Schmitt was not thinking of a quantitative or electoral minority. Such a minority, or political party or faction, could be subject of constituent power. Only a 'firm organization' (ibid.) could be placed in the position of generating a constitution by means of its constituent power. Schmitt

power stood 'outside and above' the constitution (Schmitt, 1928: 242). This was a feature it shared with sovereignty. Again, the activity of constituent power, which at one point Schmitt describes as a generating source, a *natura naturans*, approximates it to sovereignty.

Shifting away from what he had maintained in his *Politische Theologie*, Schmitt, in his *Verfassungslehre,* designated the people as a legitimate subject of constituent power and rejected the monarchical conception that legitimized the German constitution of 1871.[10] After all it was the decision of the people that had given birth to the Weimar constitution. In 1919, Germany had come to terms with the French revolution and Sieyès's conception of the people as the subject of constituent power. Sieyès had lifted that notion above and beyond positive juridical forms. In agreement with this view, Schmitt underscored the foundational nature of constituent activity. Constituent power *qua* sovereign transcended the constitution; the manner of its activity could not be prescribed constitutionally. Only when the decision of a sovereign people had been expressed could one strive to regulate its formulation and execution.

In *Die Diktatur*, Schmitt endowed Sieyès's notion of constituent power with metaphysical qualities. As *natura naturans*,

---

visualized a circle of powerful families, as was the case in the Middle Ages, or a corporate order, such as the soviets in the Soviet Union or the fascio in Italy. He did not allude to a nation's armed forces, but surely they could fit within that scheme of things. At the same time, Schmitt admitted that the theoretical construction that attributed constituent power to a minority was 'not yet clear'. An ambiguity encumbered the notion of a minority or an aristocratic group *qua* subject of constituent power. In cases like this, 'there is no definitive renunciation to invoking the will of the people, for whose true and unfalsified expression one ought first to create the preconditions' (1928: 82). One should also say that to contemplate the possibility of this third kind of constituent power implied, on the part of Schmitt, an exploration of the putschist possibilities of revolutionary conservatism (compare with Cristi, 1994: 229–50).

[10] After 1923, realizing that monarchical legitimacy was extinguished, Schmitt saw no alternative to accepting the *pouvoir constituant* of the people, and therefore popular sovereignty. As late as 1932, in opposition to Ziegler who saw the need to eliminate popular sovereignty (Ziegler, 1932: 39), he still acknowledged that democratic or plebiscitary legitimacy was the 'only kind of state justification that could be considered to be generally valid' (Schmitt, 1932: 93). The depth and sincerity of his democratic convictions would be tested in 1933 when he would implicitly come to recognize Hitler as the new subject of *pouvoir constituant*.

constituent power remained in a state of nature. From this matrix ever new forms were bound to arise. Accordingly, constituent power was the ultimate ungenerated source of all forms, the unformed (*formlos*) form of all forms (Schmitt, 1921: 142; compare with Schmitt, 1928: 80, 81). In the *Verfassungslehre*, however, Schmitt disengaged this metaphysical interpretation from constitutional theory proper. That interpretation, he now admitted, belonged to political theology. This seems to me an attempt by Schmitt to distance himself from his earlier conservative revolutionary stance which subsumed constitutional discussions under politico-theological considerations.[11]

After considering the issue of the subject of constituent power Schmitt analysed its activity. Constituent power, like sovereign power, preceded and rose, *legibus solutus*, above all positive constitutional normativity. Its activity escaped constitutional bounds, just as any measure transcends what is measured by it. In the case of sovereign monarchs, their activity could include the unilateral granting of constitutional charters. At times, prudence dictated that monarchs reach agreements with the representatives of special interests. But this did not imply a renunciation of their sovereignty. In democratic polities, the people exercises its constituent power by means of any manifestation which conveys its express will. According to Schmitt, the people as such was not a firm and organized entity, and not endowed prima facie with permanent authority. Even if its power and plastic energy could not be extinguished and could embody an infinite variety of forms, the people was not to be taken as an organized subject of

---

[11] In his *Die Diktatur*, Schmitt elaborated the groundwork for his politico-theological conception of the notion of constituent power in opposition to Egon Zweig. In his *Die Lehre vom Pouvoir constituant*, Zweig retraced the origin of that doctrine to eighteenth-century rationalism: '[T]he apex in the development and effectivity of this doctrine was reached in an epoch which brought to bear the primacy of reason within the entire circle of intellectual life. From this point of view the theory of constituent power and of the power to reform a constitution is witness, if not the product, of the Enlightenment' (1909: 4). By contrast, Schmitt thought that Sieyès's theory could only be understood as an expression of his search for 'the organizing agent which defies organization (*das unorganisierbar Organisierende*)' (1921: 142), and related such agency to Spinoza's notion of *natura naturans*. That Spinoza was able to include such a notion in his rationalist system was proof that that system was 'not entirely rationalist' (Schmitt, 1921: 142).

decision. This was the reason for its weakness and explained why its actual will could be falsified.

Constituent activity, according to Schmitt, persisted autonomously and independently of any positive constitutional legislation. This was an indication of sovereignty. Constituent power could not be destroyed, changed or altered in any way; it persevered as the extra-constitutional ground of constitutions and constitutional laws. It was not exhausted by its exercise and 'retains the ability to persevere in its existence' (Schmitt, 1928: 92). The positive constitution, as an accident supported by constituent power, could be born, suffer alterations and eventually die, but alongside and above it the *pouvoir constituant* would continue to exist.

Two radical situations envisaged by Schmitt confirmed the tie between constituent power and sovereignty. In the first place, it was possible that the constitution might undergo destruction (*Verfassungsvernichtung*). During revolutionary situations, not only the constitution and the organs of constitutional legislation, but also the species of constituent power could be destroyed (ibid.: 94). Schmitt considered the case of the German constitution of 1871, which was in effect destroyed by the German revolution of 1918–19.[12] In a case like this, the destruction affected the constitution and the specific form attained by the constituent power that sustained it. According to Schmitt, it was not the constituent power itself that perished. In no case, not even in the most extreme political situation, was it possible for the substance of power, i.e. constituent power itself, to be destroyed. What happened in Germany was that one subject of constituent power was replaced by another subject: the constituent power of the people substituted that of the monarch. Secondly, Schmitt referred to the abrogation of a constitution (*Verfassungsbeseitigung*). In this case a constitution was rescinded but there was no corresponding destruction of the *pouvoir constituant* that sustained it. A constitution which rose from an act of *pouvoir constituant* derived from it and did not itself bear within it 'the continuity of the political unity' (ibid.: 93). The latter fell on the

---

[12] Elsewhere I have analysed two other instances where a similar destruction of a constitution took place: Spain in 1936 with Franco and Chile in 1973 with Pinochet (Cristi, 1994; compare with Blumenwitz, 1981; Alvarez, 1995).

pouvoir constituant, the ultimate foundation of a constitution.

Destruction and abrogation of a constitution, the two most drastic manifestations of constituent power, confirm its conceptual kinship with the notion of sovereignty. In his *Verfassungslehre*, Schmitt was willing to concede what he had earlier rejected in his *Politische Theologie*, namely that democracy, and not just monarchy, could be an expression of political absolutism. This, however, should not be regarded as proof of his democratic conversion. On the contrary, faced with a democratic revolution that was willing to appeal to the constituent power of the people, Schmitt attempted to disarm it by acknowledging and revitalizing an old adversary – the liberal ideal of the rule of law. Schmitt's *Verfassungslehre* was a careful balancing act, which tried to offset opposed principles. The liberal rule-of-law component ought to neutralize the political democratic component and vice versa.

The recognition of the democratic political form and its constituent power had a price which Schmitt was eager to exact: the reintroducion of sovereignty as a legitimate theme for constitutional discussion. He now felt he could point without misgivings to what he called 'apocryphal acts of sovereignty'. These sovereign actions set in motion the activity of constituent power in the daily ordeal of constitutional business. They took place, for instance, when particular constitutional norms were violated. Of themselves, such violations did not imply the destruction or suppression of the constitution as a whole. On the contrary, such cases confirmed constitutional validity. According to Schmitt, particular constitutional norms were violated in order to safeguard the substance of a constitution. Those violations were only 'measures' (1928: 107) and not constitutional norms. They were justified by particular exceptional and abnormal transitory situations. What these situations demonstrated was the 'superiority of the existential over mere normativity' (ibid.). They forced the recognition of sovereignty. Sovereignty manifested itself when the legal order was violated. According to Schmitt, whoever had the faculty to violate, and thus relativize, the legal order as a whole was sovereign. An absolute form of government, monarchical or democratic, implied a sovereign prince or a sovereign people who stood *legibus solutus*, above the law. By contrast, the purpose of the liberal ideal was, according to

Schmitt, to subject the power of the state to the rule of law and expel sovereignty from its domain. For Schmitt, this ideal of absolute normativity constituted a tenuous fiction. The political and the state could be erased by legal fabrications and methods of avoidance. Acts of sovereignty would always occur. But 'these acts of inevitable sovereignty' (Schmitt, 1928: 108) were better justified when they could be seen as grounded in the constituent power of the people.

One should note that Schmitt's aversion to democracy was not superseded by his recognition of democratic sovereignty in the *Verfassungslehre*. On the contrary, he intended to make sure that, once in power, democracy could be more easily restrained than enhanced (compare with Breuer, 1984: 510). Thus, like Sieyès, he tied the doctrine of the *pouvoir constituant* of the people to the division of powers and the anti-democratic principle of representation (Schmitt, 1928: 80; compare with Kervégan, 1992: 306). According to Sieyès, the sovereignty of the people was to be delegated to their elected representatives, who in turn were not to act as popular commissars or agents. Rejection of an imperative mandate allowed the assembled representatives to assume, with autonomy and independence, what Sieyès considered to be the ultimate expression of sovereignty: the exercise of constituent power. In Hobbesian fashion, Sieyès fused sovereignty and representation, but with a difference. The people, acknowledged Sieyès, never left the state of nature. The delegation of sovereignty was only temporary and could legitimately be reclaimed at any time. This was supported by his metaphysical conception of the *pouvoir constituant* as an inexhaustible *natura naturans*. By contrast, Schmitt, in his *Verfassungslehre*, distinguished the 'positive doctrine' from the 'metaphysics' of *pouvoir constituant*. The latter belonged to the 'doctrine of political theology' (1928: 80), which ascertained a 'completely systematic and methodical analogy' with Spinoza's view on the relation between *natura naturans* and *natura naturata* (Schmitt, 1921: 142). Conscious of the radical weapons that a political theological conception of sovereignty could place at its disposal, Schmitt denied them to democracy. In his *Verfassungslehre*, he came to accept and recognize the *pouvoir constituant* of the people only because he had found a way to disarm it.

6 • The Constitution of Political Liberalism

'The constitution of the modern civil *Rechtsstaat* is always a mixed constitution' (Schmitt, 1928: 200). This statement, which introduces chapter 16 of Schmitt's *Verfassungslehre*, was the axis on which the whole argument of the book turned. With this statement in favour of a constitutional *status mixtus* Schmitt forswore his earlier advocacy of political absolutism and appeared to come to terms with liberalism.[1] I leave to biographers and historians the question of whether he was motivated by a deep conviction or by purely prudential motives (matching his well-documented propensity to make the most of opportunities). Nor do I discuss Schmitt's fidelity or infidelity towards the Weimar constitution. Certainly the *Verfassungslehre* scrutinized that constitution with an analytic eye, and it could be argued that Schmitt aimed to undermine its foundations, that he exploited its discrepancies and broadcast its repressed choices. But my aim here is to appraise the conceptual viability of Schmitt's constitutional paradigm, which deviated significantly from the ideal constitution envisaged by liberalism. The liberal ideal (but not the liberal reality) maintained a critical and negative view with respect to the political and severely limited the sovereignty of the state. 'The tendency of the liberal rule of law is to repress the political' (ibid.: 41). By contrast, Schmitt boldly acknowledged and embraced the political, and incorporated political and liberal elements side by side. His own paradigm, the one that determined the structure of his argument in the *Verfassungslehre*, was a mixture.

> The constitutions of present-day bourgeois states are always composed of two elements; on the one hand, rule of law principles

---

[1] In 1923, Schmitt expressed admiration for the Catholic Church's *complexio oppositorum*. By this he meant the Church's 'astonishing adaptability', 'feminine flexibility' and the capacity to embrace any contradiction (1923a: 10). Also in 1923 Schmitt embraced the relative rationalism of the balance theory that steers a middle course between the absolute rationalism of the French Enlightenment and Hobbes's absolute voluntarism (see Chapter 3, above).

for the protection of bourgeois freedom *against* the state, and on the other hand, the political element from which the proper stateform is to be derived. (Ibid.)

My aim, then, is to assess Schmitt's conception of a constitutional *status mixtus*, one that combined apolitical liberalism with diverse political forms.

Section I analyses Schmitt's characterization of the paradigm of modern liberal constitutions as a balanced combination of opposed principles and political forms. These abstract principles and forms come to life in parliamentary regimes. Schmitt carefully defined principles that could be measured in the Weimar regime. Contrary to what one would expect from such a harsh critic of liberalism, Schmitt was able to strike a balance between rule-of-law principles and political forms which was not distant from the contemporary fulfilment of the liberal ideal.[2] In section II, I examine Schmitt's critique of Weimar liberal democracy in *Staat, Bewegung und Volk*, a work he wrote after the Nazi takeover. Here he detected and laid out the tripartite structure of the new Nazi constitution. His argument hinged on the contrast between the new constitutional reality and Weimar's bipartite constitutional structure. I will compare the account he now gave of the *Grundkonzeption* supporting the Weimar constitution with the earlier one offered in the *Verfassungslehre*. In section III I revisit the issue of whether a continuous strategic argumentation runs through all of Schmitt's intellectual production, culminating in his involvement with the Nazis. Or did Schmitt collaborate with the Nazis merely as a matter of personal advancement, a collaboration unrelated to the body of theory he developed in his Weimar years? My concern with this issue does not address

---

[2] Stephen Holmes assumes, from biographical considerations, that Schmitt retained a proto-fascist infatuation with the state throughout the Weimar period, and that this determined his uncompromising anti-liberalism. At the same time Holmes concedes that liberal societies have successfully combined liberal and political elements in their constitutional arrangements: 'Schmitt is simply wrong ... when he says that there is no such thing as liberal statecraft, only a liberal criticism of the state. (He is wrong to declare liberalism intrinsically antipolitical even when politics is defined arbitrarily as the act of identifying a mortal enemy; for liberal societies have done this with remarkable success)' (1993: 57). My point is that, in his *Verfassungslehre*, Schmitt presents a defensible account of the concrete political conditions that underlie the full realization of the rule of law.

biographical and historical considerations. Instead I will concentrate on conceptual continuities or discontinuities.

I

The *Verfassungslehre* took the notion of a mixed constitution very seriously. By this notion Schmitt did not intend to suggest that the Weimar constitution was a mixed-up constitution or a jumbled arrangement of disparate elements. On the contrary, he was committed to proving that, while the principles that entered into its design came from opposed traditions of thought, they could still be blended in a viable working manner. Genuine harmonization required that each of the principles in the mixture be given fair recognition and that a proper balance be struck between them. The *Verfassungslehre* may be seen as a work of accommodation, the formula of a *modus vivendi* in which liberal principles were embraced by this unforgiving political and philosophical critic of liberalism. Yet Schmitt's incorporation of liberal principles did not seem insincere or contrived. On the contrary, the *Verfassungslehre* appeared to broker a genuine philosophical *rapprochement*, or at the least, a stable conceptual compromise for the Weimar *modus vivendi* to rest on. The compromise proposed by Schmitt was set out in three consecutive movements. These were summarily discussed in chapter 16 of the *Verfassungslehre*.

1. The first and most fundamental constitutional *status mixtus* proposed by Schmitt assembled liberal and political elements. 'The liberal rule of law constitution is a mixed constitution in the sense that it blends a liberal element, in itself closed and independent, and a political formal element' (p. 202). The liberal element was defined by the rule of law or *Rechtsstaat*, but as Schmitt was quick to point out, the *Rechtsstaat*, in spite of all legality and normativity, was still a *Staat*, and thus 'contain[ed], aside from the specifically liberal rule of law element, a specifically political element' (p. 125).

The liberal element proper demanded, first and foremost, 'the protection of citizens from the abuse of state power' (p. 126). The state had to be seen as 'a strictly controlled steward of society' (p. 125). This determined the two principles that found their way into every modern constitution: a recognition of fundamental individual rights (principle of distribution) and a division of public powers (principle of political organization). As a liberal element, the rule of law, the Kantian *Herrschaft des Gesetzes* (p. 127), did not entail any specific principle of political organization. All that liberalism required in this respect was the limitation and control of the state on behalf of individual freedom. This relativization of the power and authority of the state should count as the most essential ingredient in any attempt to define liberalism. Individuals were best served by closely demarcating a domain of action free of political interference.

The political element of the constitution was meant to secure the unity of the state. This question, as Schmitt understood it, was not to be taken as a normative one, but factually and existentially. The unity of the state could not be rendered by the liberal element because the tendency of liberalism was to confront the state and stand apart from it. This was what the distinction between civil and political rights presupposed. Civil rights, liberal rights *par excellence*, belonged to individuals living in a state of nature, an extra-state situation of personal freedom. Their scope was unlimited in principle. Political rights, on the contrary, were privileges that could be held only within the state. They were limited in the sense that they could not 'be claimed by aliens. Otherwise the political unity and community would cease, and the fundamental presupposition of political existence, the possibility of distinguishing between friends and enemies, would disappear' (p. 169). This concept of the political, as the possibility of distinguishing friends from enemies, placed Schmitt explicitly in the Hobbesian camp.

The political element that unified the state could adopt different forms. In agreement with classical political philosophy, Schmitt distinguished three state-forms (*Staatsformen*): monarchy, aristocracy and democracy. The juxtaposition of liberal elements and any of these political form, produced the relativization of these forms. Pure state-forms became forms of government (*Regierungsformen*).[3] Pure or absolute monarchy

---

[3] The distinction between *Staatsform* and *Regierungsform* can be traced back to Kant's distinction between a *forma imperii* and a *forma regiminis* (Kant, 1957: 13).

became constitutionally limited monarchy; pure or absolute democracy, constitutional democracy. 'The only thing that could hinder the full actualization of the principle of the rule of law is the full actualization of a political form' (p. 201). This implied that the liberal demand for the rule of law did not require the complete abrogation of sovereignty and the state, that in fact liberalism and the political could be accommodated. The limitation of sovereign state power did not entail its elimination.[4] Schmitt had in mind the thought of the so-called doctrinaires in post-revolutionary France, who 'stressed that all state power must be limited'. They were particularly concerned about the full actualization of one particular state-form, namely democracy. Guizot, for instance, referred to 'a fully actualized democracy as chaos and anarchy', and Tocqueville perceived 'the dangers of egalitarian tyranny' (p. 201). Schmitt disagreed with these liberal doctrinaires. They may have acknowledged the validity of sovereignty, but at the same time they avoided its true meaning and employed 'the diversionary notion of a "sovereignty of the constitution" (i.e. of the rule-of-law principles) ... instead of positing a concretely existing political sovereignty' (p. 201). By means of this personification of written law the doctrinaires sought to elevate the constitution above the political and evaded the issue of whether the sovereignty belonged to the monarch or to the people.[5]

The juxtaposition of liberal principles and political claims was not presented by Schmitt as a purely ideal constitutional scheme. The very substance of the Weimar constitution was 'a fundamental political decision concerning the political form and the principles of the liberal rule of law' (p. 35). In his discussion with Kelsen, Schmitt identified the fundamental political assumptions that had been repressed by a normativist reading of the Weimar

---

[4] Similarly, in Rune Slagstad's view 'the aim of the liberal *Rechtsstaat* is to bind the *Machtstaat* to general norms – not to eliminate it' (1988: 110).

[5] Tocqueville, for example, with respect to the French constitution of 1830: 'The laws of 1830, like those of 1814, point out no way of changing the constitution: and it is evident that the ordinary means of legislation are insufficient for this purpose. As the King, the Peers, and the Deputies, all derive their authority from the Constitution, these three powers united cannot alter a law by virtue of which alone they govern. Out of the pale of the Constitution, they are nothing – *hors de la Constitution ils ne sont rien*' (Tocqueville, 1961: i, 102; cf. Schmitt, 1928: 8).

constitution. As will be shown below, Schmitt thought that the principle of the rule of law could not by itself give rise to a constitution. This could only come about as the result of a decision emanating from the subject of *pouvoir constituant*, a notion which Schmitt considered to be essentially political.

2. The liberal rule of law determined that liberal constitutions be mixed in a further sense. The political element that combined with the liberal element ought not remain unblended itself. Neither a fully actualized monarchy nor a fully actualized democracy, but a mixture of these political forms ought to be joined with the rule of law. Schmitt's constitutional paradigm contained a balanced mixture of democratic, aristocratic and monarchical aspects. This constitutional *status mixtus* coincided with an old tradition which stretched back to Aristotle. Schmitt recalled Polybius, for whom the Roman constitution was a cross between democratic elements realized in popular assemblies, aristocratic elements realized in the Senate and monarchical elements embodied by the magistracies. Aquinas also thought that the *status mixtus* was the best polity. And the Catholic Church's *complexio oppositorum*, combining the monarchical rule of the popes, papal elections by an aristocratic council of cardinal and a democratic openness that allowed 'the humblest shepherd from the Abruzzi' to rise to pontifical dignity, was, for Schmitt, the paradigmatic case of *status mixtus* (1923a: 10). The rise of the modern period coincided with the conflict between absolutists and monarchomachists. Machiavelli preferred either pure monarchy or pure democracy. Any form of government that oscillated between the two would not be able to last for long. He was followed by Bodin, Hobbes and Pufendorf, who were equally opposed to mixed forms of government. By contrast, monarchomachists retrieved the idea of the *status mixtus*. Calvin, for instance, talked about the ideal of a moderate aristocracy.

The most important development in this respect took place in England, where Bolingbroke was able to 'relate the doctrine of a pendulum or balance of powers to the theory of mixed government' (Schmitt, 1928: 203). In other words, a blending of state-forms could only take effect when there was distinction of state powers – a legislative power organized democratically and the executive monarchically. Bolingbroke took the English constitution as the paradigm of 'mixed government' (as opposed to 'simple government'): 'the English king represents the monarchical element; the Upper chamber, the aristocratic element; the Lower chamber, the democratic element; an unmixed, simple form would be arbitrary and "without control"' (Schmitt, 1928: 203; compare with p. 184).[6] Schmitt detected the influence of Bolingbroke's model of mixed government in the thought of Montesquieu, Burke, *The Federalist* and Sieyès. German liberals, like von Gagern and Dahlmann, held the same view.

All this confirms that Schmitt had set political absolutism aside but had not given up his conception of the political. He acknowledged that the Weimar constitution was a liberal document which was guided by the rule of law. But of itself the rule of law did not entail a constitution or a state-form proper. Constitutions came to be and could also cease to be. Their existence depended on the political decision that brought them into being, or as Sieyès discovered, it depended on the activity of the *pouvoir constituant* or constituent power. According to Schmitt, this power, the demiurge or *natura naturans* of a constitution, 'remains always outside the realm of the rule of law' (p. 204). The distinction between constitutional liberal and political elements finds here its ultimate foundation. All attempts to situate sovereignty within the constitution itself remained abstractions that missed the reality of the political. At the same time, by stressing this old idea of the *status mixtus*, which he defined as a liberal idea espoused by liberal thinkers, Schmitt was able to rescue the monarchical and aristocratic state-forms which appeared to him to have been displaced by the predominantly democratic form of the Weimar constitution.

In order to provide philosophical underpinnings for this retrieval of the notion of a *status mixtus*, Schmitt related the community and diversity of state-forms to two polarly opposite political principles, concretely embodied in every state: the principle of identity and the principle of representation. Schmitt wrote (p. 214):

The state rests, as a political unity, on the combination of two

---

[6] In his *The Idea of a Patriot King*, Bolingbroke acknowledges that 'there must be an absolute, unlimited, and uncontroulable power lodged somewhere in every government' (1965: 18).

opposed principles: the principle of identity (namely the presence of the people as a political unity . . . when capable of distinguishing between friend and enemy) and the principle of representation, by virtue of which the political unity is constituted by the government.

On the one hand, the people was capable of unified political action. This could happen when the people attained a full realization of its identity and homogeneity (*Gleichartigkeit*). The ability to distinguish between friends and enemies became the criterion for the existence of political consciousness. The Weimar constitution acknowledged that the people was the true subject of *pouvoir constituant* and the principle of identity determined the people's political unity. In truth, there could be no state without a people and a people would always be present and make its presence felt in the constitution of the state. On the other hand, the principle of representation was based on the fact that the political unity of a people could never attain full and permanent presence, it could never be present as a actual identity. It needed always to be represented personally by individuals.

The *status mixtus* was not an ideal notion. It could not claim the conceptual rank of the principles of identity and representation. Only stark acceptance and recognition of the reality of the political was able to validate it. For the truth was that no actual state could entirely give up the principle of identity, just as none could wholly renounce representation. The principles of identity and representation were but theoretically opposed points of reference, which excluded each other only when considered in the abstract. In reality they jointly configured the diversity of existing political unities. There could be no state without some kind of representation. The need for it would seem superfluous in cases when direct democracy was rigorously exercised, when, for instance, active New England citizens met in the proverbial townhall. But in truth, even in such cases, only adult members were present and their democratic encounter lasted only while they were present together in session. At the same time, no state could dispense with the structural principle of identity. Representation could never be implemented absolutely and in a pure fashion. The people could not simply be ignored because, as a matter of fact, it would always retain a presence. In sum, Schmitt formulated the contrasted principles of identity and representation, not with a view to hinder the *status mixtus*, but better to explain its potential.

3. The constitutional *status mixtus* involved a third aspect. Schmitt observed that the blending of political forms, particularly the democratic and monarchical forms, would not be possible without aristocratic mediation. Democracy and monarchy occupied opposite poles of the political spectrum. By contrast, aristocracy 'occupies the middle point between monarchy and democracy, and because of this it embodies a mixture' (p. 218). Schmitt reiterated: 'aristocracy is, in a certain sense, a *mixed* state-form' (p. 218). Because it was not grounded on the principle of identity, it was closer to monarchy than to democracy. Like monarchy, it rested on the principle of representation; but unlike monarchy, it did not involve the exclusive and all-absorbing representation by one individual.

The aristocratic state-form was not meant to be a merely regulatory paradigm, an abstract model that balanced opposed state-forms. Schmitt's constitutional realism situated this discussion of state-forms within the context of the struggles of the bourgeoisie during the nineteenth century. When the bourgeoisie stepped into the political arena, it favoured neither identity nor representation, neither democracy nor monarchy. Its political exertions were aimed at the establishment of the rule of law, advanced as prevention and resistance 'against all forms of state absolutism, democratic or monarchical; against extreme identity and extreme representation' (p. 216). This kind of mediation fitted naturally with the aristocratic spirit, whose principle, according to Schmitt, was moderation. And moderation found institutional expression in a parliamentary style of government. 'Parliamentary rule is an instance of aristocratic rule' (p. 218). Historically, parliaments, the seat of aristocratic moderation, appeared to have been the perfect platform to expose and defend the demands claimed by the bourgeoisie. Schmitt observed that the bourgeoisie in 1848, a crucial year in its quest for political influence, was able to stake an 'intermediate position', between absolute monarchy and 'expanding proletarian democracy' (p. 309). Against monarchy, it asserted the democratic rights of parliaments and professed to be the genuine representative of the people. Against democracy and its redistributive proclivities, the bourgeoisie advocated a strong monarchical government as the best protection for individual rights and private property (p. 309).

After 1848, and particularly during the Weimar republic, parliamentary rule identified itself without residue with the democratic state-form. Here lay, according to Schmitt, the root of the crisis of contemporary parliamentarism. When deputies were to be taken as agents or commissars of the people, parliaments lost their representative capacity. According to 'old liberalism', representatives were selected because of their intellectual abilities 'to attend to the needs of the political whole as such' (p. 217). German liberals, like Dahlmann, Gneist and Hasbach, understood the British parliamentary system to operate in this manner. But the rise of democracy brought with it a decline in the representative nature of parliaments and the transformation of deputies into 'dependent agents of interest and electoral groups' (p. 217). Representation was no longer tied to the notion of sovereignty. A shift towards an emphasis on identity meant that sovereign representation (*Repräsentation*) had to yield to delegate representation (*Vertretung*).[7]

These observations defined the core of Schmitt's critique of Weimar parliamentarism. It was a critique directed against the one-sided actualization of the democratic principle. Schmitt believed that the emphasis on democracy at the expense of the monarchical element was incongruous with the design of the Weimar constitution. The bourgeoisie embraced parliamentarism to avoid being caught in Germany's political cross-currents. Schmitt did not envisage parliamentarism as an enlightened ideal but as a pragmatic manœuvre that has resulted in 'the artistic forging of a delicate balance and a mixture of political forms' (p. 310). His own interpretation of the Weimar constitution brought to light the aristocratic nature of the parliamentary regime. An aristocratic state-form moderated the system of government and allowed a balance between identity and representation, bringing justice to both democratic and monarchical tendencies. 'The aristocratic element is only a formal element among others; the parliamentary system is not a proper political form, but a balance

---

[7] Schmitt refers to Bluntschli, who writes in his *Allgemeinen Staatsrecht*: 'Public law representation (*Repräsentation*) is entirely different from private law representation (*Stellvertretung*)' (1928: 209).

between opposed forms. In order to distinguish between state powers it employs democratic and monarchical formal elements' (p. 220). The democratic element was embodied by the legislative power. Under the Weimar constitution citizens could not only select their representatives but also had the power to make plebiscitary decisions. By contrast, the monarchical element was the principle that organized the executive.[8] In parliamentary regimes, like the one instituted by the Weimar constitution, 'the faculties of a King or a state President are especially strengthened in view of the distinction and balance of powers' (p. 220). A strong government stood out as one of the enduring principles of Schmitt's conservative philosophy. The constitutional *status mixtus* fostered by the aristocratic principle ensured that strong monarchical characteristics would be able to tame democratic indiscipline.

Schmitt's *rapprochement* with liberalism after 1923 was guided by this constitutional mixture of liberal and political principles, and the aristocratic blending of opposed state-forms. The Weimar constitution, as he interpreted it, was the liberal constitution of a modern bourgeois state. In Schmitt's reconstruction, liberal constitutions 'are always composed of two elements; on the one hand, rule of law principles for the protection of bourgeois freedom *against* the state, and on the other hand, the political element from which the proper state-form is to be derived' (p. 41). Schmitt did not conceive this combination of liberal and political elements as a mechanical juxtaposition of externally added parts which left them internally undisturbed. On the contrary, the liberal element successfully relativized its political counterpart by demanding a *status mixtus*, a balance between the different political or state-forms. Even if this implied giving up political absolutism, the *status mixtus* allowed Schmitt the opportunity to offer a reading of the constitution that reversed the

---

[8] The *Reichspräsident*, Schmitt acknowledged, did not legally inherit the role or the attributions of the Kaiser. But the coincidence of similar faculties showed that 'the position of the *Reichspräsident* was analogous to that of a monarchical head of the executive' (Schmitt, 1928: 292). According to Schmitt, this was again an indication of how one determined political formal element 'combines with the principles of the liberal *Rechtsstaat* and other opposed political formal elements, and are employed for the mixture which is typical of a liberal *Rechtsstaat* constitution' (ibid.).

Weimar republic's tendency towards a fully actualized democracy by reinforcing its monarchical disposition.

Schmitt's political antennae picked up the repressed political tendencies and aspirations within liberalism. Kelsen's attempt to neutralize those tendencies, and present a purely formalized legal interpretation of the constitution, was to be strongly rejected. This politicization of liberalism was not an untried idea. Schmitt looked back and attempted to retrieve the agenda of classical liberals like Constant, Tocqueville and Hegel who were not averse to deriving conservative conclusions from liberal premises. The idealism of the rule of law was possible only when embodied in the historical evolution of political practices and institutions. I do not think that a contemporary liberal like Hayek, who closely observed the authoritarian liberal compromise struck by Schmitt in Weimar, would find it objectionable.

II

In his *Staat, Bewegung und Volk*, Schmitt undersigned the death certificate of the Weimar constitution.[9] The book opened with his acknowledgement that 'the entire body of public law of the present German state rests today on its own foundation ... The Weimar constitution is no longer valid' (Schmitt, 1933f: 5). Since the enabling act of 24 March 1933 complied at least formally with the provisions stipulated by the Weimar constitution for cases of constitutional reform (article 76), it could be argued that the Nazi regime remained under its aegis. Schmitt wrote this book to lay this view conclusively to rest. He interpreted the enabling act as having brought forth a new, if only provisional, constitution. The Weimar regime had not just succumbed politically. On 24 March 1933, its philosophical underpinnings had been also completely demolished. Many of the institutions inspired by the Weimar constitution, like the office of the *Reichspräsident*, for example, continued in place. But by the time Schmitt was writing this book they had lost their original significance. 'All the

[9] The book was published in December 1933. It was first presented at the *Leipziger Juristentag*, a law conference held at Leipzig between 30 September and 3 October 1933, and attended by more than 12,000 judges, lawyers and state officials (Koenen, 1995: 493–6; compare with Lokatis, 1992: 52–3).

principles and rules which were essential to this constitution, both ideologically and organically, have been eliminated together with all its presuppositions' (1933f: 5).

This radical interpretation of the enabling act of 24 March was motivated by a rush to detach the Nazi regime from the Weimar constitutional system. Schmitt felt he was in possession of the conceptual tools needed to sever those links. Those tools had been in his possession at least since *Die Diktatur* (Schmitt, 1921). There his aims were to distinguish the notions of commissarial and sovereign dictatorship, and to secure for the latter the recognition of the juridical status enjoyed by the former. While the commissarial dictator suspended the constitution temporarily in order better to safeguard its integrity, the sovereign dictator assumed the *pouvoir constituant* and either abrogated or destroyed the constitution in order to bring forth a new one. Even if *Staat, Bewegung und Volk* did not resort to the notions of sovereign dictatorship or *pouvoir constituant* to describe the passage to the new Nazi order, the scene Schmitt had previously envisaged for the advent of a sovereign dictator was displayed by the enabling act of 24 March.[10] Beyond suggesting that the Weimar constitution had been abrogated and that a new one had taken its place, Schmitt again acknowledged that the enabling law of 24 March was only a provisional document. This point, which was insistently repeated throughout the book, sent a clear message: now was the time to enact a definitely new constitution. Schmitt saw here that an opportunity had come for him to attempt to dictate its terms.

Staat, Bewegung und Volk was the declaration of principles of this self-appointed *Kronjurist*. In it Schmitt discussed the principles that should guide the new constitutional system. He defined the principles of the new constitution to be enacted and

---

[10] According to Schwab, Schmitt failed to mention the concept of sovereign dictatorship in his *Staat, Bewegung und Volk*, because 'Hitler came to power legally in January, and promised to proceed constitutionally to alleviate the problems at hand. Even the enabling act did not give him absolute power' (1970: 105). This does not square, however, with Schmitt's insistence that the Weimar constitution was effectively abrogated on 24 March and that the enabling act was the new, if only provisional, constitution. In truth, the reason why Schmitt did not deem it opportune to employ the term 'dictatorship' is purely tactical. Dictatorship, he acknowledged, maintained its common association with terms like 'autocracy' and 'despotism' (cf. Schmitt, 1933f: 23).

contrasted them with the *Grundkonzeption* of the former 'liberal-democratic' one. In *Staat, Bewegung und Volk*, Schmitt articulated the basic structure of the Nazi regime, the groundwork which was supposed to sustain any future constitutional arrangement. The enabling act, other enacted pieces of legislation and the daily routine of government had already staked out a landscape and cleared away an area that looked vastly different from the one depicted by the Weimar constitution. Eventually the new reality brought forth by the Nazis would need formal consecration by a new constitutional system, even though Schmitt retained his doubts concerning the whole exercise of enacting written constitutions.

The constitutional blueprint proposed by Schmitt for the Nazi regime was designed to contrast with the Weimar constitution. A detailed account of the basic structure of the Weimar constitution was supposed to confirm the novelty of his proposal, for Schmitt needed to demonstrate that his project was not contaminated by liberal-democratic principles. A comparison between the account Schmitt now gave of the basic structure of the Weimar constitution (1933f: 22–32) and the one he presented earlier in his *Verfassungslehre*, reveals that in spite of Schmitt's effort to highlight the difference from his earlier position, his basic position remained unchanged. In 1928, Schmitt emphasized the fundamentally complex articulation of the Weimar constitution, which he characterized as a constitutional *status mixtus*. By presenting it in this fashion he intended to bring to light the internal tensions of its make-up and at the same time find ways to ease up and harmonize them. The *Verfassungslehre* was a work of accommodation where Schmitt steered opposed principles to converge into a workable structure. The particular tensions, and even contradictions, within the Weimar constitution seemed to yield to his overall project aimed at bringing liberal and political elements together. In 1933, this form of political liberalism could still be identified, despite his explicit critique of liberalism and a more overt and decisive affirmation of the political.

In *Staat, Bewegung und Volk*, Schmitt described the basic structure of the Weimar regime as a dyadic arrangement. Its two basic parts, society and the state, epitomized the unpolitical and the political aspects of a polity. The unpolitical element was defined by the *Rechtsstaat*, which typically bifurcated into a distributive part, the fundamental rights of individuals, and an organic part which set limits to the state, restricting its range of action (p. 23). Individual isolation demanded the shackling of the state, the pacification of the Leviathan (p. 24). This was the aim of the liberal-democratic forces that swept through the late nineteenth and early twentieth centuries and took away from parliaments their sovereign representative nature. During the Weimar period, the parliamentary system gave up sovereign representation in favour of a merely delegate representation or *Vertretung* (p. 23). As the commissioned agent of the diverse interests pullulating in civil society, parliament did not retain the autonomy required by a genuine representative function. With the Leviathan securely tied and bound, civil society, fragmented by multiple parties embodying recalcitrantly opposed interests, faced a neutralized state which was incapable of making the necessary political decisions and drawing adversarial lines of separation from its internal enemies. 'The constitution of such a system must logically become a purely instrumental and technical weapon that everybody wields against everybody else, even the enemies of the people and the state's enemies against the friends of the people' (p. 25). But all these liberal-democratic fabrications and fictions ended, according to Schmitt, on 30 January 1933, when 'the German Reich regained its political leadership and the German state found strength to annihilate state-inimical Marxism' (p. 31).

This description of the Weimar constitution as a dyadic system corresponded to the basic distinction Schmitt drew in his *Verfassungslehre* between the liberal and the political elements of the constitution, and also to the distinction between the formal principles of identity and representation. But now in *Staat, Bewegung und Volk* one found no explicit mention of a constitutional *status mixtus*, the balanced mixture of monarchic, aristocratic and democratic state-forms that made up the political element in the *Verfassungslehre*. Nor was there explicit mention of the aristocratic state-form which Schmitt had conceived as the mediation between the democratic and the monarchical state-forms. The mediating role of the formal opposition between the principles of identity and representation was also absent. The emphasis now fell on what Schmitt perceived as the reality of the Weimar regime behind a meaningless constitutional façade. That reality was a pluralist multi-party system which encouraged the maelstrom of entrenched and irreconcilable factions on which Germany's political unity drowned. From the vantage-point of the Nazi Party in power, the Weimar regime did not rest on a constitutional *status mixtus*, a balancing act able to accommodate opposed principles and diverse state-forms. Schmitt saw it now as a liberal-democratic document from which monarchical possibilities were excluded. Left behind was the certainty he had felt of having his own authoritarian expectations fulfilled by the existing constitution. His conservative philosophy could now find no accommodation within Weimar's liberal *Grundkonzeption*.

In contrast to Weimar's bipartite scheme, the Nazi regime had developed into a basic structure made up of three elements: state, movement and the people. Distinguishable, but not separable, all three aspects of the newly created Nazi order formed an integrated totality. Those aspects could be compared to 'strands' woven together, 'running side by side each other in orderly fashion, meeting at certain decisive points, particularly at the apex, maintaining defined and articulated reciprocal contacts and cross connexions' (1933f: 12). Each element constituted, according to Schmitt,

> a specific side and a particular element of the whole. The state may then be seen, in a strict sense, as the politically static element, the movement as the politically dynamic element and the people as the apolitical element that grows under the protection and shade of political decisions.

To consider them in strict separation from each other, and not in constant hierarchical interaction, 'would correspond to the liberal dismemberment', which initiated and promoted the relativization of the state.

But there was really no balance to be struck between state, movement and people, no veritable *status mixtus*. According to Schmitt, the elements of this triad did not have an equal standing. Both the state and the people were subordinate to and borne by the movement. The movement comprised them both; it 'permeates and leads' them (ibid.). The movement, as Schmitt conceived it, owed its organization to the Nazi Party. It was a populist state-party which Schmitt took pains to distinguish from typical non-hierarchically organized liberal-democratic parties.

Schmitt assigned to the movement a mediating role. It stood between the state and the people and bore them both. Accordingly, the state and the people would be 'surpassed and decisively permeated, directed and formed' by the movement (1933f: 14). The movement, and not the state, was responsible for leadership. The movement had thus become a repository for the aristocratic and monarchical state-forms distinguished in the *Verfassungslehre*. There they were profiled as counterweights to democracy. With democracy definitely out of the picture Schmitt could now reaccommodate his conservative principles and place them at the service of a counter-revolutionary cause. The time was ripe to republish *Politische Theologie* (Schmitt, 1922a), his early revolutionary conservative tract, with a few 'non-essential' omissions.[11]

III

The issue that divides Schmittian scholarship is continuity. Those who align themselves with liberal-democratic views find a continuous line of argumentation running through all Schmitt's intellectual production – from his early *Gesetz und Urteil* to *Staat, Bewegung und Volk*, written by a then card-carrying member of the Nazi Party (compare with Scheuerman, 1996: 573–4). However powerfully argued and richly insightful, the writings that predate his involvement with the Nazis are all tainted. *Staat, Bewegung und Volk*, for instance, would make explicit the fascism that lay under the surface of the *Verfassungslehre*. It is argued that there is nothing theoretically salvageable in Schmitt's work, except perhaps his critique of liberalism, the most incisive and comprehensive within the fascist movement. By contrast, for those who share Schmitt's conservative views, his collaboration with the Nazis marks a clear break in continuity, a betrayal of the moderate views he held during Weimar and before. Works like *Staat, Bewegung und Volk* merely attempt to provide legal foundations, 'along the lines of a traditional authoritarian regime', to a 'precocious movement' in need

---

[11] In fact, the omissions were quite substantial. They amounted to about three pages of text and all made reference to the views of Erich Kaufmann.

of them (Bendersky, 1983: 242) or they constitute at most an opportunistic tactic, totally devoid of inner value. This line of interpretation will make use of psychological profiling and saddle Schmitt with character flaws – his opportunism and vanity knew no limits (compare with Schwab, 1970: 107; Bendersky, 1983: 242). This allows these conservative readers to save his Weimar production as a conservative thinker's predilection for strong state authority.

The comparison between Schmitt's *Verfassungslehre* and *Staat, Bewegung und Volk* that I have sketched in this chapter is meant to show that these interpretations do not represent antithetical points of view. The case for a break in the continuity of Schmitt's thought accords with the decisive manner in which *Staat, Bewegung und Volk* forsook the constitutional *status mixtus* he had proposed in the *Verfassungslehre* and how readily he proclaimed the demise of the Weimar constitution. To anyone holding the view that that constitution was still valid (it had not been, in fact, formally abrogated by the Nazis, who, until that moment, showed a surprising respect for constitutional procedure), Schmitt's book was bound to make one thing perfectly clear: the Weimar constitution had been destroyed and the enabling act of 24 March was the new German constitution. Furthermore, *Staat, Bewegung und Volk* demonstrated that not only the Weimar regime, but also the nineteenth-century bureaucratic state (*Beamtenstaat*) had perished in 1933.

> On this 30 January the nineteenth-century Hegelian bureaucratic state, characterized by the unity of the officialdom and the state-bearing strata, was replaced by another state construction. On that day, therefore, one might say that Hegel died. (1933f: 31–2)

Schmitt employed this striking imagery to impress on his readers the Nazi regime's novelty. The Hegelian *Beamtenstaat*, now dead, had been gravely ill since at least 1848. The Weimar republic only precipitated the process that led to its downfall. Schmitt offered a simple diagnosis: ever since the officialdom lost its autonomy and privileged position as the state-bearing stratum, and thus 'became the bureaucratic instrument of the state-bearing powers' (ibid.: 14), the state forfeited its capacity to make political decisions. The Nazi regime could not rely on a stultified machinery. The movement now offered vital leadership that could embrace in its vigorous fold both the state and the people. In the *Verfassungslehre*, by contrast, Schmitt admitted that despite the fact that the figure of the 'bureaucrat was always suspect to the radical representatives of bourgeois liberalism' (1928: 181),[12] the Weimar constitution, an essentially liberal document, 'continued the grand tradition of the German *Beamtenstaat*' (ibid.). It did so because its 'mixed character (*Mischcharakter*)' combined two principles, fundamental human rights and constitutional guarantees, and then simply ignored any possibility of conflict between them (ibid.: 181–2).

The comparative study that I have presented also gives grounds for defending the case for continuity. There are conceptual patterns and clusters of ideas that remain formally the same in spite of being put to different use on different occasions, or applied to different situations. All this is suggestive of Schmitt's postulation of a meta-legal standpoint, a substantive ground on which rests a manifold of legal phenomena and other manifestations.[13] There is a metaphysical core to Schmitt's thought whose vestiges are to be found in all his works and constitutes the main reason for his rejection of legal positivism, the view that legal systems are closed in themselves and do not need objective principles to account for their unity and systematicity. Schmitt believed, by contrast, that the condition of unity and systematicity of a constitution lay in a meta-legal foundation, in a unified

---

[12] This is one of the many occasions on which Schmitt sees fit to distinguish between two liberal factions: the new radical liberals, allied to democratic stateforms, and the old liberals who do not object to the monarchical principle.

[13] At times, Schmitt appeared to develop a political ontology alongside his political theology. A case in point was the use he made of the scholastic conception of substance, which he considered untouched by the critique of Hume and Kant (Schmitt, 1921: 55). In Jean Gerson's distinction between substance and exercise of power, 'the magic wand of Scholasticism' (compare with Schmitt, 1921: 44), he saw the basis for the modern notion of sovereignty. According to Schmitt, Gerson, a conciliarist, had come to terms with the Church's monarchical governance and the *plenitudo potestatis* of the popes. He maintained that papal power could be subject to limitations in its exercise, but in its substance it was unlimited. The modern notion of sovereignty, as the substance of state omnipotence, could be now conceived as unlimited in principle (ibid.: 193). Similarly, the distinction between substance and exercise may explain the dynamic and static aspects that Ingeborg Maus detects in Schmitt's theory of the constitution (Maus, 1976: 107–21).

ontological or substantive core.[14] Only such a foundation could hold together, as a *natura naturans*, Weimar's constitutional *status mixtus* and the Nazi regime's opposition between the state and the people.

Perhaps the best glimpse to be had of this substantivist way of thinking appeared in his early *Der Wert des Staates*, where Schmitt depicted himself as an advocate of immediacy, as one 'who only sees that every course of water, all imposing rivers and small streams, flow in the end into the sea, in whose infinity they find peace (*Ruhe*)' (1914: 110). This was the same peace that he detected in 1933, in the new preface to his *Politische Theologie*, where he noted that the urgencies of the present could obscure the peaceful being (*das ruhende Sein*) that underlay what he thought to be a great political movement.

---

[14] William Scheuerman, a defender of the continuity thesis, follows John McCormick (compare with chapter 2, n. 17) in believing that 'whereas *Dictatorship* for the most part can be read as a defence of a temporary commissarial dictatorship ... in *Political Theology* we can already detect the makings of ... a sovereign dictatorship' (1996: 588). But Scheuerman does not consider that both these works assume the distinction between the substance and the exercise of sovereignty which is the basis for Schmitt's notion of sovereign dictatorship (compare with Schmitt, 1921: 44, 105 and 194). When Schmitt's metaphysics of substance is taken into account no break in the continuity of this thought can be detected at that stage (compare Schmitt, 1922a: 22; 1922b: 42).

7 • Hayek contra Schmitt

Perhaps no one has denounced Schmitt's intellectual work so steadfastly as Hayek. He did so initially in 1944 in his *The Road to Serfdom* and was still strongly censuring Schmitt thirty-five years later in the third volume of his *Law, Legislation and Liberty*. In his view, Schmitt's critique of liberalism contributed greatly to the abrogation of the rule of law in Germany during the 1930s and to the precipitation of one of the most serious crises of European liberalism. Hayek acknowledged that the principles of the liberal *Rechtsstaat* received the most intense theoretical scrutiny in Germany during the nineteenth and early part of the twentieth centuries. It was also in Germany that the liberal *Rechtsstaat* was most decisively challenged. His acquaintance with Schmitt's legal and political theory derived from this fact. According to Hayek, Schmitt was an extraordinary German student of politics, who 'in the 1920's probably understood the character of the developing form of government better than most people and then regularly came down on what appears both morally and intellectually the wrong side' (1979: 194 n. 11). In this period, 'long before Hitler came to power', Schmitt devoted 'his formidable intellectual powers to fight against liberalism in all its forms' (Hayek, 1973: 71).[1] The success of his interpretation of the Weimar constitution, particularly after the breakdown of the Great Coalition and the consolidation of the presidial system in March 1930, and then his personal friendship with prominent conservative ideologues and active politicians, allowed him access to Hitler's regime and to become, in the words of Hayek, its *Kronjurist* (1967: 169). In his *The Road to Serfdom*, Hayek denounced Schmitt as 'the leading Nazi theoretician of totalitarianism' (1944: 187) and as the first one to embark on a philosophical investigation to uncover its essence. No longer finding meaning in the separation between state and civil society,

---

[1] For this assessment on Schmitt's position, Hayek relies on a commentary on his views by Georg Dahm, a Nazi ideologue (Hayek, 1973: 161).

he hit upon 'the essence of [its] definition' (ibid.). Later, in his *The Constitution of Liberty* and in three volumes of *Law, Legislation and Liberty*, Hayek paid special attention to his critique of the notion of the *Rechtsstaat* and to his decisionism. Schmitt's views were used as an illustration of how a legal philosophy that criticized liberalism and contravened the principles of the liberal *Rechtsstaat* was determined to lay the foundations of totalitarianism.[2]

Surprisingly, while condemning Schmitt's work *in toto* for its anti-liberal bias, Hayek also praised portions of his work, particularly his two most important books of the Weimar period. According to Hayek,

> the conduct of Carl Schmitt in the Hitler regime does not alter the fact that, of the modern German writings on the subject, his are still the most learned and perceptive; see particularly his *Verfassungslehre* (Munich, 1929), and *Der Hüter der Verfassung* (Tübingen, 1931). (Hayek, 1960: 485)[3]

He also accepted one of Schmitt's key postulates, the one that laid the groundwork for his accommodation to liberalism: the distinction between liberalism and democracy (ibid.: 104 n. 2). Related to this distinction is another one which is essential to Schmitt's authoritarian liberalism – the distinction between totalitarianism and authoritarianism. This is a doctrinal point that is also accepted by Hayek (ibid.: 103). Again, in his *Constitution of Liberty* Hayek examined the conception of law presupposed by the ideal of the rule of law. In accordance with the traditional liberal conception, law must possess the attributes of generality and abstractness. In his discussion Hayek referred to and borrowed from Schmitt's arguments in *Unabhängigkeit der Richter, Gleichheit vor dem Gesetz und Gewährleistung des*

---

[2] In Hayek's original draft of his *Law, Legislation and Liberty*, which he presented in 1970 to students at a seminar held at the University of California at Los Angeles (henceforth I refer to this text as the *California Manuscript*), he uses the following title to introduce the section in which he discusses Schmitt's legal theory, 'The Foundations of Totalitarianism in the Philosophy of Law'. This title does not appear in the definitive version.

[3] Earlier, in his *The Road to Serfdom*, Hayek had presented Schmitt's *Der Hüter der Verfassung* as the work of a 'leading Nazi expert on constitutional law' (1944: 178 n. 5).

Privateigentums nach der Weimarer Verfassung (*Independence of the Judge, Equality before the Law and Private Property Warranties according to the Weimar Constitution*) (1926). This was a defence of the generality of laws written on the occasion of a referendum on the expropriation of crown property. In Schmitt's view, as enactments of a legislative authority, laws had to be general and abstract, and could not be confused with measures or decrees. The latter were instructions that ordered state functionaries to perform certain tasks. In the same vein, Hayek maintained that the generality of laws made them 'essentially long-term measures, referring to yet unknown persons, places, or objects. Such laws must always be prospective, never retrospective, in their effect' (1960: 208). This conception of law, shared by Schmitt and Hayek, clearly placed them both within the bounds of liberalism. Finally, in the chapter of *Law, Legislation and Liberty* devoted to his model constitution, Hayek acknowledged that the view defended by Schmitt in his *Politische Theologie*, that sovereign was he who decided on the exception, had 'some plausibility' (Hayek, 1979: 125).

The aforesaid constitutes evidence that Hayek's appraisal of Schmitt's views was riddled with ambiguity. He condemned his work *in toto* because everything that Schmitt wrote appeared to him as determined by a single aim – the refutation of liberalism in all its forms. In particular, his Weimar production had to be rejected because it paved the way towards Nazi totalitarianism. At the same time, Hayek acknowledged the plausibility of some of Schmitt's ideas, particularly those developed during the Weimar period. Those views could be accommodated within a liberal framework and could thus be said to match his own standards. Hayek himself did not welcome this possibility and, as I will show below, misrepresented Schmitt's views in order to keep him at a distance. In any case, what is paramount in Hayek's treatment of Schmitt is the blanket condemnation of his ideas and the fact that he did not recognize Schmitt's attempt to accommodate his views to liberal constitutionalism. This allowed him to use those aspects of Schmitt's thought that he found 'most learned and perceptive' without the need to acknowledge that some of those views bore a resemblance, and were often remarkably akin, to his own position (compare with Scheuerman, 1995: 124–5). Hayek could thus profit from

Schmitt without having to acknowledge explicitly his debt to such a controversial author.

Hayek was right in stressing the significance of Schmitt's contribution to Nazi ideology, but was wrong in thinking that the thrust of his entire production, particularly during the Weimar period, was anti-liberal. Schmitt's main concern was the specific form attained by liberalism in the course of its history. Early liberalism had not been infiltrated by democracy and could thus still maintain an attachment to substantive values – the values of private property, individuality and the rule of law. The rise of democracy led to the positivity of liberalism. Positivism purged those liberal values and encouraged allegiance to a purely formal *Rechtsstaat*, devoid of any aim or content. Deprived of a *Weltanschauung*, liberalism lost its capacity to make political decisions and succumbed to relativism and agnosticism. According to Schmitt, the political impotence of Weimar parliamentarism was a direct result of the extinction of early liberalism and the rise of democratic liberalism. His objections were thus aimed at the latter, at a form of liberalism that had proven unable to preserve the main body of its doctrine free from democratic contamination. In this respect, Hayek's interpretation of Schmitt's work needs to be corrected. A reassessment of Hayek's view on this author should also lead to a reassessment of his own liberalism. His arguments would seem to represent the exact antagonists of Schmitt's legal and political theory. But aspects of his liberal conception considerably shorten the distance that separates him from Schmitt. It seems to me that an understanding of politically conservative liberalism, or 'authoritarian liberalism' (Heller, 1933; compare with Haselbach, 1991: 54), should help to bridge that distance.

I

Hayek shared Schmitt's understanding of liberalism as a tradition of thought that affirmed the moral sovereignty of individuals. This is the intellectual tradition that stemmed from thinkers like Locke, Kant and Mill.[4] Well-acquainted with that tradition,

---

[4] In Anglo-Saxon countries, the term 'liberal' refers to those public policies

Schmitt postulated that the first demand of liberalism was the protection of individuals. In an apt formulation, he maintained that individuals constituted the *terminus a quo* and the *terminus ad quem* of liberalism (Schmitt, 1932b: 70). An ingrained distrust of the state and the political attended this affirmation of individuality. The limitation of the power and authority of the state and its subordination to the interests of civil society was, according to Schmitt, an essential liberal demand. The liberal notion of rule of law or *Rechtsstaat*[5] was the legal procedure that guaranteed the full attainment of that demand by fostering the limitation of the political and the state.

Hayek also shared Schmitt's definition of the liberal rule of law as advancing the two general legal conditions required by a liberal polity. On the one hand, Schmitt assumed that civil society needed to be regarded as a protected sphere where individuals were accorded the freedom to develop and launch forth in every direction. As such, civil society was granted precedence over the state, and the latter was taken as instrumental to the ends individuals set for themselves.[6] The liberal rule of law, then, presupposed a clear separation between civil society and the state; and, as a separate sphere, civil society was legitimated in its demands for the least possible interference in its internal affairs. On the other hand, Schmitt maintained that the liberal rule of law

---

designed to further equality by maintaining a certain level of social welfare. Both Hayek and Schmitt would agree in defining this meaning of liberalism as more akin to social democracy and as incompatible with its classical definition.

[5] According to Hayek, these two expressions are equivalent (1960: 484 n. 35).

[6] Hayek avoids the use of the term 'state' and recommends instead the use of the term 'government': 'There is no need ... to bring in the metaphysically charged term "state". It is largely under the influence of continental and particularly Hegelian thought that in the course of the last hundred years the practice of speaking of the "state" (preferably with a capital "S"), where "government" is more appropriate and precise, has come to be widely adopted' (1973: 48). In the *California Manuscript*, one finds, in a paragraph deleted from the final version, an equally 'metaphysically charged' characterization of 'government'. Hayek writes: 'Government as the source of law and order and the protection against injustice and violence in every respect deserves that reverential respect of which in earlier time the Kings and later, at least in common law countries, the courts of justice were the symbol. The "authoritative" or "sovereign" functions (the *Hoheitsrechte* or *Herrschaft*, which play such an important role in Continental public law) possess a wholly legitimate aura of sanctity or special respect as acts of prerogative which only a specially authorized agency should enjoy.'

postulated that a state, limited in principle, should maintain a separation of its powers and competencies as a guarantee that it would remain within its own bounds. These two principles made up the heart of liberal constitutionalism. Accordingly, the structure of liberal constitutions reflected this dual condition. First, constitutions recognized the priority of individual rights. They were to be protected, but not established or generated, by the limited legislative powers of the state. This corresponded to what Schmitt called a 'principle of distribution' (1928: 126). Second, in order to make sure that the state did not overstep its limitations, its powers and competencies were to be strictly defined and separated. It was only in this latter function, as a 'principle of organization' (ibid.), that the liberal rule of law had its proper task. The classical liberal formulation of the rule of law, we are reminded by Hayek, was given by William Paley: 'the first maxim of a free state is that the laws be made by one set of men, and administered by another; in other words, that the legislative and the judicial character be kept separate' (Hayek, 1960: 173).

Hayek acknowledged that the ideal of the rule of law was 'more than constitutionalism: it require[d] that all laws conform to certain principles' (ibid.: 205). This meant that not every law enacted by a legislative authority could be considered to be a law that agreed with that ideal. More than a purely formal conception of law, Hayek required that law be defined by certain material or substantive criteria. In a liberal polity 'each individual has a recognized private sphere clearly distinct from the public sphere, and the private individual cannot be ordered about but is expected to obey only the rules which are equally applicable to all' (ibid.: 207–8). 'Laws in the substantive sense', that is, laws which conformed materially with the rule of law, were 'essentially long-term measures, referring to yet unknown cases and containing no references to particular persons' (ibid.: 208). According to Hayek, the best description of the ideal rule of law was the one given by Locke in the *Second Treatise*: 'Whoever has the legislative or supreme power in a common-wealth, is bound to govern by established standing laws, promulgated and known to the people, and not by extemporary decrees' (ibid.: 170). *Ex post facto* interference in the affairs of civil society was thereby ruled out. Laws should be abstract and general, independent of the particular will of the legislator and independent, too, of the particular ends of particular people. The persistence and endurance required by legal systems meant that only standing laws could be taken into account.

In this affirmation of a substantive conception of law, Hayek stood very much in agreement with Schmitt. In the *Verfassungslehre*, Schmitt distinguished between the rule of law as a generic notion and the liberal rule of law. The latter presupposed a state whose function was limited to 'the preservation of the legal order'; and by legal order he meant 'a *liberal* legal order, viz. one based on private property and personal freedom, one which considers the state to be the armed warranty of liberal peace, order and security' (Schmitt, 1928: 130; my emphasis). This corresponded to the substantive core embraced by early liberalism. In addition, Schmitt postulated that the conception of law required by the liberal rule of law demanded conformity with four specific criteria: generality; predictability and measurability of all political and juridical decisions; an administration subject to judicial review (ibid.: 130-2); and equality before the law (ibid.: 154-5). In his *The Constitution of Liberty*, Hayek adopted these same four criteria (1960: 207-12), and acknowledged his debt to Schmitt (p. 207 n. 9). He explicitly referred to the memorandum written by Schmitt in 1926, where he proposed that the distinction between law and measure, together with equality before the law, constituted the 'proper foundation of the *Rechtsstaat* and the most effective warranty against all despotism' (1926: 23). Schmitt defined laws as general and abstract, and measures as concrete, particular and open to the needs and interests of particular individuals or groups. The generality and persistence of law was meant equally to protect all individuals from prerogative and arbitrary authority (Schmitt, 1928: 139–41). Schmitt and Hayek agreed in assuming that the legal foundations of liberalism consisted in this objective encirclement of authority. In other words, coercive orders were in principle incompatible with the liberal idea, but they could be permitted on condition that the authorities in charge of implementing them allowed all individuals equally to foresee and calculate the course of legal actions.

Both Schmitt and Hayek acknowledged that the rule of law remained a purely procedural condition. The requirement of equality before the law and the rejection of the particular opportunities, privileges and dispensations conveyed by particular measures implied that the rule of law was indifferent to the consequences of its application (Schmitt, 1928: 154; compare with Hayek, 1960: 231–3). The emergence of substantive differences among individuals was of no concern here. The value of individual freedom would be jeopardized only by attempts to modify and correct such outcomes under the guidance of principles defined by social justice and by state intervention (Hayek, 1960: 93). In this respect, Schmitt's attacks on democratic liberalism matched Hayek's assault on the welfare state. As William Scheuerman has noted, Schmitt sought to dispose of the Weimar welfare state and thus eliminate the burdensome obligations imposed by the principle of social justice (1995: 122). The alternative to this state of affairs was summarily captured by Schmitt's formula 'a strong state and a sound economy', which sought to give capitalist managers freedom from state welfare regulation. At the same time, a decrease in state regulation could not amount to a decline in discretionary state authority. On the contrary, only a very strong state, one that strongly asserted its monopoly over the political, would be able to protect the independence required by civil society.

II

An agreement on how to define liberalism need not entail a shared commitment to its principles and practices. Schmitt was not committed to the rule of law. He came around to accept it only when he concluded that it presented no obstacles to the formation of a strong state. Strengthening the authority of the state could not be said to be Hayek's primordial aim. First and foremost, he pledged allegiance to a market society guided by liberal principles and sought to implement those principles by strict adherence to the rule of law. A strong sovereign state did not appear to have been included in his programme for the Great Society. On the contrary, his legal theory was 'mainly concerned with the limits that a free society must place upon the coercive powers of government' (Hayek, 1979: 41). He acknowledged that Locke, whose formulation of the rule of law had a decisive influence on him, was 'loath to recognize any sovereign power', and that his work should be interpreted 'as an assault on the very idea of sovereignty' (1960: 171). Even his contradictors have acknowledged 'his anxieties about the growth of discretionary state authority' (Scheuerman, 1995: 127). By contrast, Schmitt has been generally been perceived as advocating a strong state and as a critic of the rule of law. This perception can be readily verified by considering his enthusiastic support for authoritarian rule and his unequivocal condemnation of the rule of law. How could their agreement be said to be anything but superficial? How could the paleo-liberal Hayek and the proto-fascist Schmitt be said to share liberal convictions?

In an article entitled 'Was bedeutet der Streit um dem Rechtsstaat?' and known to Hayek (Schmitt, 1935; compare with Hayek, 1960: 495), Schmitt explained his views on liberalism and the rule of law. (This is important because it was written during the high point of his involvement with the Nazi movement.) His attack on the *Rechtsstaat* did not imply an espousal of the rule of force or *tel est nôtre plaisir*. What he intended was simply its replacement by 'an immediately just (*gerechten*) state' (1935: 190; compare with Hayek, 1944: 79; and Koenen, 1995: 466–7). By tracing the genesis of the *Rechtsstaat* in Germany, Schmitt was able to identify what he considered to be its most offensive features. When Robert von Mohl first defined it in 1832, his only concern was to weaken the state by subordinating it to the interests of individualist civil society. His aim was to avoid an imposition of substantive theocratic or patriarchalist requirements by the state. As a polemical notion, it was directed against two types of state: against the Christian state and against a state 'understood as the rule of *Sittlichkeit*, namely the Prussian bureaucratic state of Hegel's political philosophy' (Schmitt, 1935: 191). A reaction against Mohl and in favour of preserving a stronger state, but falling still within liberal parameters, was initiated by Lorenz von Stein and Rudolf von Gneist. Both these authors sought to reverse its subordination to civil society, but were not able to transcend the terms by which that subordination was originally defined, namely the separation of law from religion and *Sittlichkeit*, and a purely juridical understanding of law (ibid.). This would ultimately mean that the *Rechtsstaat*'s demand for a neutralized state would persevere and would confirm its instrumental value for civil society.

The definitive victory of the liberal *Rechtsstaat*, and the demise of the remnants of the Christian and the Hegelian ethical states, was secured by Friedrich Julius von Stahl, on whom Schmitt would concentrate his animosity. He blamed him for ruining and discrediting Hegel's state. Stahl's own conception of a 'Christian *Rechtsstaat*' was a sham, for it led the true Christian state 'into the *Rechtsstaat*'s conceptual snare' (Schmitt, 1935: 192). According to Schmitt, the *Rechtsstaat* that Stahl conceived was purely formal and devoid of any substantive content, Christian or otherwise. Stahl had written: 'The *Rechtsstaat* says nothing about the aims and content of the state, but defines only the manner and character of achieving those aims' (ibid.; compare with Kaufmann, 1906: 86).[7] Schmitt interpreted this view, which neutralized the *Rechtsstaat* and attributed to it a purely instrumental function, as in perfect accordance with liberalism. There were two reasons, according to Schmitt, why Stahl's conception contributed to the liberal demolition of the state. First, by placing the state at the service of the rule of law a justification was given for its subordination and ultimate devaluation with respect to civil society. Second, the instrumental function Stahl attributed to the *Rechtsstaat* led to its formalization. By becoming an 'instrument for the realization of whatever content or aim' (Schmitt, 1935: 193), as Stahl defined it, the *Rechtsstaat* became not only impervious to religion and *Sittlichkeit*, but also incapable of accommodating the political. According to Schmitt, this was not so in the case of the 'early liberal *Rechtsstaat*' (ibid.: 196). The *Rechtsstaat* envisioned by Stein and Gneist[8] had room for values and political discretion. This was no longer the case with the formalized *Rechtsstaat*, the positivist legal state (*Gesetzesstaat*), advanced by Stahl and later perfected by Hans Kelsen.

Aside from the fact, acknowledged by Schmitt in 1934,[9] that

---

[7] For Hayek, Stahl's formulation constituted 'the best-known formulation of the *Rechtsstaat* as it emerged' (1960: 483; compare with Schmitt, 1928: 125–6).

[8] In his *Verfassungslehre*, Schmitt referred to Rudolf Gneist as 'an eminent representative of the doctrine of the liberal *Rechtsstaat*' (1928: 126).

[9] In his article 'Nationalsozialismus und Rechtsstaat', published on 24 March 1934, Schmitt acknowledged that 'the *Rechtsstaat* is a state governed by a series of impersonal legal rules and not by a Führer in person ... A characteristic of the *Rechtsstaat*, the organizational separation between legislative and executive powers, had been eliminated from the national socialist state. Nowadays the executive legislates. But, according to the traditional liberal conception, where the legislative falls into the hands of the executive, there is no *Rechtsstaat*' (1934a: 715).

the Nazi regime could not be counted as a *Rechtsstaat* because it violated its fundamental principles, the objections he raised in 1935 were not much different from those he raised during the Weimar republic. In both cases those objections were directed against a formal *Rechtsstaat*, but did not directly impinge on the substantive *Rechtsstaat* defended by old liberals like Stein and Gneist. In the case of Gneist, for example, the substantive aspect that would make the rule of law operative was the participation of wealthy and instructed men in the administration of the state (Schmitt, 1928: 258). Schmitt's own understanding of what he termed 'old liberalism' was infused with aristocratic values (ibid.: 217) and this predisposed him to look favourably on it. When he stated that the 'early liberal *Rechtsstaat* . . . still subscribed to a *Weltanschauung* and was capable of a political confrontation' (1935: 196), he could not have come up with a more flattering observation with regard to liberalism. Schmitt's opposition to the rule of law was restricted to the formal rule of law demanded by the simultaneous rise of legal positivism and the welfare state in Germany. He seemed perfectly at ease with a conservative reading of liberalism, with the 'early liberalism' that could accommodate the political as such. This ease marks the composed *rapprochement* of conservative and liberal values he achieved in his *Verfassungslehre*.

In Hayek we find a puzzling account of Schmitt's position. He indicted Schmitt as an adversary of the rule of law and ascribed to him the view that the state should not be bound legally and ought to 'be released from the fetters of abstract rules' (Hayek, 1960: 239). Hayek implied that what determined Schmitt's rejection of the rule of law was legal positivism. Contrary to the proponents of natural law, who derived the validity of positive laws from rules that were not made by men but had been 'found', legal positivists denied 'the existence of rules which [were] not of the deliberate making of any lawgiver' (ibid.: 237). By stating that 'law by definition consists exclusively of deliberate commands of a human will' (ibid.), Hayek posited decisionism as the underpinning of legal positivism. While he acknowledged that legal positivists supported the notion of the rule of law, he also stated that theirs was a purely formal *Rechtsstaat*, from which every substantive content has been excised. The classical conception of the rule of law was substantive. Its main assumption was that the power of legislation had to conform to some pre-given strictures. But in Germany, particularly during the Weimar republic, a formal conception of the rule of law became dominant:

> The substantive conception of the *Rechtsstaat*, which required that the rules of law possess definite properties, was displaced by a purely formal concept which required merely that all action of the state be authorized by the legislature. In short, a 'law' was that which merely stated that whatever a certain authority did was legal. (ibid.)

What concerned Hayek most about legal positivism and its purely formal *Rechtsstaat* was that, in rejecting any meta-legal foundation, it rendered itself incapable of requiring limits to the power of legislation.

The consequences of this view could be readily seen in Germany after the First World War. In the formulation of Hans Kelsen, legal positivism

> signaled the definite eclipse of all traditions of limited government. His teaching was avidly taken up by all those reformers who had found traditional limitations an irritating obstacle to their ambitions and who wanted to sweep away all restrictions on the power of the majority. (Hayek, 1960: 238)

Possibly no liberal jurist had gone as far as Kelsen in the effort to uncouple the notions of legality and legitimacy, and thus eliminate from the legal order any reference to metajuridical notions.[10] The interventionist and constructivist policies that were based on this view were, according to Hayek, the most dangerous menace encountered by a liberal commonwealth. These were the policies that cleared the way for the welfare state and endangered the spontaneous order generated by the free actions of individuals.

---

[10] Justice, in Kelsen's view, was what a recognized authority decided to be legally binding. In a text quoted by Hayek, Kelsen stated that 'the assertion that under a despotism there exists no order of law (*Rechtsordnung*), [and that] the arbitrary will of the despot reigns, is entirely meaningless ... The despotically governed state also represents some order of human behaviour. This order is the order of law' (Hayek, 1960: 494 n. 16).

Accordingly, the defence mounted by Hayek in favour of the rule of law rested on a refutation of legal positivism and decisionism. That refutation would borrow heavily from the arguments of Schmitt, his unlikely ally, whose views he conveniently misrepresented.

III

In Hayek's view, Schmitt's anti-liberalism expressed itself most poignantly in his assault against the rule of law. But he did not acknowledge that this assault was directed, like his own, against the formalist *Rechtsstaat* of legal positivists like Kelsen, and more specifically against the constitutional positivism of Gerhard Anschütz. He did not consider that Schmitt's early decisionism and his later conception of a concrete order were proposals aimed, much like his own, against mechanical jurisprudence and the positivist manufacturing of legislation. This confused account of Schmitt's legal theory was apparent in the brief but comprehensive critical account Hayek gave of it in his *Law, Legislation and Liberty*, where Schmitt was made to appear a legal positivist and a constructivist:

> [Schmitt's] central belief, as he finally formulated it, is that from the 'normative' thinking of the liberal tradition law has gradually advanced through a 'decisionist' phase in which the will of the legislative authorities decided on particular matters, to the conception of 'concrete order formation', a development which involves 'a re-interpretation of the ideal of the *nomos* as a total conception of law importing a concrete order and community' [Schmitt, 1934b: 16]. In other words, law is not to consist of abstract rules which make possible the formation of a spontaneous order by the free action of individuals through limiting the range of their actions, but is to be the instrument of arrangement or organization by which the individual is made to serve concrete purposes. This is the inevitable outcome of an intellectual development in which the self-ordering forces of society and the role of law in an ordering mechanism are no longer understood. (Hayek, 1973: 71)

This account of Schmitt's legal theory was based on *Über die drei Arten des rechtswissensschaftlichen Denkens*, a work that Schmitt wrote one year after his embrace of the Nazi cause (Schmitt, 1934b).[11] In this work, Schmitt took a critical look at legal positivism which he saw as the conflation of two opposite modes of legal thought – normativism and decisionism. He advanced instead the notion of concrete order as an overarching system of thought akin to the natural-law theories of Aristotle and Aquinas. This he proposed as his alternative to legal positivism.

Though Schmitt formally introduced the notion of concrete order only in 1934, his employment of this idea predated its formulation. That notion lay in the background of the distinction, drawn in his *Verfassungslehre*, between an absolute and a relative concept of the constitution (compare with Herrero, 1996: p. xxiv). This distinction was in turn based on another even more fundamental one, between constitution and constitutional law. According to Schmitt, the very notion of constitution was possible only after one distinguished between constitution and constitutional law. In the domain of constitutional studies, he maintained, this was the 'starting-point of all further discussion' (Schmitt, 1928: 21). In order for a constitution not to be dissolved into a plurality of particular constitutional laws, its substantive core needed to be rescued. This substantive core could be interpreted either in concrete or abstract terms. It could appear as the 'concrete mode of existence resulting from any existing political unity' or as the 'unified and closed system of supreme and ultimate norms' (ibid.: 4 and 7). An abstract interpretation, like the one undertaken by Kelsen, was rejected by Schmitt. Kelsen defined the constitution as 'the systematic unity of juridical norms', but did not explain the 'objective principle of its unity' (ibid.: 8). In contrast, Schmitt postulated that a normative order could be derived only from precepts that were 'right in virtue of their rationality or justice' (ibid.: 9). Rationality and justice determined a concrete order of things which Schmitt sought to trace back to Aristotle's definition of the state as 'the order (τάξις) of the natural community of human beings living in a city (πόλις) or territory' (ibid.: 4).

---

[11] The book was based on two lectures delivered by Schmitt in Berlin. The first was delivered on 21 February 1934 for the Kaiser-Wilhelm-Gesellschaft zur Förderung der Wissenschaften, and the second one on 10 March during a convention of the Reichsgruppenrates der Referendare offered by the Bund Nationalsozialistischer Deutscher Juristen.

Until January 1933, the direction and content of Schmitt's legal thinking was determined by a single frame of reference – the absolute constitution defined by the Weimar constitution. This was the substantive order he had defended against positivist interpretations (like Anschütz's) that relativized and fragmented it into a plurality of constitutional laws. The decisionist elements of his thought were undoubtedly still there, but were softened by their insertion within the concrete order brought to light by the constitution. The enabling act of 24 March 1933, and its hard decisionist appeal to the notion of constituent power signified, as he himself announced, the destruction of the Weimar constitution. In his view, this was not the destruction of a relative notion of constitution. This was the destruction of an absolute constitutional order and the creation of a new one. The enabling act, by invoking the notion of *pouvoir constituant*, was its matrix. Under the prism of Schmitt's revolutionary conservatism this meant that a new order had immediately replaced the old one. His task, in the coming months and years, would be to identify and define the lineaments of the new constitutional order. As I indicated in Chapter 6, he showed that it had a basic tripartite structure: state, movement and people. He also demonstrated that the new legitimacy was not based on the will of the people or the monarchical principle, but on the *Führerprinzip*. A confirmation of this would be given in 1934:

> The new public and administrative law has put forth a foundational principle, the *Führerprinzip*, together with notions like loyalty, devotion, discipline and honour, which can only be understood from the point of view of a concrete order and community. The political unity is composed of three orders: state, movement and people. (Schmitt, 1934b: 63)

In the same book, Schmitt reflected on the notion of concrete order formation. Such a notion offered him, as the notion of the political had done before, a meta-legal standpoint from which to define and determine the sense of the two fundamental modes of legal thought: normativism and decisionism. This was in line with a tendency that had characterized his thought from the very beginning, the search for the metaphysical foundations of legal thought. It also assisted him in coming to terms with what seemed an opportunist move – his abandonment of the decisionism which he had espoused until 1933. The soft decisionism he had imputed to the figure of the *Reichspräsident* had appeared to him as the best way of preserving the political unity of the state. Legal determinacy was required for the management of business affairs with economic competitors, but it was totally unsuited for the task of identifying and confronting a political enemy. Only after the consolidation of the Nazi regime did Schmitt show an awareness of the limitations of decisionism and its relation to positivism. Decisionism appeared to him at this point as one-sided as normativism (compare with Schwab, 1970: 87), in that it lacked the objectivity needed to legitimate a stable framework for continuous political action.

Normativism represented the rule of pure rationality, the rule of abstraction and generality. It manifested, according to Schmitt, the domination of *ratio* over *voluntas*, of objectivity over subjectivity, of *lex* over *rex*,[12] and could be associated with old theological and metaphysical disputes. (Schmitt referred to the issue raised by Plato in the *Eutyphro*, namely whether the holy is loved by the gods because it is holy, or is holy because loved by the gods.) The function of law, from a normativist perspective, was the regulation of an indefinite number of cases and required, therefore, to be abstracted from the particular circumstances and intentions of each case. This indiscriminate elevation above the particular situation was challenged by Schmitt's notion of concrete order formation. Inasmuch as a rule needed to apply to a number of cases, it was surely necessary that it rose above particularity; but that elevation had to be measured. 'A general rule can only reach a limited elevation and only within a determinate frame of reference' (Schmitt, 1934b: 23). If it oversteps its measure, the one determined by the normal situation it addresses, it loses its meaning. 'A rule must follow the fluctuating circumstances for which it is formulated' (ibid.). Once the normal case is no longer obtainable, the norm that regulates it must give way to one that responds to the abnormality. A concrete order envisaged by Schmitt provided the measure of a particular set of rules. 'A

---

[12] One year before the French revolution the Parisian parliament entertained the following thesis: 'Le Roi n'a point de volonté; la loi est faite, elle doit decider; il est le premier juge' (compare with Kondylis, 1986: 95).

norm or rule does not create order. Only within the parameters of a given order does a rule have a regulative function' (1934b: 13). This was the meaning that Schmitt gave to the notion of *nomos*. '*Nomos*, just like "law" [in English], does not mean rule or norm, but law (*Recht*), which is certainly norm and decision but above all order' (ibid.: 15).

In contrast to normativism, Schmitt defined decisionism as personal rule by means of particular, concrete measures, and portrayed it as the pre-eminence of *voluntas* over *ratio*. In classical and Christian times, the decrees or commands of a decisionist figure could not be said to constitute a source of law in the sense of *Recht*. The validity of decrees rested on the authority of the one issuing them and thus presupposed the idea of order. According to Schmitt, 'in this context, pure decisions are limited and encompassed by the idea of order; decisions derive from a presupposed order' (ibid.: 25). In Chapter 2, I referred to this type of decisionism as soft decisionism. Hard decisionism, by contrast, was a thoroughly modern phenomenon made possible by the collapse of the classical and Christian conceptions of order. In Schmitt's view, the Hobbesian notion of law as command and deliberate issuing of orders adequately captured the meaning of hard decisionism. And so did the Hobbesian dictum *auctoritas, non veritas, facit legem*. Against the background provided by the state of nature, a situation of total disorder and chaos, a norm by itself could not introduce law and order. This could only be done by means of a decision. It was ultimately the explanatory and existential force of the exceptional and abnormal which sustained what was to be considered normal and ordinary. In his early work *Politische Theologie*, where he introduced 'decisionism' as a term of art, Schmitt quoted from Kierkegaard: 'The exception explains the universal so that when one wishes to study the universal all one needs to do is to consider a warranted exception. The exceptional will place everything in a much clearer light that the universal itself' (Kierkegaard, 1967: 93; compare with Schmitt, 1934b: 11). For Schmitt, then, the legally normal was defined and explained by an extraordinary will, the will of the sovereign. As an abstract concept, a sovereign was simply he who decided on the state of exception (Schmitt, 1922b: 5). In principle, there could be no definition of the exceptional. At best, one could approach this question in terms of a political theology and operate on the analogy afforded by the supreme command of God over creation. A political theology explained the unlimited power of secular sovereigns by their participation in God's omnipotence. The decision that suspended the rule of law should, in similar fashion, be explained as a miracle. According to Schmitt, nineteenth-century liberalism effectively suppressed awareness of the voluntarist foundations that grounded the rule of law. One ought simply to look behind this rationalist façade to perceive something more prosaic: the Hobbesian notion of law as sovereign command.

Employment of this distinction helped Schmitt, as a constitutional expert during the Weimar republic, to identify the decisionist elements he saw repressed by the predominantly normativist disposition of the constitution. Instead of the Reichstag, which he perceived as lacking in vigour and resolution, he pointed to the *Reichspräsident*, as the constitutional figure containing the most decisionist potential. The *Reichspräsident* was an anomaly in the Weimar constitutional design. Owing much to Weber's idea of a charismatic leader, he provided a substitute for the role previously held by the monarch. Beyond the intentions of the jurists that devised his role, the course of events was partly responsible for his elevation from what could have been a purely decorative function to sovereign ruler of the state. This ascendancy could be followed in the development of Schmitt's own views. In 1928, in his *Verfassungslehre*, he still treated the *Reichspräsident* as one constitutional organ among others, but one year later he had him raised to the exalted role of protector of the constitution (Schmitt, 1929b; cf. Neumann, 1980: 101). Schmitt followed that ascending career step by step and was perhaps solely responsible for helping to chart a decisionist course of action, clearing it from ideological obstacles and reservations (compare with Muth, 1971).

Schmitt believed that legal positivism did not constitute an original and independent mode of legal thought, but arose out of the confluence of decisionism and normativism. Legal positivism adopted a decisionist attitude when it acknowledged the preeminence of the will of current legislators. But when it subsequently demanded that the decision of a legislature 'ought to be a fixed and invariable rule and that state legislators ought to submit to the law that they themselves promulgated' (Schmitt,

1934b: 35), decisionism gave way to normativism. The legislator's decision did not have to be grounded in a pre-established order or in natural law. It could be understood, therefore, as a pure decision. For this reason Schmitt believed that the positivist *Rechtsstaat* reduced to a purely legal state, a *Gesetzesstaat*, that could satisfy any form of state, democratic or anti-democratic,[13] for it was devoid of substantive content.

By adopting the notion of concrete order Schmitt's legal thought joined the natural-law tradition and veered away from the residual positivism he now saw ingrained in decisionism. Legal positivism meant 'the rejection of the "extralegal", of all law (*Recht*) that was not the result of human statute, whether it be divine, natural or rational law' (Schmitt, 1934b: 31). By contrast, the notion of a lawful order, typical of the 'Aristotelian and Thomist natural-law theories' (ibid.: 7), was a dimension of being that embraced both decisionism and normativism as their condition of possibility. The closest modern antecedent of that notion was Maurice Hariou's theory of the institution, but it could ultimately be traced to Hegel's notion of *Sittlichkeit* (ibid.: 45–57). He interpreted the Hegelian state as resting neither on the sole sovereign decision of a prince, nor on an empty 'norm of norms'. Rather, it ought to be seen as 'the concrete order of orders, the institution of institutions' (ibid.: 47). While the notion of concrete order displayed a supra-personal character, norms appeared to be impersonal rules while decisions were always merely personal resolutions (ibid.: 13).

When Hayek, in the passage quoted above on p. 158, discussed Schmitt's 1934 distinction between three forms of juridical thought, namely normativism, decisionism and the notion of concrete order formation, he interpreted the latter as an arrangement resulting from the deliberations and conscious decisions of

---

[13] Joseph Raz, for instance, has perceived the compatibility of the rule of law, as Hayek understands it, with non-democratic systems ('The Rule of Law and its Virtue', *The Law Quarterly Review*, 93 (1977), 196): 'A non-democratic legal system, based on the denial of human rights, on extensive poverty, on racial segregation, sexual inequalities and religious persecution may, in principle, conform to the requirements of the rule of law better than any of the legal systems of the more enlightened western democracies. This does not mean that it will be better than those western democracies. It will be an immeasurably worse legal system, but it will excel in one respect: In its conformity to the rule of law.' Compare with John Gray, 'Hayek on Liberty, Rights and Justice', *Ethics*, 92 (1981), 77–8.

particular individuals. He read that notion as equivalent to what in his system are deliberately constructed organizations and the notion of law as *thesis*. The latter was opposed to his own view of spontaneously grown institutions and the notion of law as *nomos*. The concrete order envisaged by Schmitt could then appear to serve as a vehicle for decisionism in so far as organizations and the notion of law as *thesis* presupposed the agency of personally active individuals. But Hayek disregarded the meta-legal and suprapersonal sense that Schmitt wanted to ascribe to the notion of concrete order. By doing so Hayek was able to defend a diametrically opposed conception of order which he described as a system of abstract relations and interactions. Abstract reason and not the will would then become the dominant factor. Reason would only contemplate the unfolding of a spontaneous, natural order resulting from an evolutionary process, the involuntary outcome of customs and established practices, and not of human design. Hayek, however, misrepresented Schmitt's notion of order as containing purely decisionist elements.[14] This misrepresentation was functional to his system of thought for it allowed him to believe that a great distance separated him from Schmitt. In like manner, his own self-understanding tended to overlook the decisionist potential that lay dormant in his own conception of order.

Schmitt's expressed intention to move away from advertising decisionism as his favoured mode of legal thought, and emphasize instead the meta-legal conditions of its exercise, ought to be taken seriously. His earlier posture was determined by what he saw as an extraordinary weakening of the role of state authority, the result of the German revolution of 1918–19. His argument in *Die Diktatur* and *Politische Theologie* took into account a postrevolutionary situation and the immaturity of the Weimar constitution. Not having yet attained the status of an absolute constitution meant that the situation was still fluid and left room for further constitutional or, more ominously, extra-constitutional experiments. Schmitt conceived the notion of a sovereign dictator and espoused hard decisionism as a way to legitimate

---

[14] Schmitt's notion of concrete order was not refractory to decisionism and was intended to serve as a channel for the decisions of a sovereign. As a substitute for the monarchical principle, the 'leadership principle' (*Führergrundsatz*) could not operate in a void but needed the context of a concrete order formation, in this particular case the Nazi movement (Schmitt, 1934b: 63).

such experiments. Only in 1926 would he fully acknowledge the validity of the constitution (1926: 27; compare with Maus, 1976: 115).

IV

Hayek defended the view that democracy and liberalism were unrelated answers to completely unrelated questions. This same view was espoused by Schmitt and used by him as a way of accommodating political options akin to decisionism within the liberal discourse. The strong state advocated by Schmitt in the 1930s was supposed to respect the autonomy of civil society. Hayek appeared to be saying the same thing when he wrote:

> Liberalism and democracy, although compatible, are not the same. The difference is best seen if we consider their opposites: the opposite of liberalism is totalitarianism, while the opposite of democracy is authoritarianism. In consequence, it is at least possible in principle that a democratic government may be totalitarian and that an authoritarian government may act on liberal principles. (1967: 161; compare with Hayek, 1960: 103)[15]

That a liberal polity, one limited by abstract general rules, could be open to authoritarian rule did not appear contradictory to Hayek. Like Schmitt, he too distinguished sharply between civil society and the state. Like Schmitt, again, he distinguished between authoritarianism and totalitarianism in strict adherence to the views expressed by Heinz Otto Ziegler in his *Autoritärer und Totalitärer Staat*, a work heavily influenced by Schmitt. The autonomy and independence reserved to the state grounded its authoritarian potential. Again like Schmitt, Hayek opposed central planning and any form of state intervention in economic matters. The role of the state ought to be negative, never affirmative of any positive outcomes or ideal patterns of production or

---

[15] Hayek acknowledged that he followed Heinz O. Ziegler in opposing totalitarianism to liberalism, and authoritarianism to democracy (Hayek, 1960: 442 n. 1). Ziegler, in turn, derived this view from Schmitt. Ziegler wrote: 'One may distinguish two different oppositions: total state ... as opposed to liberalism; the authoritarian state as opposed to modern democracy' (1932: 15–16).

distribution. It ought to be limited to a merely protective function. Hayek's idea of a spontaneous order presupposed civil society's capacity for self-regulation and autonomous administration. This should confirm the complete dethronement of politics within that sphere (compare with Hayek, 1976: 102–3; 1979: 149–50). Still, the negative tasks ascribed to the state were to be determined and sustained by the action of the state itself. It was thus positively and actively that the state ought to restrict and limit its action to a merely negative one, so that the depoliticization of civil society could turn dialectically into the state's active preservation of its monopoly over the political as such. Whenever the normal working of civil society became in any way imperilled, so that its spontaneous order was converted into an organization, the knowledge of such a situation and the decision to alter the spontaneous order of civil society lay beyond its powers in so far as they were recognized as being of a political nature. Hayek admitted that the power to declare a state of emergency belonged to the state. And it did not escape his attention that there was some plausibility in Schmitt's contention that 'whoever has the power to proclaim an emergency and on this ground suspend any part of the constitution is the true sovereign' (Hayek, 1979: 125). It appears as if Hayek was unable to exorcise the notion of sovereignty. Hayek offered a series of precautionary measures aimed at avoiding a relapse into an unbalanced decisionist posture. I will not discuss here whether these measures were effective or not. I will only say that decisionist elements were potentially incorporated into his system in so far as the separation between state and civil society was essential to it.

Hayek reiterated his support for a politically conservative liberalism and expressed a preference for strong but limited government. This concurred with the necessary limitation and relativization of state power demanded by individuals who claimed sovereignty and the spontaneous order that arose from their free and sovereign activity. In accordance with liberalism, Hayek first postulated unbounded individual freedom and the recognition of rights that were prior to the state. Individuals possessed a domain of action over which they alone could claim absolute sovereignty, and which demanded limitations on constructivist state interference. Second, while Hayek emphasized the typical liberal limitations on the state, he did not object to the formation of a strong state. He thought that strong authoritarian governments could ensure the necessary depoliticization of civil society.[16] His liberalism was thus politically conservative for it presupposed the possibility of postulating both a strong state and a liberal society. Possibly no one better expressed this conceptual dichotomy than Benjamin Constant when he wrote: 'le gouvernement en dehors de sa sphère ne doit avoir aucun pouvoir; dans sa sphère il ne saurait en avoir trop' (compare with Röpke, 1948: 28; Friedrich, 1955: 531). It should come as no surprise that Hegel, together with Hayek and Schmitt, expressed a close affinity with Constant's political philosophy. And just as Schmitt was an attentive reader of Hegel, so Hayek was an attentive reader of Schmitt.

---

[16] In the *California Manuscript*, Hayek appeared to be amenable towards dictatorship. In a passage that he *expressly* deleted from the final version, he wrote: 'There may even exist today well-meaning dictators brought to power by a real breakdown of democracy and genuinely anxious to restore it if they merely knew how to guard it against the forces which have destroyed it.' Hayek visited Chile in 1978 and *personally* warned General Pinochet about the dangers of 'unlimited democracy' (*El Mercurio*, 18 November 1978; I owe this reference to Mario Sznajder). During his second visit, he stated in a interview for a Santiago newspaper: 'a dictatorship may impose limits on itself, and a dictatorship that imposes such limits may be more liberal in its policies than a democratic assembly that knows of no such limits' (*El Mercurio*, 19 April 1981). It seems to me that Hayek was ostensibly defining the military regime of General Pinochet as a strong but limited state (compare with Dyzenhaus, 1996: 47).

8 • The Concept of the Political

I

In 1927, while still working on his *Verfassungslehre*, Schmitt published an article entitled 'The Concept of the Political'. In *Verfassungslehre*, he deviated from standard liberal views and included, as an essential element of the discussion, an account of the political aspects of the constitution. Schmitt was well aware of the liberal proportions of the Weimar constitution and was eager to keep the discussion of the political separate from his constitutional theory. This was surely the reason why he chose to deal with the concept of the political in a separate publication. This would confirm the sincerity of his *rapprochement* to liberalism.

Schmitt expanded his article into a book in 1932 (Schmitt, 1932b). This augmented edition included an article written in 1929, entitled 'The Era of Neutralizations and Depoliticizations'. In 1933, after the Nazi takeover, Schmitt published a new revised edition of the book (Schmitt, 1933g). Heinrich Meier claims that Schmitt substantially revised his original argument in both these editions – in 1932, to distance himself from what he saw as concessions made to the liberal point of view in the original article; in 1933, to respond to, but also to signal his agreement with, Leo Strauss's review of the 1932 edition (Meier, 1995).[1] Meier notes how Strauss, writing in 1932, deconstructed Schmitt's argument by analysing the revisions he had made. In 1927, still caught in 'liberalism's aspiration of autonomy' (1927: 12), Schmitt defined the political by assigning to it an autonomous domain, separate from economics, morality,

---

[1] According to Meier, Schmitt and Strauss held a hidden dialogue with one another in 1932–3 – a dialogue between Schmitt's political theology and Strauss's political philosophy under which lay substantive agreement. Both authors attempted a radical critique of liberalism. 'What primarily interests Strauss in writing on the *Concept of the Political* is to complete [Schmitt's] critique of liberalism' (Meier, 1995: 11).

aesthetics and other cultural domains. In 1932, by contrast, he sought to eradicate this residual liberal perspective and defined the political by its degree of intensity. 'Both religion and the fact of the political resist the parcelling of human life into "autonomous provinces of culture"' (p. 30). The political domain was thus granted the right to intervene in other cultural domains, which were now understood as more specific and subservient to the political. Meier interprets this change as determined by the rise of the total state and its challenge to liberal neutralization and depoliticization.

Meier next shows how Strauss sought to unscramble Schmitt's relation to Hobbes in order to understand better his political thought and enhance his own radical critique of liberalism. Strauss's illuminating concluding remarks read: 'A radical critique of liberalism is thus possible only on the basis of an adequate understanding of Hobbes. To show what can be learned from Schmitt in order to achieve that urgent task was therefore the principal intention of our notes' (1932: 119). What, then, did Strauss learn from Schmitt? According to Meier, he learned from his mistakes, from Schmitt's inadequate understanding of Hobbes. And this could only compromise any radical critique of liberalism. One could not succeed in gaining a horizon beyond liberalism, if one disregarded Hobbes's overall liberal (i.e. antipolitical) intention. When he left the state of nature behind and traded civil obedience for strong state protection, his aim was not the affirmation but the negation of the political. Hobbes's fear of the political and his craving for security betrayed his allegiance to bourgeois moral ideals. With Hobbes as an ally Schmitt's 'critique of liberalism occurs in the horizon of liberalism' (ibid.).

Furthermore, Schmitt ignored Hobbes's contribution to the neutralization of political theology. According to Strauss, that process was inaugurated by both Hobbes and Descartes as they sought to underwrite the metaphysical basis of full state protection and thereby advance the cause of a security-conscious bourgeoisie. Enlightened morality and the nineteenth-century economic point of view accelerated the process of depoliticization and neutralization. Technology had now completed a process that could only be understood within the horizon of liberalism. Strauss fully shared Schmitt's abhorrence of a depoliticized world and 'the illusory security of a status quo of comfort and ease'

(Meier, 1995: 41). Like Hobbes, he also believed that the survival of a bourgeois lifestyle depended on posting constant reminders of the horrible insecurity of the state of nature. But Strauss could not go along with an attempt that grounded the political in an anthropology steeped in theological dogma, even less if this theology was passed as Hobbesian. Schmitt's rejection of bourgeois moral ideals stemmed from a theologically (Augustinian) motivated 'relinquishment of the security of the status quo' (ibid.: **39**) that was foreign to Hobbes.

Provoked by this objection, Schmitt's 1933 'reply' underscored the politico-theological nature of his thought and further emphasized the subordination of reason to faith, of knowledge to action. The necessity of the political had its foundation in original sin, a topic Schmitt had already sounded in his *Politische Theologie* of 1922. The 1933 edition contained an admission that was absent in the earlier versions: 'The denial of original sin destroys all social order' (Schmitt, 1933g: 45; Meier, 1995: 53). The inevitable choice between God and Satan forces us to decide between political friends and enemies. Thus, Meier concludes, 'political theology is the apt and only appropriate description of Schmitt's teaching' (ibid.: 76). This was not discernible in the earlier versions of *The Concept of the Political*, but it can be readily explained: 'Carl Schmitt envelops the center of his thought in darkness because the center of his thought is faith' (ibid.: 68). The political theologian in Schmitt came to full light in 1933 after Strauss's effective prodding.

Meier is convincing in arguing for a shift in Schmitt's conception of the political between 1927 and 1932; or when he shows how Schmitt retouched his argument in 1933 in reply to Strauss's objections; or again, when he reveals how Schmitt, in response to Strauss, revived and underscored the politico-theological themes he had developed during the early Weimar years. But the claim that political theology is 'the apt and *only* appropriate description of Schmitt's teaching' does not match the multifaceted and shifting nature of Schmitt's thought. It fails to account for his intellectual output as a professor of constitutional law and his activity as a constitutional jurist during the Weimar period. In his *Verfassungslehre*, for instance, he distinguished between the 'positive doctrine' and the 'pantheistic metaphysics' of *pouvoir constituant*; the latter, he admitted, belonged to the 'doctrine of political theology,' and was something not to be handled within the parameters of constitutional theory (Schmitt, 1928: 80). It also fails to account for Schmitt's distinction between pure and consistent liberal individualism, which he equated with anarchism, and a politically conservative liberalism, one that could simultaneously champion a strong state and a free economy.

Such considerations void Meier's discovery of a major shift in Schmitt's position between 1927 and 1933: a shift was possible only if in 1927 he had rejected, or cryptically veiled, the political theology he was to embrace openly in 1933. Meier does not consider the possibility that Schmitt again espoused it because it matched the revolutionary tempo stirred up by the Nazi regime. Political theology was only one of the weapons in his intellectual armoury. From the Church's rich *complexio oppositorum*, he had borrowed its 'astonishing accommodation' and 'feminine flexibility' (Schmitt, 1922a: 10).

II

In Strauss's view, Schmitt's critique of liberalism did not advance far enough, for it remained trapped within the horizon of bourgeois liberalism. Schmitt was on the right track when he confronted 'the liberal negation of the political with the position of the political' (Strauss, 1932: 103), but was mistaken to think that Hobbes was his ally in that respect. Hobbes's only desire was to negate the political. He sought to escape the state of nature, the *status belli*, and embrace the security and peace enforced by the state. After all, this was the man who betook himself to Paris in 1640 at the prospect of civil war. He appeared to prefer 'the horrors of the state of nature to the spurious joys of society', but this was meant only as an admonishing reminder. 'The bourgeois existence which no longer experiences these terrors will endure only as long as it remembers them' (Strauss, 1963: 122). When Hobbes left the state of nature behind and traded civil obedience for strong state protection, he knew that this was not the end of the political. His fear of the political and craving for bourgeois security led to the affirmation of the political as the only effective way to ensure its negation. In his political philosophy, negation was inextricably entwined with affirmation, just as liberalism was indispensably bound with authoritarianism.

Strauss reminded Schmitt of his expressed intentions to return 'to the true beginning ... the genuine *ritornar al principio*, the return to intact, noncorrupt nature' (Schmitt, 1932b: 93). He reminded him that by this he had meant 'the relinquishment of the security of the status quo' and the return to 'cultural or social nothingness' (ibid.; Strauss, 1932: 115). Strauss reminded Schmitt that he was still moving within the horizon of political theology and had thus not fully buried his revolutionary determination. As Meier notes, he duly acknowledged this objection by retouching his 1933 edition of *The Concept of the Political*. Strauss, he would also confess, 'saw through me and X-rayed me as nobody else has' (Meier, 1995: p. xvii).

Strauss was right in detecting that Schmitt was shackled to liberalism. But Meier is wrong in thinking that Schmitt, who readily owned his underlying revolutionary determination, would give up his entente with liberalism. A view of liberalism as politically conservative and the need to distinguish it from the radical stand assumed by anarchism was discernible in the three editions of Schmitt's *The Concept of the Political* (Schmitt, 1927; 1932b; 1933g). In a section that discussed the anthropology underlying the different state conceptions, Schmitt associated anarchism's negation of the state with its radical affirmation of the natural goodness of human beings. In contrast, for liberalism, which also affirmed the goodness of human nature, depoliticization was 'nothing more than an argument by means of which the state [was] made to serve society' (Schmitt, 1927: 22; 1932b: 60; 1933g: 42). Schmitt recognized that classical liberalism was not as radical as anarchism, that its negation of the state and the attempt to neutralize it had only 'a determinate political sense and [was] addressed against a determinate state and a determinate state form' (1927: 23; compare with 1932b: 61; 1933g: 42). This view matched the *rapprochement* to liberalism that guided his interpretation of the Weimar constitution in the *Verfassungslehre*, a work contemporary with his 1927 article on the political. The liberal negation of the state only denied its priority and proclaimed its subordination to the interests of civil society. Schmitt also conceded that liberalism had 'neither instituted a positive theory of the state nor its own form of state (*Staatsform*)'

(1927: 23). The way it dealt with the unavoidable, for in the end the political proved impossible to ignore, was by requiring a 'division and balance of powers, i.e. a system of limitation and controls over the state, that one could never refer to as a theory of the state' (ibid.), or as a 'political building principle' (1932b: 61; 1933g: 43). The development of a liberal theory of the constitution alongside a conservative theory of the state, formed the core of what I have referred to as Schmitt's authoritarian liberalism.

A confirmation of this political conception of liberalism was Schmitt's distinction between 'nineteenth-century liberalism' and the 'pure and consistent notion of individualist liberalism' (1927: 27; 1932b: 68–9; 1933g: 49–50). While from the latter one could not gain a 'specific political idea' (ibid.), the former was capable of adopting a political stance. This was the kind of liberalism one could legitimately refer to as politically conservative liberalism for it embraced a variety of non-liberal elements and ideas. In fact, it was coupled with the 'entirely illiberal, because essentially political forces of democracy' (ibid.). And it could come as no surprise that in the 1932 and 1933 editions, these democratic forces would be seen by Schmitt as advancing the total state (1932b: 68; 1933g: 50). Thus, Schmitt's critique of liberalism was addressed primarily against its dehydrated configuration, the humanitarian version. By fomenting a generalized attitude of distrust against the state and the political, it compromised the minimal role it retained, namely the protection of individual freedom and private property. This attitude could give rise to a theory of the constitution, but not to a theory of the state.

The discredit endured by the modern state was illustrated by Schmitt with contemporary pluralist theory. The pluralism of Cole and Laski, inspired by the corporatism of Gierke and Figgis, negated the sovereignty of the state and proposed instead autonomy and devolution of power to associations like unions, churches, sports clubs and other intermediate associations. None of them could be said to be sovereign or absolutely decisive. According to Schmitt, the historical event that had made the greatest impression on Laski was Bismarck's defeat in his struggle against the Catholic Church. This proved to him that even 'a state as strong as Bismarck's was not sovereign and omnipotent' (1927: 13; 1932b: 42; 1933g: 25). Another example was Franz

Oppenheimer's proclaimed 'extirpation of the state' (1927: 31; 1932b: 75; 1933g: 58). His radical liberalism even denied the state the role of armed protector of civil society. The political methods employed by the state implied robbery, economic onslaught and all kinds of criminal behaviour. Civil society and its economic methods meant exchange, reciprocity, equality and peace. Oppenheimer thus reversed Hegel's conception which had placed the state, the empire of *Sittlichkeit* and objective reason, above selfish civil society (Schmitt, 1927: 31; 1932b: 76; 1933g: 59). Like Hegel, who was in principle opposed to popular sovereignty and blamed it for the excesses of the French revolution, Schmitt adopted an anti-democratic position. Again like Hegel, who thought that only a state that was strong could adopt a more liberal attitude, Schmitt espoused the view that a strong state was a pre-condition for a free economy.

III

In 1927, embracing liberalism meant, first and foremost, distinguishing it from the apolitical anarchism of pure individualism and espousing conservative liberalism. It also meant trimming its association with democracy and grafting other political configurations, monarchic or aristocratic. Schmitt's *Verfassungslehre* presupposed a political accommodation with liberalism. After distinguishing monarchy, aristocracy and democracy as three forms of state (*Staatsformen*), Schmitt wrote: 'The principles of liberal freedom are able to accommodate any form of state, so long as the limits imposed by the rule of law on governmental power are observed and the state is not conceived as absolute' (1928: 200). By essentially separating it from anarchism and democracy, Schmitt assumed a notion of liberalism that did not negate the state as such, but only an absolute state.

In 1932, Schmitt took further steps towards a strong state by emphasizing the dictatorial disposition of the office of the *Reichspräsident*. He did so in an attempt to forestall what he perceived as the end result of a democratic state, which he defined as 'the total politicization of the entire expanse of human existence' (1932a: 93). Underscoring a dictatorial solution did not entail, in Schmitt's case, giving up the basic liberal tenet, the dualism of state and civil society. On 10 July, a few weeks after Papen became Chancellor, his *Legalität und Legitimität* unequivocally embraced a fundamental liberal requirement – the depoliticization of civil society. In Schmitt's view, the condition for the realization of this requirement, 'for the necessary depoliticization and the restoration of the domains and spheres of a free life', was a 'stable authority' (1932a: 93). Schmitt thus streamlined his conception of liberalism and came close to the views espoused by the economists of *Ordoliberalismus*. This development was discernible a year before in his *Der Hüter der Verfassung*. But now it came more graphically to light due to changes introduced to the 1932 re-edition of his 1927 article on the concept of the political. It has been shown above how in 1927 Schmitt rejected the view that liberalism could be simply equated with anarchism. There was a species of liberalism that was identical with anarchism and pure individualism. But there was another species which did not aim at the extirpation and abolition of the state, for it did not concur with the anthropological postulate of the intrinsic goodness of humankind. For this other kind of liberalism the abolition of the state was not necessary. Schmitt wrote:

> For the liberals, by contrast, the goodness of humankind signifies nothing more than an argument by means of which the state is made to serve society; it only means that society is good and that the state is only its distrustingly controlled subordinate. (1927: 22)

In the 1932 edition, he maintained basically the same view, but dropped and added crucial terms which confirmed his *rapprochement* to the neoliberal standpoint. The same text now read:

> For the liberals, by contrast, the goodness of humankind signifies nothing more than an argument by means of which the state is made to serve society; it only means that society has its own order in itself and that the state is only its distrustingly controlled subordinate, bound to precise limits (1932b: 60)

A comparison of these two texts shows, in the first place, a substitution of the phrase 'society has its own order in itself' for the phrase 'society is good'. This change coincided with what Schmitt had advanced in his *Der Hüter der Verfassung*. There he had developed a conception of a strong state, strong enough to maintain its independence with respect to the free development of the forces that constituted civil society. Only a strong state could restrict its social interventions to a minimum and allow 'that society and the economy could adopt in their respective spheres the necessary decisions according to their immanent principles' (Schmitt, 1931: 78). This view of the state coincided with requirements demanded by German neoliberals and Schmitt had no reservations in complying with them. Second, he added the phrase 'and bound by precise limits', defining in this way a condition that the state ought to respect. This again conformed with his conception of a strong state, a state that would stay within its own limits and would not invade, in quantitative totalitarian fashion, the domain of society.

In 1933, Schmitt re-edited *The Concept of the Political* for a second time.[2] The section under consideration was again altered, but this time the alterations were minimal. The text would now read as follows:

> For the liberals, the goodness of humankind only signifies an argument by means of which they make the state serve society, because society has its own order 'in itself' and the state ought to be only its distrustingly controlled instrument, bound to precise rules. (1933g: 42)

What is relevant here is that Schmitt saw that alterations were needed and that he decided to modify the text. But he did so in a way that changed it only superficially and left its meaning undisturbed. This was the same passage he had substantively altered in 1932 with a clear objective in mind. Now, four months into the Nazi regime he saw no need to deviate from that previous objective, namely the strengthening of a state in order to secure the

---

[2] The 3rd edition of *The Concept of the Political* came out in May 1933, again a revised edition which this time was meant to reach a wider public. After his participation in the committee that prepared the *Reichsstatthaltergesetz* and the publication of the official commentary on that law, Schmitt came to be known as the regime's *Kronjurist*. In total 29,000 copies were printed and sold (Lokatis, 1992: 51).

spontaneously generated order of society.[3] And this was in spite of the fact that, three pages below, prompted by Strauss's objections, he would retrieve his revolutionary determination (1933g: 45; compare with Meier, 1995: 53). Schmitt had crossed the Rubicon with his neoliberal agenda intact.

---

[3] There is another set of changes pointing in the same direction (compare with Schmitt, 1927: 16; 1932b: 49; 1933g: 31).

9 • The Bridge over the Rubicon

The first time Schmitt mentioned the notion of total state during the Weimar period was in his *Der Hüter der Verfassung* (*The Protector of the Constitution*), whose preface was dated March 1931. He used that notion to highlight what he considered to be the latest phase in the 'dialectical development' of the modern state. This development had its point of departure in the 'absolute state of the seventeenth and eighteenth centuries', and then, mediated by the 'neutral state of the nineteenth century', it reached its final destination with the twentieth-century 'total state which identifies state and society' (1931: 79). As his argument proceeded, it became clear that the identity that characterized the total state meant a weakening, and not a strengthening of state authority. In this respect, the total state was diametrically opposed to its earlier configurations. It demanded the interpenetration of state and civil society, and thus denied the complete independence and autonomy on which rested the authority of both the absolute and the neutral states.[1] In his *Legalität und Legitimität* (1932a), the notion of total state was again mentioned and explicitly contrasted with that of the authoritarian state. In this case, Schmitt acknowledged the work of Heinz Otto Ziegler. The notion of authoritarian state in contrast to the total state was the theme of Ziegler's book entitled precisely *Autoritärer oder totaler Staat* (1932). The next time Schmitt made public reference to this notion was in his keynote address entitled 'Strong State and Sound Economy', presented at a meeting of the

---

[1] Lutz-Arwed Bentin has pointed out that 'the total state in the philosophy of Carl Schmitt would correspond in practice to an authoritarian regime, and not to the totalitarian dictatorships of National Socialism or Soviet Stalinism' (1972: 114). This statement ought to be qualified for Schmitt himself would not have considered Hitler's regime to be totalitarian dictatorship comparable in any way to Soviet Stalinism. On the contrary, his collaboration with the Nazi revolution assumed that democracy, the seed of totalitarianism, had been superseded, that the Weimar constitution has been effectively abrogated and that Hitler was the authoritarian figure that would strengthen the German state.

Langnamverein.² This time he reversed his position and extended the use of the term 'total state' to include the authoritarian state he sponsored. This was to be understood as a qualitative total state, as opposed to the purely quantitative total state which he equated with twentieth-century democracy.

On each one of these occasions, Schmitt brought up the topic in the context of a broader discussion, namely the development of Germany's constitutional design after the revolution of 1918–19, and more pointedly after the inauguration of a presidential government on 28 March 1930. On that day, *Reichspräsident* Hindenburg appointed Heinrich Brüning as Chancellor without prior consultation with the political parties. The new government could function as a non-parliamentary regime that rested on Hindenburg's own authority. The legal basis for his decision was article 48 of the Weimar constitution. This event marked the collapse of what Schmitt called the 'legislative state' in Germany and the beginning of a presidential regime that departed from the parliamentary system as it had come to be known and practised in the Weimar republic.

In a 1929 article entitled 'Der Hüter der Verfassung' (1929b), which he expanded in 1931 into the book of that same title (1931),³ Schmitt sought to justify Hindenburg's presidential regime not merely as a legal configuration sanctioned by the constitution but also as the republic's only politically viable option. Up to that point, much of Schmitt's work as a jurist had been devoted to demonstrating the need for an enhanced political role for the *Reichspräsident*. A consistent use and application of article 48 of the constitution was the procedure he suggested. This, he thought, would break the hegemony of a parliamentary

---

² Between March 1931 and November 1932, Schmitt devoted a lot of attention to the discussion of this notion. In December 1931, he published an article in *Europäische Revue* which contained the section of *Die Hüter der Verfassung* which dealt with the issue of the total state. The article was appropriately entitled 'Die Wendung zum totalen Staat' ('The Turn towards the Total State'). Earlier that year he had referred to that notion in his *The Concept of the Political*, whose preface was dated October 1931. This book was a revised version and expansion of his 1927 article 'The Concept of the Political', which contained no references to that notion.

³ According to Bentin, key sections of *Der Hüter der Verfassung* were written in collaboration with Johannes Popitz. Through Popitz's mediation it was made known to the public in the pages of *Germania* (Bentin, 1972: 126).

system gone astray and restore the fine balance between legislative and executive functions procured by the parliamentary tradition before it was corrupted by the advancement of democracy. The entrenchment of a presidial system could be characterized as more than a provisional step aimed at solving the conjunctural difficulties of Weimar parliamentarism. What was at issue here compromised the very existence of the modern state. Like a dying star, the state had experienced a voluminous expansion in size, matched by a commensurate loss of prestige, power and authority.[4] By overstepping its limits and becoming involved in what were the exclusive concerns of civil society, the state had lost its autonomy and independence and advanced with accelerated pace towards its own extinction. Hindenburg's presidial regime intended to save the state by reinforcing its executive functions at the expense of the legislative power. According to Schmitt, this action could only be interpreted as the restoration of a balance disrupted by the influx of democratic party politics.[5] The total state was Schmitt's description of this predicament, which resulted in the modern state's slanted evolution. Schmitt charted the course of this evolution and for that purpose he distinguished four distinct state configurations: the judicial, executive, legislative and administrative forms of the state. These were functional descriptions which corresponded to four historical

---

[4] In his article 'Staatsethik und pluralistischer Staat', Schmitt saw a confirmation of the state's loss of prestige and authority in the success of the political theory of pluralism (1930). Pluralism flourished particularly among English theorists of the state. Schmitt mentioned the work of Ernest Barker, G. D. H. Cole and Harold Laski, who negated 'not only the state as the highest comprehensive unity, but also its ethical claim' (1930: 29). He referred to an article by Barker whose title said it all, 'The Discredited State'. In that article, Barker wrote: 'It is perhaps not an untrue saying, that the State has generally been discredited in England. Indeed, foreign lawyers have been known to say that the State has never existed in England. Notions like *imperium* and *majestas* have not flourished in these islands, except in the Byzantine days of Henry VIII . . . A Sovereign and majestic State, a single and undivided *imperium*, lifted above the conflicts of society, neutral, mediatory, impartial, such as Hegel conceived and such as German theorists still postulate – this we have not known' (Barker, 1914: 151).
[5] According to Bendersky, Schmitt's political involvement as a constitutional adviser for the government began in 1929, after the publication of his article 'Der Hüter der Verfassung' (Schmitt, 1929b). This involvement was mediated by his association with Johannes Popitz and General Schleicher (Bendersky, 1983: 113–14).

embodiments: the feudal state, the seventeenth- and eighteenth-century absolutist state, the nineteenth-century parliamentary state and the twentieth-century democratic state which he also called the 'administrative' or 'total' state.

The aim Schmitt had in mind in drawing this manifold distinction was a description of the political regime that had evolved under the aegis of the Weimar constitution.

> With the distinction between the legislative state, the judicial state, the executive state and the administrative state, the theory of the state and the constitution acquires the specific indicators that help better and more clearly to understand the concrete peculiarity of the legal system and its present situation. (Schmitt, 1932a: 19)

These configurations did not constitute four specific instantiations of a common generic nature. The administrative or total state was not properly a state but served as the portrayal of its dissolution. What was common to the first three configurations was the dualist structure constituted by the separation of the state from civil society. The dissolution of the state occurred, according to Schmitt, when the dualism maintained by the separation between civil society and the state dissipated.

I

The description of the 'specific indicators' necessary to explain the concrete structure of his contemporary political and constitutional situation was the task Schmitt sought to accomplish in *Der Hüter der Verfassung* and in *Legalität und Legitimität*. He proceeded, first, to define what he understood by judicial state or *Juridiktionsstaat*. This configuration became discernible when the core of a regime came to rest on the function of jurisdiction. The feudal state and current Anglo-Saxon political systems exemplified this kind of state (compare with Schmitt, 1931: 75). In Germany, those jurists who idealized the role of the American Supreme Court as the defender of the constitution longed to see the Weimar regime move in that direction. Many voices were heard during the sessions of the Weimar Assembly's constituent commission extolling the American system and the institution of 'judicial review' (Schmitt, 1931: 13). But those institutions corresponded to a tradition alien to Germany and continental Europe generally.[6] In Schmitt's view, 'thoughtless adaptations and mythical representations' were to be avoided at all cost (ibid.: 14).

The role of the American Supreme Court could only be understood in the context of a judicial state. Such a state could arise when the constitution was interpreted in terms 'of fundamental civil rights, namely personal freedom and private property' and the need to protect them judicially from interference by the legislative, executive and administrative functions of the state (ibid.). In particular, the aim of the institution of 'due process of law' was the protection of civil society's economic order from invasive parliamentary legislation. In the American system, judicial review consisted 'principally in its ability to protect general principles. Thus, it turns the Court into the protector and defender of the existing social and economic order' (ibid.: 18). Compared to this powerful judiciary body, the German Supreme Court, the *Reichsgericht*, was confined a more modest role, for it could not compete with the faculties of an enlarged legislative power. In accordance with the more moderate view he had adopted in 1923, Schmitt dismissed the possibility of espousing an absolutist interpretation of the role assigned to the legislative. He now maintained that the view 'that discovers an almighty sovereign and even the subject of constituent power in article 76 [of the Weimar constitution]' had to be rejected (ibid.: 16; compare with Schmitt, 1929a: 37–8). But even if that interpretation could be sustained, it was clear to him that article 76 granted faculties to the legislative power that could not be subject to judicial review.[7]

---

[6] Schmitt referred to John Commons who observed the 'unique position' occupied by the American Court 'in world history' (Schmitt, 1931: 13 n.1). This institution could not therefore be adapted to the different social and political circumstances of continental Europe.

[7] In its sentence of 4 November 1925, for instance, the *Reichsgericht* reaffirmed the notion that the legislative power could alter the constitution by an ordinary act of legislation. It stated: 'the prescriptions of the constitution can only be abrogated by a properly approved legislative reform act'. That same sentence limited the control that that tribunal could exercise over legislation to the simple laws of the Reich and did not extend it to constitutional reform laws promulgated in accordance with article 76 of the Weimar constitution. By contrast, Schmitt observed that in *Marbury* v. *Madison* US (1803), Chief Justice Marshall favoured the view that 'the constitution controls any legislative act repugnant to it' (Schmitt, 1931: 15 n. 2).

In addition to this historical argument, which pointed to the German judiciary's secular inability to compete with the legislative power for the role of protector of the constitution, Schmitt appended a conceptual consideration. The dangers from which a constitution needed protection were 'determinate' dangers which arose from 'determinate' quarters. The protector could not grant 'abstract' security, but ought to take into account 'determinate, concrete dangers' (Schmitt, 1931: 24). In other words, the protection of the constitution, which defined the state's highest function, was a political function. Were this role to be assumed by the judiciary, this would inevitably lead to its own politicization.

II

The next two configurations described by Schmitt – the executive and the legislative state – arose as typically modern phenomena. The executive state, or *Regierungsstaat*, ought to be seen in relation to the rise of the modern absolutist state, which was characterized by the predominance of a strong executive power. Parliamentarism, marked by the hegemony of the legislative functions, determined the ascent of the legislative state or *Gesetzgebungsstaat*. (According to Schmitt, the constitutional monarchies of the nineteenth century matched this state configuration.) Both these state-forms possessed a dualist structure defined by the separation of the state from civil society. This implied the depoliticization of civil society and the convergence of all political functions in an independent and autonomous government. I will first examine Schmitt's conception of the executive state, the strongest of these two state-forms and the one he ended up extolling as a plausible alternative to the paralysing parliamentarism of the Weimar republic.

The modern absolute state, built on the ruins of the old feudal juridical state that disintegrated in the course of the sixteenth century, was Schmitt's paradigmatic executive state. Putting an end to the wars of religion, it gave rise to the ideal circumstances for the imposition of a centralized order of government. According to Schmitt, the executive state's *modus operandi* was defined by 'the *ratio status*, the often misunderstood reason of state', whose concern was not normativity itself but the conditions of its realization

(1931: 75-6; compare with Schmitt, 1921: p. viii). The modern regime of absolute princes lent the executive state its pathos. Princely attributes like *'majestas, splendor, excellentia, eminentia, honor* and *gloria'* (Schmitt, 1932a: 13), enhanced their representative role in the sense of *Repräsentation*. The subsequent erosion of the validity of *Repräsentation* was heralded by the ascendancy of republican virtues during the latter part of the eighteenth century. The rise of *vertu* meant the displacement of *honneur* and the demise of all representative qualities. *Repräsentation* was then 'unmasked' by democracy and exposed as 'mere theatre'. The democratic 'presence' of the people was opposed to the 'representation' of absolutist princes and their court (ibid.: 13). The idea of a 'wise and incorruptible *législateur*' accrued to the democratic fund of ideas and served to introduce the next political configuration, the nineteenth-century legislative state.

The executive state found its proper expression 'in the sovereign personal will and authoritarian mandate of an executive head of state' (ibid.: 9). It could be seen as the appropriate outlet for decisionist attitudes. The executive state, in Schmitt's view, held in high regard the ability to command and extract obedience. The authority exerted by such a state put an end to 'lawyers' pleas, typical of jurisdictional states, as well as the endless discussions of parliamentary legislative states' (ibid.: 13). This was the only state configuration that fully acknowledged the juridical value of the 'decisionism of an immediately executable decree' (ibid.).

Two phases characterized the departure from the tradition of the strong executive state: one was determined by a liberal demand, the other by a democratic demand. First, the nineteenth-century legislative state sought to encircle the authority of the executive state by way of a normativist system. Liberalism saw in the strong state of absolutist monarchs a threat to the individualist values of liberty and private property. As a guarantee that those values would be respected it demanded state neutrality and the replacement of the rule of men by the rule of law. But what it got was a division of powers, which meant that monarchs, dislodged from legislative functions, could still retain the control of the executive (compare with Kelsen, 1929: 81). Second, the liberal demand was superseded by a democratic demand that led to the formation of the twentieth-century state of total administration.⁸ By emphasizing the democratic principle of identity, the distinction between state and civil society was compromised. The state was put in charge of the supervision and direction of the spontaneous order of the market, untouched by the nineteenth-century legislative state. This meant a loss of autonomy and independence for the state, which naturally led to the weakening of its authority. In Schmitt's view, the current crisis of the Weimar republic was ultimately a crisis of authority.

Schmitt defined the legislative state as the state 'ruled by impersonal, general and predetermined norms, by lasting norms of determinable and measurable content, where law is detached from its application to the concrete case, where the legislator is detached from the officials that execute it' (1932a: 8). Typical of the legislative state was the distinction between laws and measures or decrees, between law and its execution. It was also on this conception of law that Schmitt based his distinction between normativism and decisionism. The legislative state, and its parliamentary embodiment, realized the ideal of the *Rechtsstaat*. The old Aristotelian dictum that laws and not men ought to rule implied that sovereignty and power were extinguished. Whoever claimed exercise of sovereignty and power could do so only 'according to the law or in the name of the law' (ibid.). Schmitt envisaged the legal system imposed by the legislative state as hermetically closed. Its claim to validity excluded and made it refractory to any external appeal to legitimacy, and thus to any recourse to a right of resistance. Legality meant 'making superfluous and rejecting not only legitimacy (both monarchical and the plebiscitary will of the people) but also any sovereign or higher authority' (ibid.: 14). This also implied a perfect congruence between justice and legality, which made the possibility of abusive legislation inconceivable.

---

⁸ The *Rechtsstaat* espoused by nineteenth-century liberalism was marked by a reference to substantive values (individual freedom and private property). The twentieth-century democratic movement also constituted a substantive *Rechtsstaat* but the values espoused by social democrats like Hermann Heller and Max Adler were equality, social justice and social homogeneity. These were the values that would serve as the legitimation for the welfare state. In an attempt to avoid the inevitable clash between these substantivist conceptions, Kelsen adopted a hybrid view of democracy, one 'determined by the value of freedom and not by the value of equality' (1929: 93), and a formalized view of liberalism, from which he purged substantive values. Schmitt's distinction between liberalism and democracy purported to expose Kelsen's contradictory legal liberalism (compare with Dyzenhaus, 1994).

Schmitt would thus conclude that legality was conceptually opposed to legitimacy.

Disconnected from the external check provided by legitimacy, the legal system became dependent on an elaborate mechanism of procedural checks and balances. But in spite of its closed proceduralism, the whole system still depended on an external tacit foundation – trust. It was trust that sustained the notion that a procedurally tied legislator would guarantee the protection of the substantive values of individual liberty and private property. Prior to the First World War, that trust was certified by a bicameral system, a federal system and a monarch supported by the army and the bureaucracy.

> Trust is the presupposition of any constitution that organizes the *Rechtsstaat* as a legislative state. Without trust the legislative state becomes an elaborate form of absolutism, the unlimited duty of obedience becomes open oppression and the sincere renunciation to the right of resistance becomes irresponsible turpitude. (Schmitt, 1932a: 24)

While this trust towards the legislative bodies persisted, and circumstances remained stable and peaceful, the theoretical difficulties affecting the notion of the legislative state did not have a practical import. According to Schmitt, the German democratic revolution of 1918–19 was responsible for distorting and ultimately bringing down the whole system of parliamentary rule by dissolving the institutional supports of that trust. Legality could now serve as a serviceable framework for any imaginable aim. This 'illusion' meant that procedures could be found to open a legal window that accommodated 'even the most radical and revolutionary aspirations, objectives and movements, which could then attain their goal without an appeal to violence or subversion' (ibid.: 14–15). It was this illusion that kept the Nazis' bid for power within legal bounds. And, as Schmitt himself would later acknowledge, this would in truth prove to be a mere illusion.[9] In

---

[9] As was shown above in Chapter 1, an article published in the *Deutsche Juristen-Zeitung* on 1 April 1933, contained Schmitt's affirmation of the revolutionary nature of Hitler's government. The government was now decisively defined, according to Schmitt, 'by the political leadership of the Chancellor of the Reich' (1933c: 457), which meant that legality had been surpassed.

his view, the avowal of political legitimacy took precedence over legality and over questions concerning constitutional requirements and reservations. A new set of political circumstances demanded that the Weimar legal system be superseded and that a whole new legal system be put in place. As he would put it in his address to the *Langnamverein* a few months later, there was the need to 'create new arrangements, new institutions, *new constitutions*' (App.: p.230).

Both the executive and legislative states depended on the separation between the state and civil society. Constitutional monarchy was able to preserve that dualism, but the ascent of democracy introduced a logic of identity that consolidated the will of the state and the will of the people. A new concept of law emerged which Schmitt defined as follows: 'in a democracy law is the will of the people present at a point in time. In practice that boils down to the will of the majority of enfranchised citizens at any point in time' (1932a: 27). Acknowledging this democratic ascendancy, Weimar parliamentarism deviated from the standard set by the constitution, which, in Schmitt's interpretation, was defined by the model of legislative state. In practice, the regime strayed away from the conditions imposed by such a model and made the transition to a different one. Schmitt could then claim that it was Weimar parliamentarism, and not Hindenburg's new presidial regime, that had veered from the standard set by the constitution. Weimar parliamentarism facilitated the transition towards a new political situation, the administrative total state. This state was inimical to the principles that defined Weimar parliamentarism, though not to its practice. By contrast, the presidial regime inaugurated by Hindenburg not only coincided with the Weimar constitution, but was also its best principled defence. The new regime could be said to be both legal and legitimate.

III

In *Der Hüter der Verfassung*, Schmitt still found the nineteenth-century legislative state capable of yielding a strong state. Weimar's legislative state retained a dualist structure which assured its autonomy and independence, the foundation of its strength. This situation would last as long as a balance was maintained between the executive and the legislative functions. To highlight this balance Schmitt disregarded the formal nature of the distinction between state configurations and contemplated their concrete, historical instantiations. Seen from this perspective the functions that gave rise to the different state-forms never appeared in isolation. Evidence for their coexistence and amalgamation was to be found in the fact that in every state sentences were passed, orders and commands were given, rules and norms were enacted, and measures were taken for the management of state business. In accordance with the views expressed in the *Verfassungslehre*, Schmitt appealed to the notion of *status mixtus* to describe this coexistence of forms:

> In classifications and typifications of this nature one should always consider that there can be no pure legislative state just as there can be no pure judicial state, or a state that is nothing but executive power or administration. As far as it goes, every state is a combination and mixture of these configurations, a *status mixtus*. (1931: 76)

This coexistence and balance between state configurations did not preclude the possibility of describing concrete states on the basis of the 'central sphere' of state activity (ibid.). It was fair to say, for example, that the nineteenth-century constitutional state ought to be described as a legislative state, for in it the notes that defined both the judicial and the executive states were subordinate to the legislative function. But Schmitt's primary interest was to point out the common features that typified the historical embodiment of those state functions, namely the dualism of state and civil society. Observance of that dualism meant that the nineteenth-century state resulted from 'a balance between two kinds of state: it was at the same time an executive state and a legislative state' (ibid.: 75). First, the separation of the state from civil society ensured the formation and endurance of a strong state, strong enough to keep at bay the many religious, cultural and economic differences that divided a state-free society. According to Schmitt, the realization of a 'common opposition to the state relativized those differences and did not impede social integration' (ibid.: 73). Second, a strong state could also be a neutral state, neutral with respect to religion and the economy and 'respectful of the autonomy of these vital and objective domains' (ibid.). In this respect, the nineteenth-century state was 'neither absolute nor strong enough to render any non-state business meaningless' (ibid.). The balance between state and non-state competences allowed the persistence of dualism. The state, as a *stato neutrale e agnostico* and bereft of any metaphysical commitment, was able 'to build a state-free economy and an economic-free state' (ibid.). The neutrality of the state was a result of its strength. Only a strong state could hand over to civil society, without fear or jealousy, the management of its own affairs. Schmitt recognized that

> the tendency of the liberal nineteenth century was, when possible, to limit the state to a minimum, to prevent it from intervening and interfering with the economy, to neutralize in relation to society and its conflicts of interests, so that society and the economy could adopt in their respective spheres the necessary decisions according to their immanent principles. (ibid.: 78)

Accordingly, he saw no objection in allowing the market to operate according to its own 'automatic mechanism', thus assuring the highest economic prosperity (ibid.: 78; compare with Fijalkowski, 1958: 27). But this liberal order could only survive if placed under the aegis of a strong state.[10] A fundamental alteration occurred when the dualist structure of state and civil society lost its antithetical tension. By yielding to democracy and intervening in society's spontaneous order the state became a 'welfare state' and in the process lost its autonomy and independence, its neutrality and strength.

A year later, in his *Legalität und Legitimität*, there would be a significant shift in Schmitt's estimation of what constituted a strong state. As in *Der Hüter der Verfassung*, he again tried to determine where 'the centre of gravity of the decisive will' could be located and which was 'the type of supreme will that stepped forward decisively at the crucial moment' (1932a: 10). He also acknowledged the possibility of an indeterminate situation, where coexistence and amalgamation of state configurations would be

---

[10] For Schmitt, strengthening the state meant bracing the hand of the *Reichspräsident* as a countervailing force against the 'pluralism of powerful social and economic interest groups' (1929b: 234; 1931: 159).

observed. He observed that perhaps only during 'momentary interim periods' was a 'happy balance' to be attained between the different and autonomous state powers and functions (ibid.).[11] But the omission of any reference to the notion of *status mixtus*, and the cursory manner in which the whole question of combining state-forms was dealt with, indicated a shift in his view that a strong state could be accommodated within the confines of parliamentarism and the legislative state. The happy balance attained in the nineteenth century between executive and legislative functions could not be duplicated. Confronted with the weakness demonstrated by the legislative state in its inability to withstand the democratic avalanche leading to the total state, he saw the only alternative was to turn back to a strong executive state and abandon the first part of the constitution which regulated the parliamentary and federal structure of the republic (1932a: 98; compare with Muth, 1971: 111; Breuer, 1993: 158). This coincided with his support for the authoritarian disposition of Papen's regime inaugurated on 1 June 1932,[12] and his mounting frustration with the aims and results of democratic party politics.

Schmitt's forsaking of the notion of *status mixtus* to describe the combination of state-forms should be examined in the light of his *Verfassungslehre*. There, the notion of *status mixtus* was employed in connection with the possibility of mixing the political forms distinguished by Aristotle (monarchy, aristocracy and democracy). Their conjunction was seen as a paradigm that could be extended to the whole constitution. The intermixing of the different political forms advanced the convergence of the political as such with the normativist elements proper to the *Rechtsstaat*. Schmitt's programmatic statement – 'the constitution of the modern civil *Rechtsstaat* is always a mixed constitution' (1928: 200) – was shown to be the key to his theory of the constitution (see Chapter 6). But now Schmitt stated that 'the traditional tripartition between monarchy, aristocracy and democracy, with

---

[11] In the *Verfassungslehre*, Schmitt concurred with Lorenz von Stein's view that, in terms of moderation, balance and *juste milieu*, Louis-Philippe's constitutional monarchy (1830–48) constituted 'the ideal type of liberal state' (Schmitt, 1928: 308).

[12] Schmitt expressly noted that he completed his book on 10 July 1932, that is, a few weeks after Papen had become Chancellor and ten days before the Prussian *coup* of 20 July (1932: 7; compare with Muth, 1971: 103).

their modifications, should be of no use here' (1932a: 10). Forsaking the notion of *status mixtus* was also a sign that Schmitt no longer pursued a convergence between political forms and the *Rechtsstaat*. The *Rechtsstaat* seemed now to constitute a formalist system, closed in itself and unable to take the political into account. The intersection of legitimacy and legality, which typified his theory of the constitution in 1928, was now abandoned. Legitimacy, not legality, would now take precedence.

> Today the normativist fiction of a closed system of legality clearly and unequivocally collides with the legitimacy of an actually existing and rightful will. This is nowadays the decisive antagonism, and not the tripartition between monarchy, aristocracy, oligarchy or democracy, which is for the most obscure and confusing (1932a: 10–11).

It is plain to see that Schmitt's interest in a description of state-forms and the difficulties he found in combining them prefaced his concern for the preservation of the state as such. In his estimation, the state's very existence was compromised by the rise of democratic party politics and the state-form that democracy demanded and advanced, namely the administrative or total state. Democracy, furthermore, was responsible for weakening the unitary and decisive will of parliament. Parliament had become the 'scenario of a pluralist system' (1932a: 90), so that party politics meant that the will of the majority shifted according to unstable compromises between a plurality of heterogeneous organizations. This situation seriously compromised the legislative state's capacity to survive. For it to survive as a *state* it was essential that state sovereignty be enhanced and a sharp separation from civil society be maintained. The total state obliterated that separation and imperilled the autonomy and independence necessary for the state to function. This development need not have occurred if the parliamentary regime had been truly successful in preserving a *status mixtus*, i.e. an inner balance among its constituent elements, particularly between its executive and legislative functions, and not allowed the exorbitant development of the latter. Because the Weimar regime failed to do this, Schmitt proposed the retrieval of an executive state as a solution to the crisis currently faced by the Weimar republic. The crisis resulted from the extinction of the authoritarian ethos and the decisionist temper that could sustain a strong state.

IV

The task of saving the state by reinforcing its executive functions did not mean cancelling the autonomy of civil society and the substantive liberal values it embodied – individual liberty and private property. In *Legalität und Legitimität*, Schmitt concurred with Heinz Otto Ziegler's condemnation of democracy as the matrix of the total state and, like Ziegler, he also espoused a strong and stable authority as necessary 'for the restoration of the free spheres and domains of life' (1932a: 93). Ziegler, who quoted profusely from *Der Hüter der Verfassung* and substantially reiterated Schmitt's argument, had no qualms in pointing out that the crisis of the contemporary state stemmed from a 'fundamental absence of authoritarian factors' (1932: 27), which in turn derived from the entrenchment of the principle of popular sovereignty. This principle legitimized 'total and absolute democracy' (Ziegler, 1932: 8; compare with Bentin, 1972: 109). Democracy's interest demanded the plebiscitary mobilization of civil society and did not endeavour to secure the existence of autonomous, independent and personally responsible state authorities. By emphasizing identity and the elimination of the distinction between of state and civil society, the principle of democracy provided the philosophical foundations of the total state.[13]

A few months later, Schmitt would substantially reiterate this view in his address to the *Langnamverein*. This conference was convened by big business in a show of support to Chancellor Papen's policies of minimum state intervention and maximum dependence on private initiative.[14] One might assume that Schmitt

---

[13] According to Ingeborg Maus, Ziegler interpreted Schmitt's views as favouring this form of democratic total state (Maus, 1976: 152, n. 151). It seems to me, on the contrary, that Ziegler was simply making Schmitt's own long-standing anti-democratic assumptions explicit. Schmitt had learnt to live within the democratic framework secured by the Weimar constitution and was not prepared, for prudential reasons, to give up this *modus vivendi*.

[14] In Heller's view, Papen was both the representative 'champion of the authoritarian state' and a committed 'adversary of the welfare state' (Heller, 1933: 296).

was invited to address this forum only because he shared its liberal views on the economy. In fact, Schmitt's views on a strong state and a free economy coincided with the 'new liberalism' of a number of German economists like Alexander Rüstow, Walter Eucken and Wilhelm Röpke (compare with Friedrich, 1955; Bentin, 1972; Haselbach, 1991). Like Schmitt and Popitz, this 'conservative liberal' school of thought (Bentin, 1972: 145 n. 16) held the view that only a strong state could guarantee the self-regulation of the market, that only a strong state could initiate the required depoliticization and ensure the creation of state-free spheres. In agreement with Schmitt, Rüstow, for instance, acknowledged that:

> the old liberalism had to deal with an exceptionally strong state, and what it demanded of that state was not weakness but the clearing of a space for its own development under the protection of a strong state ... At any rate, the new liberalism that is justified today demands a strong state, a state that rises above the economy ... (1932: 69)[15]

By contrast, the interventionist state, 'which Carl Schmitt in agreement with Ernst Jünger called "total state"' (Rüstow, 1932: 66), was seen by Rüstow as an example of a weak and impotent state (compare with Bentin, 1972: 109–10). In his address to the *Langnamverein*, Schmitt also recognized that depoliticization involved political decisions. The state of total politicization or quantitative total state, already mentioned in *Legalität und Legitimität* (Schmitt, 1932a: 96), could only be confronted by a similarly total state capable of making the political decisions required to depoliticize civil society:

> In this respect the total state is at the same time an especially strong state. It is *total in the sense of quality and energy*. The fascist state calls itself 'stato totalitario', and by this it means that the new powers of coercion belong exclusively to the state and promote its escalation of power. A state does not allow forces inimical to it, or those that limit or divide it, to develop within its interior. It does

---

[15] I thank Prof. Piet Tommissen for allowing me access to two letters that Alexander Rüstow addressed to Schmitt on 5 July and 28 August 1930 (compare with Tommissen, 1988: 90). The 5 July letter shows that Rüstow was well-acquainted with Schmitt's work and that he knew him personally.

not contemplate surrendering new powers of coercion to its own enemies and destroyers, thus burying its power under such formulae as liberalism, rule of law, etc. It can discern between friends and enemies. In this sense, as has been said, every true state is, and always has been, a total state. (Appendix: p. 217)

Schmitt did not hesitate to identify the strong state he proposed with the *stato totalitario* of Italian fascism.[16] Ziegler had already presented the Italian fascist state as both totalitarian and authoritarian (1932: 37). Schmitt followed suit but made the distinction sharper by introducing the notion of total quality and energy as opposed to democratic total quantity. The *stato totalitario* of fascism was total only qualitatively speaking. It had done away with popular sovereignty and thus retained the capacity to concentrate power in itself and monopolize it. As Ziegler described it, the fascist state was not an executive instrument of the national will that manifested itself through liberal-democratic channels. Instead it represented in itself the unity and duration of the nation (Ziegler, 1932: 37).

Schmitt's expressed sympathy for the fascist state could not translate into support for the Nazis. Since mid-August 1932, Hitler had proclaimed his opposition to the Papen regime and become a defender of parliamentarism and democracy.[17] In spite

---

[16] Schmitt's correlation of a strong state with the fascist *stato totalitario* did not necessarily detract from the liberal significance of his proposal. Faced with the alternative, communism or fascism, many certified liberals veered towards fascism which they adopted as an emergency makeshift. In 1927, Ludwig von Mises, a leading liberal economist and spokesperson of the Austrian school of economics, acknowledged that the economic programme of fascism was 'altogether antiliberal and its policy completely interventionist' (1985: 49). At the same time, he wrote that fascism would never succeed 'in freeing itself from the power of liberal ideas', and that liberalism would 'continue to have an unconscious influence on the Fascists' (ibid.). He concluded: 'Fascism and similar movements aiming at the establishment of dictatorships are full of the best intentions and ... their intervention has, for the moment, saved European civilization. The merit that Fascism has thereby won for itself will live on eternally in history' (Mises, 1985: 51. For a different reading of this text, compare with Nicholls, 1994: 30, n. 34).

[17] 'Overnight the NSDP became a zealous defender of the parliamentary democracy Hitler had hitherto excoriated. In the Prussian *Landtag* the Nazi deputies joined in late August with the Social Democrats and Communists in passing bills aimed at restoring the authority of the State parliament and ending Papen's emergency rule in that state' (Turner, 1985: 274).

of the fact that a majority in the audience had become disillusioned with Papen and now considered Hitler's rise to power inevitable, Schmitt was hopeful that a strong authoritarian government could stop the Nazis. The pro-democratic stand they had assumed could only worsen the advanced quantitative totalitarianism promoted by the Weimar republic. He thought that General Schleicher represented the best chance for the realization of his authoritarian ideas (compare with Bendersky, 1983: 172).

Schmitt's address proceeded then to ask two questions: How had the Weimar republic reached this condition of total weakness? How was it possible to move away from such a condition? The first question received a direct answer. The drive towards the quantitative total state was the result of the German party system that now monopolized the political and completely absorbed the life of individuals.

> Each party realizes in itself the totality, totally absorbing their members, guiding individuals from the cradle to the grave, from kindergarten to burial and cremation, situating itself totally in the most diverse social groups and passing on to its membership the correct views, the correct ideology, the correct form of state, the correct economic system, and the correct sociability on account of the party. (App.: p. 219)

In agreement with comments made by Springorum in his prefatory remarks, Schmitt blamed the method whereby parties nominated the list of candidates without input from the electorate. He also condemned the ideological rigidity of the five German parties. They gave the electorate a choice between 'five fully incompatible, opposed and closed total systems, which espouse ideologies, forms of state and economics ... whose coexistence [made] no sense' (App.: p. 220). A system like that made the formation of a governing majority impossible. It contributed to the consolidation of a purely quantitative total state that drew no distinction between state and civil society. Chaos would have already ensued were it not for the office of the *Reichspräsident*. Schmitt, as always, relied on the strong leadership of the *Reichspräsident* as the main support of law and order.

The answer to the second question presupposed reaffirmation of the fundamental condition negated by Weimar's quantitative total state, namely the separation of state and civil society. The 'dreadful coalescence' of the state and all kinds of non-state interests could be remedied by a 'painful surgical intervention' (App.: p. 221) and not by a gradual process of slow growth.[18] This would ensure the necessary depoliticization of civil society, a key liberal requirement. Only a strong state could achieve this, with the support of a non-partisan bureaucracy and professional armed forces.[19] This was familiar territory, for it coincided with the separation of state and civil society he espoused in his late Weimar writings. But what followed constituted a departure. Schmitt posed the following question: 'What would be required, from the *side of the economy*, to allow for the possibility of a strong state and a sound economy?' In a bold move, Schmitt set the duality of state and civil society aside and replaced it by the following tripartition in the domain of economics:

> We will draw a three-fold distinction in the domain of economics and replace, with a *tripartition*, the two-fold antithesis between state and free individual economy, state and private sphere. First, the *economic sphere of the state*, the sphere of genuine state privilege ... Second, in opposition to that domain, the sphere of the free, individual entrepreneur, i.e. the *sphere of pure privacy*. Third, the intermediate *non-state, but still public* sphere. For decades we have endured an unfortunate conceptual confusion that understood anything public as a state concern. This meant that one of the greatest achievements of the German people – real autonomous administration (*Selbstverwaltung*) – could not be rightly understood anymore ... In the domain of economics, however, it would be necessary to set the record straight with respect to the notion of *autonomous economic administration*. (App.: pp. 224–5)

As Haselbach points out, up to this point, Schmitt 'had followed the ordoliberal [i.e. neoliberal] programme almost to the letter ... [T]he state was not to interfere in the market' (1996: 3). But the

---

[18] This preference for 'painful surgical interventions', as opposed to the organic reform and slow growth favoured by traditional conservatives, could be read as a sign that Schmitt was veering towards the more radical agenda espoused by revolutionary conservatives.

[19] Contrary to 'the radical representatives of bourgeois liberalism', Schmitt had never regarded the bureaucracy and the armed forces with suspicion (1928: 181).

tripartition of state/private sphere/autonomous administration altered the liberal duality state/private sphere (compare with Koenen, 1995: 493–4). That duality determined the distinction strong state/free economy, and its companion piece, Popitz's distinction between centralization and autonomous administration. By introducing autonomous administration as distinct from the private sphere, Schmitt was suggesting a corporatist structure, one that appeared to follow the social doctrines of Pius XI.[20] But his proposition was vague and muddled and could easily pass for the state-oriented corporate order promoted by fascism. In any case, whether Catholic or fascist, what appeared to be a serious incongruity in his address was that he first adopted a neoliberal programme based on the duality strong state/free economy, and then sought to bolster it by the inclusion of a third intermediary element – autonomous economic administration. Whatever reasons he had for doing so, there is one that clearly stood up. Schmitt wrote: 'Without an autonomous economic administration, in the sense of that intermediate sphere, a real new order would be hardly thinkable'. But the state that was 'to bring about this new order ought to be ... extraordinarily strong' (App.: pp. 226–7).

At this point, Schmitt raised the issue concerning the Papen–Gayl reform espoused by Springorum in his prefatory remarks. Schmitt was not in principle opposed to constitutional reform. In *Legalität und Legitimität*, he had tested the inner consistency of the constitution (Schwab, 1970: 87) and found it wanting. He proposed a reform or, as he put it, a 'reshaping of the constitution', in order to stop a further erosion of residual authority (Schmitt, 1932a: 97). Nor was he opposed to the idea of a second chamber *per se*. His opposition to the Papen–Gayl plan stemmed from what he considered to be a misdirected attempt at stregthening the authority of the state. The second chamber proposed by the regime would not of itself strengthen the state. Instead, the causal sequence ought to be reversed. 'Only a strong state [could] bestow on this second chamber the respect and

---

[20] The idea of a professional order proposed by the papal encyclical *Quadragesimo Anno* (1931) had a corporatist orientation. It espoused the spontaneous formation of union-guilds and corporate or professional associations. Contrary to the state supervised corporatism sponsored by fascism, Catholic social corporation was meant to replace in a subsidiary fashion the productive functions assumed by the state.

authority required by its members to free themselves from professional (*ständischen*) allegiances ... No upper house and no second chamber [was] possible without a strong state' (App.: p. 229). With a democratically elected lower chamber in place, a corporative upper chamber had no chance of making a difference. The new corporatist order defined by the autonomous economic administration deviated from the constitution's democratic orientation. Schmitt expressly declared that autonomous administration had nothing to do with economic democracy. Economic democracy was a mixture of politics and economics that corresponded to what he had denounced as the quantitative totalitarian state.[21] While economic democracy could be incorporated by the institutions of the Weimar constitution, Schmitt's proposed autonomous administration introduced a corporatist system which was inches away from the propositions of Italian fascism. Ultimately, not a piecemeal reform of the constitution but its overhaul would be the aim of a strong state. 'We need, in the first place, a strong state that is capable of acting and ready for its great tasks. Were we to have it, we would then create new arrangements, new institutions, *new constitutions*' (App.: p. 230). The foundations of the bridge that allowed him to cross the Rubicon on 24 March 1933 had been laid on this earlier occasion.[22]

---

[21] In his *Verfassungslehre*, he had acknowledged that the notion of autonomous administration or *Selbstverwaltung* was part of Gneist's idea of integrating the aristocracy to the administration of the state (Schmitt, 1928: 132). But what Schmitt now understood by autonomous administration went far beyond that proposal.

[22] Ernest Fraenkel noted, in relation to Schmitt's *Langnamverein* address: 'In view of this speech it cannot be said that Schmitt's conversion to National-Socialism a few weeks later represented any significant inconsistency' (1941: 61; compare with Maus, 1976: 154).

Conclusion

In an hour-long interview aired by the German *Südwestfunk* on 6 February 1972, Schmitt held that he crossed the Rubicon immediately after the promulgation of the enabling act of 24 March 1933 (Tommissen, 1975: 105–6). Before that day, Schmitt acknowledged, he had not looked for contacts within the Nazi regime nor had he considered entering the party. But his swift conversion and radical commitment to the regime, in evidence in his 1 April article for the *Deutsche Juristen-Zeitung* (Schmitt, 1933c) and in the collaboration that began that same day at the offices of the Interior Ministry, indicated a long-standing readiness and conviction. By December 1936 this collaboration would end under a cloud of suspicion. He would have to give up his interest in domestic issues and shift his attention to theoretical questions and international affairs. According to Schwab, 'Schmitt, disillusioned and frightened, signaled in his writing on the *Leviathan* that he was reconnecting himself to the pre-1933 Schmitt. The bridge to his past was his "Starker Staat und gesunde Wirtschaft" which appeared in print in January 1933' (Schmitt, 1938: p. x). But what Schwab sees as Schmitt's bridge to the past can more properly be interpreted, I think, as his bridge to the future. The *Langnamverein* address displayed his reservations with respect to the democratic and procedural dispositions of Weimar liberalism. Those reservations he had never abandoned and they would determine his collaborative work with the Nazi regime. In his view, Weimar liberalism was unable to secure the political unity of the state. The pluralist tendencies that it unleashed promoted the antipolitical attitudes which weakened state authority.

Schmitt's *Langnamverein* address adopted the idea of a strong state and a free economy. A process of depoliticization and the segregation of the state from non-state spheres was implied, which in turn required 'a clean and clear distinction between state and state-free spheres' (App.: p. 221). In adopting this view Schmitt sanctioned the constitutional requirements demanded by nineteenth-century competitive capitalism and supplied by classical liberalism. This coincided with his earlier rejection, in *Der Hüter der Verfassung*, of the twentieth-century 'total state which identifies state and society' (Schmitt, 1931: 79). Such identity meant a weakening, and not a strengthening, of state authority. The total state criticized by Schmitt was diametrically opposed to earlier state configurations. It demanded the interpenetration of state and civil society, and denied the complete independence and autonomy on which rested the authority of the classical liberal state. Again, in his *Legalität und Legitimität*, Schmitt echoed another centrepiece of classical liberalism, namely the distinction between law and measure, and attacked the democratic administrative state, i.e. the quantitatively total state, for obliterating such a distinction. This motivated his warning that Weimar democracy was heading towards dictatorial rule by decree (Schmitt, 1932a: 87) and explains his attempt to recapture nineteenth-century capitalism and the liberal separation of state and civil society.[1]

In his *Langnamverein* address, while affirming the early liberal state–society duality, Schmitt also noted its insufficiency. 'The old nineteenth-century opposition, the opposition drawn by our liberal forebears between state and free individuals, is insufficient' (App.: p. 224). To save the dual structure of strong state and free economy espoused by Popitz and liberal economists like Rüstow, Schmitt sought to strengthen this structure by adding a third intermediary element. A tripartite structure resulted which included a sphere of state privilege, a sphere of free entrepreneurs and an intermediate non-state (but still public) sphere. This third sphere incorporated the notion of autonomous administration

---

[1] An argument similar to Schmitt's can be found in Hayek (Hayek, 1960: 208). William Scheuerman, however, notes that 'whereas Hayek's valorization of the distinction between individual command and general norm culminates in a theory of so called economic "libertarianism", it helps Schmitt embrace fascism' (Scheuerman, 1993: 273). He further conjectures that in 1932 Schmitt assumed that there was 'no going back to an early liberal state–society constellation' (ibid.: 273). This is a mistake. In 1932, Schmitt supported the authoritarian policies of Papen and Schleicher because he saw in them a return to the classical liberal formula (a formula that included a strong state and a free economy) and an end to democratic progress. Furthermore, in his *Langnamverein* address, fascism appeared to be instrumental in bringing about that classical liberal formula.

(*Selbstverwaltung*) which mediated between the state and private entrepreneurs. As a sphere of autonomous administration, distinct from the sphere of free enterprise, it resembled a corporatist structure and had affinities both to the professional order suggested by Pius XI in *Quadragesimo Anno* (1931) and to the fascist corporate order. In no way was this intermediary body to gain independence and autonomy from the state. On the contrary, Schmitt proposed it as a way to strengthen the authority of the state. It is at this point, and not earlier in his *Legalität und Legitimität*, as seen by Scheuerman, that Schmitt would explicitly introduce a fascist solution to the problems faced by Weimar capitalism.

A year later, in *Staat, Bewegung und Volk*, Schmitt's proposed guideline for the future Nazi constitution, he would again reject the liberal bipartition between state and free individuals, 'between state power and individual freedom, state and state-free society, politics and the nonpolitical private sphere' (Schmitt, 1933f: 23). An immediate opposition of both spheres would bring about their collapse. In the *Langnamverein* address the introduction of an intermediate corporate order aimed at eliminating that opposition. The same intention guided Schmitt's proposals in *Staat, Bewegung und Volk*, but now he had to respond to a totally changed situation. Since March 1933, the Nazi party had occupied the whole of the German political landscape and its prominence had given it enormous power and influence. This made it necessary to reassess earlier recommendations to ensure the persistence of a strong state. Schmitt explicitly reiterated his faith in a 'strong state' (ibid.: 33). Its strength would derive from the preservation of its traditional political functions and would be further enhanced by linking it to the notion of *Führertum* (ibid: 33). According to Schmitt, the monarchical principle, which energized the pre-revolutionary German state, had resurfaced in the figure of the Führer. Next, the role of the intermediate corporate order was reaffirmed. Referred to simply as 'the people', it made up the non-political ingredient of the new structure and was again conceived as the locus of autonomous administration (*Selbstverwaltung*). The articulation of this intermediate nonpolitical domain was achieved by means of a corporate or professional economic order as well as a communal autonomous government. Schmitt reiterated that something like the fascist corporate state 'could occupy this sphere of non-state, but public autonomous administration' (ibid: 13).

So far Schmitt had remained committed to the views he had maintained in his *Langnamverein* address. The novelty in his approach came from his introduction of the 'movement', something which he had not and could not have envisaged prior to March 1933. In the revised scheme, the movement was embodied by the Nazi party and was assigned the task of mediating between the state and the people. Schmitt took care to stress that the Nazi party was 'in no way a "party" in the sense of the superseded pluralist party system' (ibid.: 20). He noted that the law against the creation of new parties of 14 July 1933 assured its prominence and forestalled all attempts to reintroduce Weimar's party pluralism. The political convergence of state and party became a priority in Schmitt's agenda. The party could not endanger the political unity of the state. 'The Nationalist Socialist German Workers' Party is, as upholder of the idea of the state, inseparably tied to the state' (ibid.: 20).

Missing in all of this was any reference to the sphere of the private entrepreneur, the third element of the tripartite structure postulated by the *Langnamverein* address. One should not conclude from this absence that Schmitt had now abandoned the proposals regarding a free economy made before the *Langnamverein* convention in November 1932. The Nazi regime, having eliminated the communist and socialist opposition, had done away with the principal ideological obstacle to a free-market economy. The capitalist system remained intact and both Papen and Popitz, committed supporters of a free economy, were now highly placed collaborators within the Nazi regime. A potential menace could still be posed by the Nazi party, particularly after gaining such prominence. Schmitt could not easily forget Hitler's opposition to the Papen regime and the violent anti-capitalist rhetoric deployed by the Nazis in the summer of 1932. From this perspective, *Staat, Bewegung und Volk* should be interpreted as an attempt to integrate the Nazi party into a constitutional scheme hegemonized by the state. To allow the party to assume a stance opposed to the state could mark the return to the old pluralist system. Schmitt thus denied party status to the Nazi party. What is significant in all this is Schmitt's continued attempt to strengthen the authority of the state and its traditional attendants – the army and the bureaucracy. The party or movement, in spite of a rhetoric that elevated it to the heavens, was to be effectively squeezed between the state and the people. Schmitt expressed confidence that the recognition of diversity would not lead again 'to an unhappy pluralist sundering of the German people according to creed, race, class, ranks and interest groups'. Political unity was secured now by a 'strong state' that rose above every multiformity (ibid.: 33). An autonomous and independent state marked the continuity of Schmitt's concerns. The concrete order formation 'state, movement and the people' coincided, in its basic intentions, with the 'new order' envisaged in his *Langnamverein* address (cf. Maus, 1976: 130–1; Haselbach, 1991: 81–3).

The argument presented in this book has chronicled the development of Schmitt's pre-1933 theory of the state and the constitution, the front line of a broader campaign aimed against the German democratic revolution of 1918–19 and the Weimar constitution. According to Schmitt, classical liberalism was able to maintain a clear line of separation between civil society and the state, which had the effect of preserving the latter's independence and autonomy. But the German democratic revolution meant an irreparable weakening of the state. By giving free rein to the pluralist tendencies buried in civil society it allowed the occupation of the state by party politics and the consequent dissolution of its unity. The Nazi destruction of the constitution in 1933 was hailed by Schmitt as a reversal of that historical process. To think that a piece of paper could personify the sovereignty formerly held by the representative figure of the monarch was, according to Schmitt, a dangerous illusion. Ascribing sovereignty to the constitution and the ideal of the rule of law was the illusion peddled by humanitarian liberals in their campaign to discredit the state and the political. But it was simply a mistake to think that a constitution could of itself warrant the realization of the juridical (*Recht*). The realization of the juridical was first and foremost the achievement of the *pouvoir constituant* whose activity, according to Schmitt, could not be contained within strict constitutional bounds. The original *pouvoir constituant* would always transcend the constitution, which ought to be regarded as a merely derivative *pouvoir constitué*.

Schmitt introduced his notion of dictatorship as proof of the opposition he saw 'between the norm to be realized and the method of its realization' (Schmitt, 1921: viii and 194; compare with Schmitt, 1914: 52). The exercise of sovereignty, but not its substance, was limited by the system of legality. The omnipotence of the state remained latent but ready to break through when circumstances so required. The proceduralism of humanitarian liberals affirmed the self-sufficiency of legality and the ideals of a purely procedural republic, and assumed that they could do away with the political and the state. Schmitt reminded them of Barère, the 'Anacreon of the Guillotine', who spoke on 5 April 1793 in support of the creation of the Committee of Public Safety: 'on parle sans cesse de dictature' (1921: 150). Then and now dictatorship, or any other form of political agency, created the situation which allowed for the realization of the juridical. 'Every juridical norm presupposes the homogeneity of a normal situation for its validation' (ibid.: 137). This was Schmitt's response to juridical liberals like Kelsen for whom the basis for the validity of a norm could only be a norm and not a more basic moral conception (Schmitt, 1928: 9). In Schmitt's view, in order to ensure the objectivity of a legal system, Kelsen detached legality from what he considered to be the subjective, and ultimately arbitrary nature, of moral valuation. For Schmitt, Kelsen's liberalism assumed a moral relativism which robbed a constitution of the possibility of defining its essence, and thus of distinguishing between constitution and constitutional law, between *pouvoir constituant* and *pouvoir constitué*.

One should understand Schmitt's distinction between liberalism and democracy in the light of what he stipulated as the conditions for the realization of the juridical. This distinction presented him with a more realistic way of looking at constitutional affairs. It also gave him the conceptual means to come to terms with the Weimar constitution, for he could identify what he saw as its essence. Democracy was the constitutionally designated political method for the realization of the constitution's liberal principles. Monarchy had been abrogated by the German revolution, and democracy now embodied the unavoidable political disposition of the constitution. Schmitt would continue to adhere to his view that procedural liberalism meant the negation of the political and the state, but he acknowledged that not all liberals were anarchists and that, as a matter of fact, there were liberals who did not wish to 'radically negate the state' (1927: 23). In fact, nineteenth-century liberalism was sensible to the reality of the political and thus succeeded in reaching a formula of cohabitation with the monarchy. This mixed condition (*status mixtus*), a balance between executive and legislative functions, provided the institutional basis for the formation of a state that was strong and could still be trusted by political liberals whose aim was to ensure the autonomy of civil society and the operation of a free economy.

In spite of Schmitt's recognition of democracy as a method for the realization of liberal principles and the rule of law, he did not surrender his deep anti-democratic sentiments. Hoping to defuse the democratic intent of the doctrine of the *pouvoir constituant*, he drastically downsized the people's agency and allowed it only a passive role. The people could not govern, deliberate or discuss political issues. All it could do was 'to answer affirmatively or negatively to a question put to it' (Schmitt, 1932a: 93). Democracy was to be plebiscitary not participatory. Furthermore, as direct democracy emphasized the identity of rulers and ruled and shunned representation, it helped to impair the autonomy of the state. In view of this, Schmitt tried to compensate for what he saw as the exaggerated influence attained by direct democracy within the Weimar republic. Monarchical legitimacy had perished and a democratic regime was now entrenched. By resurrecting the notion of *status mixtus* he sought to revive the repressed monarchical and aristocratic constitutional components as a way of balancing the preponderance of democratic components. His *Verfassungslehre* proposed an interpretation of the Weimar constitution as a mixed constitution. Alongside the typical limitations to state interference imposed by juridical liberalism, there was enough room for the manifestation of the political in the form of a balanced mixture of democratic, aristocratic and monarchical elements. By emphasizing the monarchical elements he thought that he could considerably strengthen the hand of the *Reichspräsident*. If the apex of the state were occupied by a strong figure empowered with the prerogatives of a dictator, the democratically elected *Reichspräsident* would acquire monarchical standing and guarantee the unity of the state. Only those who were blinded by the ideals of procedural liberalism would condemn as dictatorial this affirmation of a strong state that did not compromise the development of a free liberal economy.

Under the aegis of a strong state, the disintegrating effects of the market would cease to be detrimental to Germany's political unity. Schmitt had thereby enriched his conceptual resources and added flexibility to his conservative views. Pure humanitarian liberalism and its negation of the political did not, as he saw it, exhaust the liberal spectrum. A politically conservative liberalism could lead to the simultaneous affirmation of an authoritarian state and a free liberal economy.

This view of an authoritarian liberalism, of a species of liberalism willing to revisit classical statecraft and wield its political might, guided Schmitt's *Langnamverein* speech. But Stephen Holmes criticizes Schmitt for declaring that liberalism is 'essentially antipolitical even when politics is defined arbitrarily as the act of identifying a mortal enemy; for liberal societies have done this with remarkable success' (1993: 57). Schmitt's mistake was not to take into account the 'Augustinian strand' that runs through liberal thought. This should nullify his attempt to saddle liberalism with a 'naive optimistic anthropology' (ibid.: 59). But Holmes here does not take Schmitt's distinction between anarchism and liberalism into account.[2] While humanitarian liberalism comes close to anarchism, classical liberalism, in its defence of private property and individual autonomy, was seen by Schmitt as open to the political. Private property and individual freedom were substantive values that needed the protection of a state. The essentially torn and deeply divided nature of civil society needed the unity and stability of a strong state to allow it to withstand its own injurious, and yet inevitable, fluctuations. Only a strong state could ensure that a free economy would be left to carve out its own destiny.

Much of what appears bewildering and contradictory in Schmitt rested on the metaphysical symbiosis of dynamicity and staticity, pluralism and unity. This was the *complexio oppositorum* that separated and brought together the state and civil society. Around the distinction between the juridical and the realization of the juridical, and that between the substance of power and its exercise, likely to be dismissed as 'scholastic subtleties'

---

[2] Thus, Holmes writes: 'Similarly, Schmitt's tendency to link liberalism to anarchism inadvertently alerts us to the positive attitude toward lawful state power shared by all classical liberals' (1993: 261).

(Schmitt, 1921: 194), Schmitt built his last line of defence. On these rested a string of other axiomatic distinctions which shaped the architecture of his theory of the constitution (*pouvoir constituant* and *pouvoir constitué*, law and measure, absolute and positive constitution) and his theory of the state (the polarity state/civil society, the separation of executive and legislative powers). This metaphysical appurtenance of dynamicity and staticity, pluralism and unity was meant as the conceptual structure that would ease the inevitable transition to a substantively liberal society. According to Schmitt, a well-ordered liberal society was one founded on substantive values like private property and individual freedom (Schmitt, 1928: 8 and 130).[3] In the course of history, other national communities had been able to entrench and institutionalize a substantive liberal order that did not dissolve into factions. To attain such an order Germany required a strong state, one that could crush the powerful factions that menaced it from within. Only a strong state could be trusted to minimize the power to be exercised over individuals. As Condorcet acknowledges, once those *associations puissantes* are dismantled, 'il faut bien peu de force pour forcer les individus à l'obeissance' (Schmitt, 1921: 204).

One question remains. Is Schmitt the twentieth-century Hobbes or is he the systematic theorist of fascism, buried for a long time under the debris of Nazism? If the latter were the case, there would be no philosophically valid reason to recommend the study of his work. Only historians of ideas would benefit from the clarity and articulation of his thought when trying to make sense of the fascist hotchpotch. But if the notion of a Hobbesian Schmitt were to be seriously entertained, his work would demand philosophical attention, for it would signify a sweeping re-evaluation of liberalism. Possibly this is what has led Holmes sharply to separate Schmitt from Hobbes and approximate him to Mussolini (1993: 42). Based on Strauss's interpretation, Holmes thinks that only by disregarding Hobbes's overall liberal intention could Schmitt enlist him as a political ally. But the stark portrait

---

[3] According to Helmut Schelsky, the point of departure of Schmitt's scientific and political conceptions was a 'liberal *Grundeinstellung*' (1983: 30). In agreement with Schelsky, Schwab describes Schmitt as a '"traditional bourgeois liberal" who opted for a strong state in order to protect life and property' (1938: p. xxi).

of the state of nature in the *Leviathan* was meant as an incentive to leave its ills behind and force individuals to trade civil disobedience for strong state protection. Hobbes advocated the denial of the political, not its affirmation. His fear of the political and a craving for security betrayed an allegiance to the bourgeois moral ideals that Schmitt despised. By contrast, Schmitt's bellicism and exaltation of myth were 'Mussolini, not Hobbes' (Holmes, 1993: 42). In 1923, for instance, Schmitt approvingly cited Mussolini's speech before the March on Rome: 'We have created a myth, this myth is a belief, a noble enthusiasm; it does not need to be a reality' (Schmitt, 1923c: 76). This clearly contrasted with Hobbes's rationalism.

Yet in 1937 Schmitt turned to the clear-headed Hobbes for a discussion of the mythical. He recognized that Hobbes 'was not a mythologist nor a mythic figure', and that only with the image of the leviathan did he come close to a myth (Schmitt, 1938: 85). Strauss had evoked a liberal Hobbes and now Schmitt, in agreement with Schelsky and Tönnies, interpreted the *Leviathan* preponderantly as a *political* and not as a scientific treatise (1938: 11 and 94). Its purpose was not so much to present an impartial account of human nature, but to help us distinguish political friends from political enemies, the kingdom of light from the kingdom of darkness. Only in this political context did it make sense to invoke the mythical. With the help of the mythical one could visibly conjure up enmity or friendship. Like Plato's well-bred dogs, Hobbes's state as leviathan was meant to be both dangerous and gentle. It was meant to inspire terror to its enemies, the aristocratic Frondes and the *associations puissantes*, and to bring peace and quiet to its bourgeois friends. Schmitt recognized that Hobbes's attempt misfired and that the mythical weapons he had forged 'did not serve his cause' (1938: 85). But when he himself again summoned the mythical he did so because he identified with Hobbes's cause, the cause of liberalism. Like Gentz, Schmitt could appreciate the 'liberal demands' of his epoch 'as soon as he could only free himself from the fear of a revolution' (1925b: 23).

Certainly, Schmitt did not espouse the cause of humanitarian liberalism. Such was the enlightened conviction of the aristocratic Montesquieu when he wrote: 'je suis homme avant d'être François, parce que je suis nécessairement homme, et que je ne suis François que par hasard.' And then he added, 'si je savois quelque chose utile à ma patrie, et que fût ... préjudiciable au Genre humain, je la regarderois comme un crime' (1949: 980–1).[4] In contrast, Schmitt adopted, during the last years of the Weimar republic, authoritarian liberal views that sought to secure property rights and a market economy within the confines of a territorial state and an ethnic community. Substantive liberal values like private property and individual freedom required political protection. That protection would be diluted and rendered ineffective by an appeal to humanitarian ideals and a disregard for national politics. As an abstract notion, 'the concept of humanity excludes the concept of the enemy' and is thus unfit to be combined with a political point of view (Schmitt, 1932b: 54–5). But as a concrete notion, the concept of humanity proved that it could suffer political employment. In the eighteenth century, for example, the concept of humanity served as a 'polemical negation of the then existing aristocratic-feudal order' (ibid.: 55). And during the Weimar period, it could serve to conceal the class-based interest of welfare policies. Those redistributive policies contradicted the substantive liberal values defended by Schmitt. It was thus natural for him to regard German communists and socialists as his political enemies.

In 1933, Schmitt triumphantly proclaimed the proscription of the Communist party, which he declared to be 'an enemy of the state and the people' (1933f: 5). Out of 'its own weakness and neutrality', Weimar humanitarian liberalism had not been able to defend those substantive liberal values and 'identify the mortal enemy of the German people' (ibid.: 5). The Nazi regime abolished humanitarian neutrality, 'understood as the incapacity to distinguish between enemies and friends, ethnic comrades and strangers' (ibid.: 5–6). But the Nazis also declared Jews to be their political enemies, and did so based on horrendously perverted

---

[4] But then Montesquieu, in contradiction to cosmopolitanism, and more in agreement with his aristocratic stance, came closer to Schmitt's pessimism when he affirmed: 'si les hommes étoient parfaitement vertueux, ils n'auroient point d'amis ... [U]n homme véritablement vertueux devroit être porté a secourir l'homme le plus inconnu comme son ami propre' (1949: 1129–30). Thus, from the fact that we need friends it follows that human beings are not perfectly virtuous. And not being perfectly virtuous, human beings will not come to the help of strangers as if they were their friends (compare with Sandel, 1996: 342).

prejudices. Without hesitation, Schmitt embraced their racist policies. This fateful decision would ruin the integrity of his character and his reputation as a scholar. It was one thing to expose the insincere political blindness and impartiality of humanitarian liberalism; quite another to betray without remorse its most noble ideals.

Like Hobbes, Schmitt rejected cosmopolitan ideals and the intrinsic goodness of humankind. In his view, the original corruption of human nature forced us to identify the agents of evil, brand them as enemies and secure the good will and co-operation of friends. If we all lacked intrinsic goodness and virtue, this meant that the political was unavoidable. Like Hobbes, Schmitt identified an autocratic strand within liberalism, but by Schmitt's time in Germany the danger to liberal society had become so acute that reincarnating the leviathan would be insufficient to save it. Schmitt conjured up a darker vision than Hobbes and thereby warned us against engaging in any false optimism about the natural tendencies of liberal society. His critique of humanitarian liberalism should caution us about weaknesses of liberal theory at the end of the century. The preservation of a liberal society which maintains and sustains freedom requires us to look beyond liberalism to forms of social solidarity which are not wholly dependent on exclusive private property and economic growth, and are more open to participatory forms of democracy.

Appendix

Strong State and Sound Economy:
An Address to Business Leaders[1]
Carl Schmitt

I

Gentlemen! I shall deal with the issue 'Strong State and Sound Economy' from the *point of view of the state*. You have heard the remarks of your Chair, Dr Springorum, concerning a series of economic projects and possibilities. *Dr Springorum* also mentioned the projects and plans of my dear friend Popitz,[2] that have to do with the administrative aspects of that issue. Aside

---

[1] This is a translation of Schmitt's address to a conference of the *Langnamverein* entitled 'Sound Economy in a Strong State', held in Düsseldorf on 23 November 1932 and published in its proceedings (Schmitt, 1932c: 13–32). Schmitt's address was untitled. This translation uses the text published in the *Langnamverein* proceedings, but adds the title Schmitt gave it when he republished it in *Volk und Reich* (Schmitt, 1933a). It appeared in January 1933, 'only days before President Hindenburg appointed Hitler chancellor of Germany' (Schmitt, 1938: p. x). In February 1933, sections of Schmitt's address were reproduced in an article entitled 'Weiterentwicklung des totalen Staats in Deutschland' published in *Europäische Revue* (Schmitt, 1933e). It was among the essays that appeared in Schmitt's *Verfassungsrechtliche Aufsätze* (1958).
  The *Langnamverein* was an association of Ruhr industrialists whose full name, *Vereins zur Wahrung der gemeinsamen wirtschaftlichen Interessen in Rheinland und Westfalen* (Association for the Furtherance of the Joint Economic Interests of the Rhineland and Westphalia), forced its abbreviation to be 'Long Name (Langnam) Association' (Abraham, 1981: 122).
  The 23 November meeting of the *Langnamverein* had been convened as a show of support for Papen's policies before he tendered his resignation on 17 November. At the time of the meeting, Papen was only Acting Chancellor. After the conference, one of its participants wrote: 'The *Langnamverein* convention ... originally conceived within the framework of the Papen program and intended to support him revealed [instead] the fact that almost all of industry supports the appointment of Hitler, no matter under what circumstances' (quoted in Abraham, 1981: 321–2; compare with Turner, 1985: 302).
[2] According to Bentin, Johannes Popitz, Prussian Finance Minister and

from these predominantly economic or administrative aspects, it is necessary to pay attention to state matters, and thus by necessity to the political. I do not intend to engage in politics, but I must refer to political matters because the state is something political, and a strong state is, in a particularly intensive way, a political formation. I share Dr Springorum's opinion when he said that only a strong state can remove itself from non-state affairs.[3] The process of depoliticization and the creation of state-free spheres is a political process. I would like to make this my point of departure.

Two years ago I addressed this conference at this same place. Your meeting then bore the motto 'Courage to Action'. On that occasion I allowed myself to say that beautifully designed organizational reform plans were not as relevant as real political forces, how to identify them accurately, and then recruit them in some fashion. Above all, the regime was supposed to use all *legal means*. My assumption was that those legal possibilities were strong, much stronger than one would have then surmised. This view has not been largely disproved since that time. In these two years we have come to recognize the practical usefulness and energy of article 48. Admittedly, a strong opposition has been launched to discredit and defame article 48. This ought to prove that even today article 48 is a good, practical and indispensable instrument of a strong government.

Schmitt's close friend, should be credited as 'proper author of the Schmittian notion of "a free economy in a strong state"' (Bentin, 1972: 125). Schmitt's lifelong friendship with Popitz began in Berlin in 1929 (Schmitt, 1958: 8; compare with Noack, 1993: 102–7).

[3] Fritz Springorum was at the time managing director of the Eisen- und Stahlwerk Hoesch AG of Dortmund, treasurer of the Ruhrlade and chair of the *Langnamverein*. In his prefatory remarks to the audience of 1,500 participants, Springorum expressed support for Papen's blueprint for a strong state. He acknowledged that, at first sight, it appeared likely that business would favour a weak state. A strong state could impose 'all kinds of fetters on private business through taxes, credit policies and social policies' (Springorum, 1932: 5). But in reality only a strong state was able to set limits to its own activity and did not overreach its high functions. Springorum praised Papen's proposed constitutional reforms, which he thought would strengthen the state. He also suggested that the Chancellor should continue in office and cautioned against implementation of a job-creation programme by the government. The best employment programme lay in the 'return to the sound economic methods of private capitalism' (Springorum, 1932: 11; compare with Turner, 1985: 303).

It is reasonable to raise the question whether in these two years anyone truly showed the courage to action that was then demanded of you. Could we, in this respect, acknowledge any achievement? We often get the general impression that the state has grown weaker and the circumstances have worsened and become more chaotic. It seems to me that one may respond affirmatively to the question whether, with respect to courage to action, one single achievement is to be acknowledged. The *Prussian coup of 20 July*[4] went to the core of the Weimar constitution's worst design defect – the dualism between the Reich and Prussia – and rectified it on a crucial point. This has to be acknowledged as an achievement and as proof of courage to action. Subsequently this achievement became, if I may say so, rapidly relativized and even paralysed. Here lies another danger for a strong state. The danger came to light during the trial held before the *supreme court in Leipzig* (there were actually twelve trials).[5] As soon as a genuine courage to action is exhibited and a strong state, requested for so long, really steps forward, the strangest confederates and all those interested in the status quo are found together united in their resistance. The coalition that developed during this trial against the Reich used Leipzig as a scenario. Factions and dismissed ministers combined together with Bavaria and Baden – the states that make a lot of noise with respect to their statehood. The *federal party-state* revealed itself in full daylight. The Bavarian representative referred to the dignity of Bavaria as a state, and described the Leipzig supreme court as an interstate body. He went as far as to compare it to the

---

[4] President Hindenburg appointed Franz von Papen as Chancellor on 1 June 1932, and on 4 June dissolved the *Reichstag*, invoking article 35 of the constitution. On 20 July Papen, with article 48 at his disposal, placed Prussia under martial law and dissolved its government. This event became know as the Prussian *coup* of 20 July (compare with Bendersky, 1983: 154–7; Noack, 1993: 137–54). Even though Schmitt did not share Papen's constitutional reform plans, he openly supported his government (Muth, 1971: 107) and participated, as a juridical expert, in designing a strategy for the Prussian *coup* (Huber, 1988: 38). It could not have been a surprise when during the cabinet session of 25 July Papen announced that Schmitt would officially represent the government before the supreme court at Leipzig.

[5] According to Bendersky, '[b]y the time the trial before the supreme court in Leipzig finally opened on October 10, the number of plaintiffs had expanded to include the states of Baden and Bavaria, as well as the Center and SPD factions of the Prussian Landtag' (1983: 160).

so-called 'World Court' at The Hague. But when I asked how could this state of Bavaria, showing up hand in hand with dismissed Prussian ministers and Prussian parliamentary factions, disregard the first assumption in interstate affairs and international courtesy, namely non-intervention in the affairs of another state, the reply was: 'We welcome federal friends wherever we find them.' These are significant words and, as it were, the insignia of the federal party-state. You should be sure, gentlemen, that when a necessarily strong state actually arises, the most heterogeneous federal friends join together to see that it does not become too strong.

Therein lies the great *lesson of this Leipzig trial*. I refer to it in the singular because, for the most part, what went on in it has not become part of the political consciousness of the German people. At present, the grotesque coexistence of three governments[6] in the capital of the German Reich, Berlin, makes a mockery of the German state and is a natural and adequate consequence of judicial politics. Were we actually to enter into a new era of trials like the one held at the supreme court in Leipzig, I fear then we would not need to refer to a 'strong state'. This is a clearly discernible danger for anyone who pays attention to the lessons of German constitutional history and the development of the contemporary federal party-state. During three wretched centuries the *political unity* of the German people had *collapsed* and, lest we forget, in accordance with the methods of *judicial politics*! Those were the days of the Imperial court in *Wezlar* and the Imperial privy council. To my dismay I saw the shadow of that period appear again at Leipzig. We should hope that it soon disappears, never again to return.

That sole achievement, the one obtained on 20 July, was distorted by the Leipzig verdict. Aside from this, a retrospective look at this latest year indicates that a general conception has become pervasive and that the actual leadership methods, and the management of the relations between the state and the economy, are generally seen as not viable. The worst spiritual confusion in this respect should have disappeared by now. For approximately

---

[6] The three governments Schmitt is referring to were: the government of the Reich, the government of Prussia and the commissarial Prussian government headed by Papen (compare with Noack, 1993: 143).

ten years now, the whole of Germany and the whole planet has echoed the call: *Away with politics!* The solution to all problems was said to be the elimination of politics and the elimination of the state. All matters should be decided by technical and economic experts according to allegedly purely objective, technical and economic points of view. Innumerable articles and brochures published by famous authors and economists of many nations repeated this a thousand times between 1919 and 1924. In the mean time we have known about conferences of experts and scientists. Mountains of valuable material have been stored in Geneva, Berlin and other capitals of the world, and the decision on important issues lies buried under this kind of objectivity. It turns out that this sort of depoliticization may be politically useful in deferring unpleasant problems and necessary changes through allowing any resolute will to exhaust itself.

After those approximately five years of radical demands for exhaustive non-politics, an idea has seeped through – all problems may be political problems after all. In Germany we experienced a *politicization* of all economic, cultural, religious and other dimensions of human existence. This would have been inconceivable in the nineteenth century. After years of attempting to reduce the state to economics, it now appears that economics has been entirely politicized. One can now fully grasp the effective and illuminating formula of the *total state*. I will examine it in more detail, for it surely does not only provide the key to help clarify the issue of the relations between the economy and the state, but it also indicates the direction from where the solution may come. A total state exists. One may angrily and indignantly reject the formula 'total state' as barbaric, Slavic, un-German or un-Christian, but that will not make it disappear from view. Every state is anxious to acquire the power needed to exercise its political domination. The surest sign of a real state is that it proceeds in that manner. Presently, we are all under the impression that power has expanded. Every state has expanded its power by technological means, more precisely, by the techno-military instruments of power. Modern technical means give governments of even small states such power and effective possibilities that old notions concerning state power and the possibility of resisting it fade away. The traditional images of street marches, barricades, etc. are child's play in light of contemporary coercive methods. A state is forced to acquire modern weaponry. If it were to lack the strength or the courage to do so, another power or organization will do so and will thus become the state.

The proliferation of technical means also allows for the possibility of *mass propaganda*, which may be more effective than the press and other traditional means of influencing public opinion. In present-day Germany, there still exists a widely respected freedom of the press. In spite of all emergency decrees, the scope for the free expression of opinions is quite broad; nobody thinks of censuring the press. But every state must control the new technical means – film and radio. There is no state so liberal as to reject intensive censure and control of radio, film and other visual media. No state can afford to yield these new technical means of mass control, mass suggestion and the formation of public opinion to an opponent. The formula 'total state' accurately describes the contemporary state's undreamt-of new means of coercion and possibilities of the greatest intensity. We barely conceive of the effect these will have since our vocabulary and imagination are still deeply seated in the nineteenth century. In this respect the total state is at the same time an especially strong state. It is *total in the sense of quality and energy*. The fascist state calls itself *stato totalitario*,[7] and by this it means that the new powers of coercion belong exclusively to the state and promote its escalation of power. A state does not allow forces inimical to it, or those that limit or divide it, to develop within in its interior. It does not contemplate surrendering new powers of coercion to its own enemies and destroyers, thus burying its power under such formulae as liberalism, rule of law, etc. It can discern between friends and enemies. In this sense, as has been said, every true state is, and always has been, a total state.[8] The novelty is only

---

[7] Schmitt's interest in Mussolini and Italian fascism sprang from his fascination with myth (Mehring, 1989: 86) and his desire to revitalize the state (Breuer, 1993: 131). In 1929, in an article entitled 'Wesen und Werden des faschistischen Staates' (a review of Erwin von Beckerath's book with that same title), Schmitt wrote: 'The fascist state decides not as a neutral but as a higher third. That is its supremacy. Whence does its energy and new force come from? From national enthusiasm, from Mussolini's individual energy, from the war veteran movement ... The fascist state will again be a state of ancient probity, with visible leaders and representatives, and not the façade and antechamber of invisible and non-responsible rulers and financiers' (Schmitt, 1940: 113–14).

[8] Compare with Schmitt's assertion in his *Verfassungslehre* that 'the modern

new technological power, whose political meaning one should clearly acknowledge.⁹

There is, however, another meaning of the expression 'total state'. Unfortunately this is the one that can be applied to the present-day German state. This kind of total state is one that penetrates all domains and all spheres of human existence, one that knows of no state-free sphere because it can no longer discriminate. It is *total in a purely quantitative sense, in the sense of pure volume and not in the sense of intensity or political energy*.¹⁰ This is what defines Germany's party-state. Its volume has been expanded to a monstrous degree. It concerns itself with all possible affairs. There is nothing which is not somehow related to the state. Not even a bowling club can continue to exist without maintaining a good relation with the state, that is to say, to a certain party and funds. This totality, in the sense of volume, is the opposite to force and strength. The present German state is *total due to weakness* and lack of resistance, due to its incapacity to resist the onslaught of parties and organized interests.¹¹ It must

---

state is a closed political unity and essentially the status, namely the total status that relativizes all other status within it' (Schmitt, 1928: 173).

⁹ Quaritsch laments Schmitt's casual use of the same label 'total state' to refer to two 'opposed realities', the authoritarian strong state and the weak totalitarian state (1988: 24, 41; compare with Koenen, 1995: 198–205). It is possible, though, that Schmitt purposely referred to his and Ziegler's notion of authoritarian state as 'total state' to emphasize its affinity with Mussolini's *stato totalitario* (compare with Heller, 1933: 296).

¹⁰ Schmitt referred for the first time to the notion of a quantitative total state in his *Legalität und Legitimität* (Schmitt, 1932a: 96). He adopted Ziegler's view that total politicization meant a 'quantitative expansion' of the state, and not a strengthening of its power and authority (Ziegler, 1932: 7).

¹¹ Only a strong state could rise above contradictory interests. Alexander Rüstow's description of the strong state as 'a state that rose above groups and above interests, that could extricate itself from entanglement with economic interests' (1932: 68) coincides with Schmitt's conception. As Haselbach observes, Rüstow's call for a strong state ought to be seen in the context of *Ordoliberalismus*, Germany's neoliberal movement of the 1920s and 1930s: 'The point of departure of a "new liberalism" was the revocation of the fusion between the state and the economic spheres. Rüstow espoused the separation of state and society. Like nineteenth-century entrepreneurial capitalism, society should again regulate itself with respect to the market and the price system' (1991: 40). Anthony Nicholls notes that Rüstow's lecture at the 28 September 1932 meeting of the German Association for Social Policy (*Verein für Sozialpolitik*) was 'a landmark in the prehistory of the social market economy. Rüstow's words certainly made a

yield and satisfy everyone, while simultaneously pleasing contradictory interests. As I have indicated, its expansion is the consequence not of its strength but of its weakness.

II

How is it that we got into this condition of total weakness?

If we take a closer look, we see that we do not have a total state but a *plurality of total parties*. Each party realizes in itself the totality, totally absorbing their members, guiding individuals from the cradle to the grave, from kindergarten to burial and cremation, situating itself totally in the most diverse social groups and passing on to its membership the correct views, the correct ideology, the correct form of state, the correct economic system, and the correct sociability on account of the party. Old liberal-styled parties, which are not capable of such organization, are in danger of being pulverized by the millstones of the modern total parties. The drive towards total politicization appears to be inescapable.

Coexistence between these total visions, which on their way to parliament dominate the state and turn it into the aim of their compromises, leads to that remarkable indiscriminate quantitative *expansion of the state* in all directions. A strong well-organized *plural party system* interposes itself between the state and its government on the one side, and the mass of citizens on the other, and manipulates the *monopoly of politics* – the most astounding of all monopolies, the monopoly of political mediation, the monopoly of the transformation of interests, which of course must exist, into the will of the state. The need to submit to this political monopoly which is the case with every vital concern and every major social organization today in Germany, modifies and falsifies all constitutional institutions. This political monopoly of a series of strong political organizations is more important than any economic monopoly. These organizations will tolerate a strong state only if this state can be exploited for their purposes.

---

great impression on his listeners, among who was at least one future Minister of Economics in the Federal Republic of Germany' (1994: 48). But Nicholls fails to mention Rüstow's explicit agreement with Schmitt's views on the total state.

The principal tool of this political monopoly is the nomination of the *list of candidates*. Every election depends on the list of candidates. The electorate cannot nominate candidates on its own. Today, the great majority of voters is completely dependent on approximately five party lists. Elections are no longer direct. The representative is nominated by the party and not chosen by the people; so-called elections are fully mediated statements that voters address to a party organization. The number of parliamentary seats that accrue to each list is thus the only remaining question. I submit that this process, as it plays itself out today, does *not constitute an election*, not just an immediate election but no election at all. What goes on here? We have five party lists dictated by five organizations; the masses mount, if I may say so, five already prepared saddles, and one still refers to the statistical recording of this process as 'an election'. What does this mean? One must gain full awareness of this question lest Germany perish through the use of those very methods. The choice between five fully incompatible, opposed and closed total *systems*, which espouse opposed ideologies, forms of state and economics, and whose coexistence makes no sense, is absolutely *monstrous*. Five organized hostile systems, each of them total and all of them coexisting – and the people must choose between them five times each year! Whoever can clearly grasp what that means and then understand that each time the entire German people must choose between five opposed ideologies, economic systems and forms of state, cannot expect that a functioning and active majority may ever ensue from such a procedure – a majority, even a loosely connected one, united for the formation of a political will. A process like this can only give rise to five political systems and organizations which endure an unstructured, indeed, hostile coexistence, and whose aim is mutual subjugation and deception. There should be no delusions on this matter.

Such methods of constituting a political will lead to a purely quantitative total state that draws no distinction between the economy and the state, the state and culture, or even between the state and other spheres of human and social existence. Elections are no longer elections, representatives are no longer the representatives that the constitution conceives. The representative is no longer an independent, free person, representing the common welfare over and against partisan interests. The representative is the partisan that marches in step and knows how to cast a ballot; debates and ballots in the popular assembly become an empty farce. Just as the representative is no longer a representative, so too *parliament* is no longer parliament. The present-day *Reichstag* is not the *Reichstag* of the Weimar constitution. The non-confidence vote is not the non-confidence vote understood by a rational parliamentary system, because today it does not have the capacity or the willingness to form a functioning and responsible government. All these constitutional institutions have become frail and have entirely lost their meaning. If the one last column of our constitutional order – the *Reichspräsident* and the government appointed by him and carried by his confidence – were not to stand, chaos would probably exist already in full view and in outward appearances, and even the semblance of order would have vanished.

III

How can we get out of this situation? The state's weakness, due to the reasons mentioned, has led to the confusion of the state and the economy, to the confusion of the state and other non-state spheres. Only a *very strong state* would be able dissolve this dreadful coalescence with all kinds of non-state businesses and interests. That would have to be a painful surgical intervention and not an 'organic' process in the sense of slow growth. If slow growth were allowed, rank growth and weeds sprout faster and multiply more readily than the healthy strains they now cover and obstruct. A process of depoliticization, the segregation of the state from non-state spheres is, to repeat, a political procedure. In today's circumstances, disengagement from politics is a specifically political act. It cannot be generated by party-political motives, whether of an economic, cultural or confessional nature; it can only originate from the state as a whole. The first requirement is a clean and clear distinction between state and state-free spheres. Distinction, not separation! But distinction ought to be the point of departure.

And first, because we are dealing here with a process that is primarily political, one ought to start with the state. The state ought to be again a state. The first prerequisite is obviously a *bureaucracy*, which is not a prop or an instrument of party-political interests or aims. It seems to me that the significant coalescence of state and party, characteristic of present-day Germany, is more the result of flawed knowledge and perception than of bad will. The peculiar coexistence between well-acquired rights and the right to political activity is not generally acknowledged as intrinsically impossible.[12] Otherwise it would have long since been dismissed both morally and juridically. We face here a simple alternative: *either* well-acquired rights and the forswearing of all political activity, *or* vice versa. There is no third alternative. Until recently, our way of thinking was a notion that was not familiar and for which we only have a technical expression, a somewhat awkward foreign term: incompatibilities, that is, *irreconcilabilities*.[13] Whoever refuses to see that well-acquired bureaucratic rights are incompatible with party-politics, will refuse to accept that it is usually the state, communities and other public associations, who pay a party's employees and collaborators, and that thereby bureaucrats turn out to be something else than what the constitution prescribes. Here, it is evident that there is a need for unequivocal distinctions. Until now we have not clarified the necessity of those incompatibilities. On the contrary, one may define contemporary Germany as the land of unlimited compatibilities, where everything may be reconciled with everything else, where one and the same person may simultaneously be a member of the Reichstag, of a provincial assembly, a representative of the Council of State, a high state functionary, a party chairperson, and a multitude of other offices. This is precisely the characteristic expression and product of the type of quantitative total state that exists today in Germany; it can neither define itself as state nor distinguish itself from what is not

---

[12] According to Schmitt, only an autonomous and independent bureaucracy would be be able to counterbalance the effects of unstable party coalitions (compare with Schmitt, 1928: 172; 1931: 101). He noted that articles 129–30 of the Weimar constitution protected the bureaucracy against parliamentary interventions by means of institutional guarantees like tenure and intangible well-acquired rights. (Article 129 of the Weimar constitution stated that 'the well-acquired rights of public functionaries are inviolable' and extended these rights to the armed forces. Article 130 stated: 'Public functionaries serve the whole state and not one party'.)

[13] The issue of incompatibilities is discussed in Schmitt's *Verfassungslehre* as a theoretical consequence of the separation of powers (1928: 189–91).

state. Who will then be able to distinguish between spheres, when state and non-state domains and functions are combined in such a grotesque manner? For once, we could at least look at this problem of incompatibilities right in the eye. In Germany, we have preserved an island in this sea of unlimited compatibilities, and today every German feels that safeguarding the *armed forces* unpolluted by party politics is the equivalent to having saved Germany and the state. The armed forces were able to elude that murky flood. This can also be an encouraging paradigm for the rest of German bureaucracy. It demonstrates that non-partisanship and a disposition towards the state are still possible and are not at all utopian.

If the specific instruments of state power, the armed forces and the bureaucracy, remain undisturbed, a strong state is still conceivable. But then I would consider it unfortunate if one were to take away the only legal instrument of coercion that is still retained for genuine cases of emergency – article 48. The coexistence of the total parties that have occupied the state can never lead to state power, that is, to a strong state. In virtue of its original meaning, the democratic-parliamentary system ought to generate a state capable of acting, ruthlessly if necessary, in cases of emergency, a state that enjoys the unified agreement and consent of the entire people. In Germany's present-day circumstances this aim cannot be reached, and with conditions such as they are it cannot be reached in the foreseeable future. On the contrary, our type of party-state, with its plurality of total parties, precludes any genuine power. It unites itself against any attempt at securing a strong state and leads to a combination of impotence and the annihilation of power. The bearers of this situation still retain enough power to want, and to be able to, block others from acquiring power. To me, this negative resolve not to permit the emergence of a strong state explains the present battle against article 48 and the attempts to destroy this last indispensable instrument of the state.

From the side of the state, present-day conditions are in fact more difficult. The responsibility lies not in the democratic methods for the formation of the state will, but in the peculiarities of the total party-state as they exist now in Germany. But Germany is no longer a democratic state. A state is self-contradictory, particularly a democratic state, if it no longer has the right to bring up its young militarily and educate them as good soldiers. *There can be no meaningful universal electoral rights without a necessarily corresponding universal military service.* In the past this was obvious to every democrat. But this is the most effective of all the endeavours aimed at the destruction of the German state – the separation of electoral rights and military duties, thus leading universal *electoral* rights, without the necessary correction provided by universal *military* duties, to its most absurd consequences. This caricature of a democratic state determines that the democratic parliamentary methods for the formation of the political will, possibly good under other assumptions, bring about an impotence that is destructive of power. One word, at least, with respect to the inseparable connection that exists between the question of military duty and the military readiness of the German people. I know the both the factual and legal difficulties of this issue, which is also unfortunately a foreign affairs issue, but here, in the demilitarized Rhine, that is, in the dishonoured zone, that should not remain unsaid.

What would be required, from the *side of the economy*, to allow for the possibility of a strong state and a sound economy? Here again some new distinctions should be drawn. The old nineteenth-century opposition, the opposition drawn by our liberal forebears between state and free individuals, is insufficient. There is still today a very significant domain of the singular individual which is in essence, I believe, economic activity. But today one can no longer oppose the state with the private individual, with the isolated private entrepreneur. Both would instantly fall to the ground. In opposition to the collective image of the modern state it is necessary to insert an intermediate domain between the state and the singular individual. I use here a distinction drawn in recent years by young constitutional jurists. It is valuable and useful, not for the purpose of setting up new organizations but in order to begin with the right knowledge. We will draw a threefold distinction in the domain of economics and replace, with a *tripartition*, the two-fold antithesis between state and free individual economy, state and private sphere. First, the *economic sphere of the state*, the sphere of genuine state privilege. Certain activities of an economic nature belong to the state – certain commercial entitlements are, for instance, absolutely necessary, and in certain forms, like the postal entitlement, have always existed. These are legitimate state enterprises, which ought to be clearly featured as monopolies and distinguished from the rest of the economy. Second, in opposition to that domain, the sphere of the free, individual entrepreneur, i.e. the *sphere of pure privacy*. Third, the intermediate *non-state, but still public* sphere. For decades we have endured an unfortunate conceptual confusion that understood anything public as a state concern. This meant that one of the greatest achievements of the German people – real autonomous administration (*Selbstverwaltung*) – could not be rightly understood anymore.[14] It is known how, in the wake of party politicization, autonomous municipal administration has reached a critical point. Everyone is aware of this crisis in our autonomous administration. In the domain of economics, however, it is necessary to set the record straight with respect to the notion of *autonomous economic administration*. 'Autonomous economic administration' may be an ambiguous, possibly a misleading slogan. Like in any ambiguity, here too, under this description, the unclear and obscure aims of every kind of party-politician may find refuge.

What is advanced here as economic autonomous administration, and as the distinction between state and public spheres, is completely different from the 'economic democracy' propagated a few years back by a certain side. That economic democracy explicitly espoused a *mixture of economics and politics*; it also wanted to acquire economic power within the state by means of political power, and subsequently increase its political power by means of the economic power it had thus acquired. By contrast, when I refer here to economic autonomous administration [or economic self-management] I mean something different, something that aims at a distinction and a separation. There is an economic sphere that belongs to the public interest and should

---

[14] In his *Verfassungslehre*, Schmitt employed the notion of autonomous administration as Gneist understood it, namely administrative jurisdiction as an honorary activity placed in the hands of wealthy and instructed citizens. Here, however, Schmitt adopted Popitz's views. Popitz extolled the virtues of municipal autonomous administration, which 'demands, in a practical sense, strengthened and unified state supervision (the "companion piece of autonomous administration"). This supervision should emanate from the central state and not from the federal states. Centralization and autonomous administration do not exclude each other, but are mutually required' (Bentin, 1972: 20).

not be seen as separate from it. Still, this is a non-state domain that can be organized and administered by these same business agents, as it happens in any genuine autonomous administration. Today, we already gather under the insufficiently clear expression 'autonomous economic administration' a number of things: industrial and commercial chambers, non-voluntary unions of every sort, associations, monopolies, etc.; we have mixed economic enterprises, where again the expression 'mixed economies' is misused when applied to pure state socialist or state capitalist corporations that organize themselves privately as stock companies or companies of limited responsibility. Finally, we have monopolies of every kind chartered in the public interest but administered autonomously by commercial agents. A major confusion still reigns here, which is characteristic of the present and that we always encounter. The state appears as an economic agent in all conceivable outfits: in public law and private law, as state, as treasury, as majesty, as company of limited responsibility and as stockholder. The state is thus disguised and concealed, making it absolutely necessary to refer to it in simple, solid and non-ambiguous legal forms and methods and to ask that it appear openly as state when 'the state' is at issue. Should it require a commercial privilege, it should use it openly as a state privilege and not misuse it in an unclear combination of private legal forms.

One may already refer today to an *autonomous economic administration* and to an intermediate sphere of a public but non-state economy as an order that exists in a number of initiatives. Naturally, those are often contradictory initiatives, and, of the formations just mentioned, some will be good and promising, others bad and bizarre. We are dealing here with a basic outline that has to be considered and kept in view. Without an autonomous economic administration, in the sense of that intermediate sphere, a real new order would be hardly thinkable.

IV

If the gist of basic outline is clear, we can proceed to raise the question: how can one today render the distinction between state and economy effective? Increasingly one thing is evident: only a strong state can depoliticize, only a strong state can openly and effectively decree that certain activities, like public transit and radio, remain its privilege and as such ought to be administered by it, that other activities belong to the above mentioned sphere of self-management, and that all the rest be given to the domain of a free economy. A state that is to bring about this new order ought to be, as was said, extraordinarily strong. Depoliticization is a political act in a particularly intense way. How can we achieve a strong state that may be capable of such *tour de force?* At present, it is evident that the state, today only intermittently and momentarily a state, needs to gain particularly solid authoritarian foundations by means of new arrangements and institutions. In connection with this I refer to the proposals, also mentioned in the exposition of Dr *Springorum*, for a new type of second chamber, an upper house, as it is sometimes referred to, a combination of state council, state economic council and other elements, or for the creation of something similar. But if I have understood the expositions of your Chair, a certain – I would not say scepticism – reserve and a certain lack of unconditional optimism was expressed, when he mentioned the problem of the opposed interests dividing industry and agriculture.[15] It can be very useful to bring organized interests together, to unite them in guilds [*Gremien*] for the purpose of a round-table session and then to await the decisions of this guild. However, I would like to remind you of the following: interests, particularly business interests, may unite or may separate. That cannot be changed. Whoever organizes interests as such, simultaneously organizes opposed interests and possibly increases, by means of the organizing, the intensity of the opposition. When these organized interests come to the table, and once serious conflicts of interest ensue – the conflicting case is precisely the case that is of interest here, for it is obvious that we will reach agreement on irrelevant matters – the assembly will soon dissolve into its component parts. The danger of secession or the exodus of one group is

---

[15] In his prefatory remarks, Springorum lamented the fact that the recent economic crisis had pushed the different sectors of the economy apart instead of bringing them together. He mentioned the conflicts his own sector had had with agriculture over quota fixing in foreign trade and suggested that agriculture and industry should have a round-table discussion on matters concerning trade policy (1932: 10).

constant. I remind you of the experiences that we had with the *Business Advisory Board* in October 1931. One would have to say that it broke apart too soon. I would also remind you of the notorious experience that has been had with more or less each and every union of various professionally (*berufsständisch*) organized groups: if a unified resolution is to pass, unconditional parity must be eliminated and the possibility of a veto or of being outvoted must be allowed. When every professional branch has a firm quota and its electoral weight stays forever the same, the result is predictable; majority resolutions make no sense in those cases. That would give majority resolutions, where a coalition of shoemakers and bakers could outvote beekeepers; or, as was once the case, where professional musicians were the decisive factor in the conflict of interest case between steel and coal.

In order to avoid politicizing a most interesting consideration concerning professional associations, and also to avoid illusions, I would suggest that the great, and also somehow idealized, medieval *history of the professional associations* (*Berufsstände*) and their organization offers us the following lessons: first, these medieval Estates (*Stände*) did not constitute a politically unified will of themselves. They faced a monarch or a prince and only in this way was the constitution of a politically unified will possible.[16] Second, the Estates never passed resolutions as a collective association of professions and never voted as separate Estates. No Estate was outvoted by the majority of the other Estates. The outvoting of one Estate was not possible in a system of professional associations and would be meaningless. Third, the medieval Estates did not vote at all in the way we do. Within each Estate our problem with the 51 per cent majority did not arise. On the contrary, a certain unanimity arose of itself in a way that, for corrupted human beings like us, cannot be explained without procedural manœuvring. In any case, there is no historical basis

---

[16] In 1938, Schmitt would praise Hobbes's strong state for overcoming 'the anarchy of the feudal estates' and the church's right of resistance as well as the incessant outbreak of civil war arising from those struggles' (1938: 71). He also noted that during the nineteenth century, Hobbes's old adversaries, 'the "indirect" powers of the church and of interest groups, reappeared ... as modern political parties, trade unions, social organizations ... They seized the legislative arm of parliament ... and thought they had placed the leviathan in harness' (p. 73).

which would allow this whole system to function with our methods. Our arithmetical conception of the 51 per cent majority, that puts the remaining 49 per cent in the shade, was certainly not available. However, our modern electoral ways boil down to that. One should not disregard the difficulty of these matters in the call for a second chamber.

The issue of a *second chamber* is brought forward today primarily as a way of strengthening a state that is not strong enough and lacks authority. A second chamber would furnish it with the authority it requires, obtaining it from anywhere, from authority residuals of an earlier epoch, let alone as an advance. In my view, *the sequence ought to be reversed*. Only a strong state can bestow this second chamber the respect and authority required by its members to free themselves from professional (*ständischen*) allegiances, and dare to submit to a unified collective resolution in a way that externally preserves their respectability and nobility without immediately being chased away by their unsatisfied clients. No upper house and no second chamber is possible without a strong state. Here, a strong state is also the first presupposition. From it proceeds the ordering effect that overcomes the confusion and antagonism of the diverse interests, and orders them like a magnet attracts iron filings. Otherwise they would at best organize a pathetic duplicate of today's Reichstag. In the history of the modern constitutions this second chamber, i.e. the chamber that is not generated by universal ballot, has normally had until today the role of limiting and slowing down. It ought to preserve duration and continuity in the face of the first chamber, the unstable and revolutionary-minded chamber generated by the universal vote of the essentially dispossessed masses. Among us the first universally elected chamber is incapable of any action. Should a new second chamber be conceived of as a constraint and counterpoise of a first chamber that is incapable of action, it becomes an institution that is unclear in itself. Something that is in itself incapable of action cannot and need not be further constrained. But should the second chamber strengthen or replace the missing capacity to act of the first chamber, then the latter will probably receive a new impulse and again throw its weight around as popular representative. The second chamber will then share the destiny of the state business council, so that the question arises whether it is good and convenient to lend in this manner new life to such a first chamber. So long as the point of view of the democratic electoral system remains decisive for legality and legitimacy, an elected chamber will unavoidably either abrogate the second chamber or make it into its mere shadow and reflection. These considerations should not, as was indicated, disprove the thoughts of a second chamber, but only interpolate cautionary restraints against hasty institutions.[17] I know how useful a second chamber can be, I would not like to reject or dismiss it as an ultimate goal. However, in view of the difficult circumstances of present-day Germany, I must turn my attention to our immediate present and to our immediate future as far as it may be assessed. We need, in the first place, a strong state that is capable of acting and ready for its great tasks. Were we to have it, we would then create new arrangements, new institutions, *new constitutions*.

In my opinion now is the time, and we no longer have many chances or much latitude for great constitutional experiments. I would go as far as saying, if I may express my own personal private opinion, that the German people has no professional competence for constitutional legislation, in the present meaning of constitutional legislation. I consider that not a fault or an inferiority of the German people. Mostly, we produce imitations of French-styled or Soviet constitutions. And when we draft and constitutionally establish new institutions, according to an organizational scheme of clever and deep kind, we probably obstruct a clearing that ought to remain free. We have before us the example of Weimar's improvisation. A constitution is swiftly prepared, and then in a few minutes, when it is required, lies ready-made on the table. But once it is there it is not easy to discard it. It is then a source of *legality*. It may be that today the German people does not need legality as much as it did in the past, and that it also does not believe so much in legality. Do not forget that a modern state and its bureaucracy function according to the point of view of legality. The authorities listen only to legal prescriptions. Legality is – as distinguished from law (*Recht*) in a

---

[17] In Heinrich Muth's view, one should not read this criticism of a corporatist second chamber, Papen's 'pet project', as a sign of a rift between Schmitt and the regime. Schmitt's objections had to do with a long-standing and unresolved dispute within the Catholic camp (Muth, 1971: 125).

'pathetic' sense – the manner in which modern bureaucracies and the modern civil service function. I speak here very soberly about the political meaning of legality, and in this sense the notion has still a very special value, and particularly so for the strong state. When we now improvise a new legality and posit, next to the current institutions of the Weimar constitution which its creators took as no more than an *emergency setting*, new institutions, we thus create new legalities and thereby new protective walls for various interests which will immediately take refuge under the new legal walls.

I believe therefore that it is better first not to create authority through new institutions, so to say in anticipation. We live in a situation that is similar, even if more acute, to the one we lived in two years ago. The government should make use of all *constitutional means,* but also of *all* constitutional means, which stand at its disposal and that prove to be necessary in chaotic circumstances. It should try to establish immediate contact with the real social forces of the people. The tasks are indeed great. In the introductory words of the Chair, a list of those important matters was already mentioned. The duty to labour service, to settlement, to military exercises and to the military service for the youth, and many other things, are such great and powerful tasks that a government which employs those means to that end, and is able to unite with the forces of the social self-organization of the German people, may have the success that every decent German recognizes. Success comes from immediate labour, from the solution of a genuine labour task. That is possible and not mere utopia. *Authority stems only from success and achievement.* Not the other way around. One should not begin with a proclamation of authority. Nobody will be fooled by this. I must work, show what I can do, and this possibility belongs to work. When besides other strictly constitutional institutions, that may wish to intefere but whose interference is to be eliminated, new methods, guilds (*Gremien*) or even individual persons prove their worth, then a new authority rises, for which, I believe, the readiness of the German people to follow and honestly to recognize an honest success is great. The problem of the constitutional legalization of new institutions will not then constitute an insuperable difficulty.

This is how I envisage the road ahead. The assumption is that work shall start immediately. Another assumption is that the vast and strong productivity of the German people, which in the course of centuries of German history has always stood out in the most astounding way, is rendered fruitful. Our own experience during the last decades still reminds us how the capacity for autonomous organization always proved successful: during the war and the post-war period, during mobilization and demobilization, in good and bad times. This capacity for work and for autonomous organization does not require today the party-political costume in which it is forced to perform in disfigured fashion. If a decisive and ready for action government were to retrieve this connection and immediately seize these forces, what is necessary would then also be possible.[18] Extensive organizational plans for constitutional reform should not be given up. But today they should be deferred. *The forces are here. They are only awaiting a call.* Were they to be seized, rational distinctions would then again be possible, particularly the distinction between state administration, autonomous economic administration and the individual domain of freedom. On the basis of such distinctions, the German people would, over and above party divisions and particularisms, gain its political unity and a strong state.

---

[18] According to Bendersky, this should be read as Schmitt's 'wholehearted' support for General Schleicher's proposed national front government 'extending from the Socialists and Catholics to the left wing of the Nazi party'. Schleicher's project included social reform and a massive public works programme to generate employment (Bendersky, 1983: 183). In Turner's view, Schleicher had virtually no support among Germany's business leaders, who favoured Papen's reliance on private enterprise. Schleicher was perceived as being 'soft on labour' and 'as a potential quasi-socialist in military garb'. Hans Zehrer, one of his conservative revolutionary admirers, referred to him as a 'red general' (Turner, 1985: 304–5). Is it then conceivable that Springorum invited the wrong man to address the *Langnamverein* convention?

References

Works by Carl Schmitt

1914 *Der Wert des Staates und die Bedeutung des Einzelnen*, Tübingen: J. C. B. Mohr (Paul Siebeck) Verlag.

1919 *Politische Romantik*, Munich and Leipzig: Duncker & Humblot.

1921 *Die Diktatur. Von den Anfängen des modernen Souveränitätsgedankens bis zum proletarischen Klassenkampf*, Munich and Leipzig: Duncker & Humblot, 1928.

1922a *Politische Theologie. Vier Kapitel zur Lehre von der Souveränität*, Munich and Leipzig: Duncker & Humblot, 1934.

1922b *Political Theology. Four Chapters on the Concept of Sovereignty*, Cambridge, Mass.: MIT Press, 1985.

1922c *Politische Theologie. Vier Kapital zur Lehre von der Souveränität*, Munich and Leipzig: Duncker & Humblot.

1923a *Römischer Katholizismus und politische Form*, Munich: Theatiner Verlag, 1925.

1923b *Die geistesgeschichtliche Lage des heutigen Parlamentarismus*, Berlin: Duncker & Humblot, 1961.

1923c *The Crisis of Parliamentary Democracy*, trans. by Ellen Kennedy, Cambridge, Mass.: MIT Press, 1985.

1924 'Die Diktatur des Reichspräsidenten nach Artikel 48 der Weimarer Verfassung', appended to *Die Diktatur. Von den Anfängen des modernen Souveränitätsgedanken bis zum proletarischen Klassenkampf*, Munich and Leipzig: Duncker & Humblot, 1928.

1925a *Politische Romantik*, 2nd edition, Berlin: Duncker & Humblot, 1968.

1925b *Political Romanticism*, tr. by Guy Oakes, Cambridge, Mass.: MIT Press, 1986.

1926 *Unabhängigkeit der Richter, Gleichheit vor dem Gesetz und Gewährleistung des Privateigentums nach der Weimarer Verfassung. Ein Rechtsgutachten zu den Gesetzenentwürfen über die*

Vermögensauseinandersetzung mit den früher regierenden Fürstenhäusern, Berlin and Leipzig: Walter de Gruyter.

1927 'Der Begriff des Politischen', *Archiv für Sozialwissenschaft und Sozialpolitik*, 58, pp. 1–33.

1928 *Verfassungslehre*, Berlin: Duncker & Humblot, 1965.

1929a 'Zehn Jahre Reichsverfassung', *Verfassungsrechtliche Aufsätze*, edit. by Carl Schmitt, Berlin: Duncker & Humblot, 1985, pp. 34–40.

1929b 'Der Hüter der Verfasung,' *Archiv des öffentlichen Rechts*, Neue Folge, 16, pp. 161–237.

1930 'Staatsethik und pluralistischer Staat', *Kant-Studien*, 35, pp. 28–42.

1931 *Der Hüter der Verfassung*, Berlin: Duncker & Humblot, 1969.

1932a *Legalität und Legitimität*, Munich & Leipzig: Duncker & Humblot.

1932b *Der Begriff der Politische*, Berlin: Duncker & Humblot, 1963.

1932c 'Gesunde Wirtschaft im starken Staat!', *Mitteilungen des Vereins zur Wahrung der gemeinsamen wirtschaftlichen Interessen in Rheinland u. Wesfalen*, 1, pp. 13–32

1932d 'Der Missbrauch der Legalität,' *Tägliche Rundschau* (July 19).

1933a 'Starker Staat und gesunde Wirtschaft,' *Volk und Reich*, 2, pp. 81–94.

1933b 'Machtpositionen des modernen Staates,' *Deutsches Volkstum*, 15, pp. 225–30.

1933c 'Das Gesetz zur Behebung der Not von Volk und Reich', *Deutsche Juristen-Zeitung*, 38 (April 1), pp. 455–8.

1933d *Das Reichsstatthaltergesetzt*, Berlin: Carl Heymanns Verlag.

1933e 'Weiterentwicklung des totalen Staats in Deutschland', *Verfassungsrechtliche Aufsätze*, edit. by Carl Schmitt, Berlin: Duncker & Humblot, 1985, pp. 359–66.

1933f *Staat, Bewegung und Volk*, Hamburg: Hanseatische Verlag.

1933g *Der Begriff des Politischen*, Hamburg: Hanseatische Verlag.

1934a 'Nationalsozialismus und Rechtsstaat', *Juristische Wochenshrift*, 63, pp. 713–18.

1934b *Über die drei Arten des rechtswissensschaftlichen Denkens*,

Hamburg: Hanseatische Verlag.

1935 'Was bedeutet der Streit um den Rechtsstaat?', *Zeitschrift für die gesamte Staatsrechtswissenschaft*, 95, pp. 189-201.

1938 *The Leviathan in the State Theory of Thomas Hobbes. Meaning and Failure of a Political Symbol*, Foreword and Introduction by George Schwab. Translated by George Schwab and Erna Hilfstein, Westport: Greenwood Press, 1996.

1940 *Positionen und Begriffe im Kampf mit Weimar, Genf, Versailles. 1923-1939*, Berlin: Duncker & Humblot, 1988.

1958 *Verfassungsrechtliche Aufsätze aus den Jahren 1924-54. Materialien zu einer Verfassungslehre*, Berlin: Duncker & Humblot, 1985.

Secondary Literature

Abraham, David. 1981. *The Collapse of the Weimar Republic. Political Economy and Crisis*, Princeton: Princeton University Press.
Alvarez, Alejandro. 1995. *Die verfassunggebende Gewalt des Volkes unter besonderer Berücksichtigung des deutschen und chilenischen Grundgesetzes*, Frankfurt am Main: Peter Lang.
Anderson, Perry. 1992. 'The Intransigent Right at the End of the Century', *London Review of Books*, September 24, pp. 7-11.
Anschütz, Gerhard. 1933. *Die Verfassung des Deutschen Reichs vom 11. August 1919*, Darmstadt: Wissenschaftliche Buchgesellschaft, 1963.
Barker, Ernest. 1914. 'The Discredited State', in Ernest Barker, *Church, State and Education*, Ann Arbor: The University of Michigan Press, 1956.
Becker, Josef. 1961. 'Zentrum und Ermächtigungsgesetz', *Vierteljahreshefte für Zeitgeschichte*, 9, pp. 195-202.
Bendersky, Joseph. 1983. *Carl Schmitt. A Theorist for the Reich*, Princeton: Princeton University Press.
——1987. 'Carl Schmitt at Nuremberg', *Telos*, 72, pp. 91-129.
Beneyto, José María. 1993. *Apocalipsis de la modernidad. El decisionismo político de Donoso Cortés*, Barcelona: Editorial Gedisa.
Bentin, Lutz-Arwed. 1972. *Johannes Popitz und Carl Schmitt. Zur wirtschaftlichen Theorie des totalen Staates in Deutschland*, München: C. H. Beck Verlag.
Bielefeldt, Heiner. 1994. *Kampf und Entscheidung. Politischer Existentialismus bei Carl Schmitt, Helmuth Plessner und Karl Jaspers*, Würzburg: Königshausen & Neumann.

Bielefeldt, Heiner. 1996. 'Deconstruction of the "Rule of Law": Carl Schmitt's Philosophy of the Political,' *Archiv für Rechts- und Sozialphilosophie*, 82, pp. 379–96.
Blumenwitz, Dieter. 1981. 'Die neue Verfassung der Republik Chile,' *Jahrbuch des öffentliches Rechts. Neue Folge*, 30, pp. 618–61.
Böckenförde, Ernst-Wolfgang. 1988. 'Der Begriff des Politischen als Schlüssel zum Staatsrechtlichen Werk Carl Schmitts', in *Complexio Oppositorum. Über Carl Schmitt*, edit by Helmut Quaritsch, Berlin: Duncker & Humblot, pp. 283–99.
Bolingbroke. 1965. *The Idea of a Patriot King*, S.W. Jackman (ed.), Indianapolis: Bobbs-Merrill.
Breuer, Stefan. 1984. 'Nationalstaat und pouvoir constituant bei Sieyès und Carl Schmitt,' *Archiv für Rechts- und Sozialphilosophie*, 70, pp. 495–517.
——1993. *Anatomie der Konservative Revolution*, Darmstadt: Wissenschaftliche Buchgesellschaft.
Brodführer. 1933. 'Das Staatsnotrecht in modernen Verfassungsleben. Aus einem Vortrage, gehalten Ende März in Weimar von Prof. Carl Schmitt,' *Deutsche Richterzeitung*, 25 (September 25), pp. 254–5.
Caldwell, Peter. 1995. 'National Socialism and Constitutional Law: Carl Schmitt, Otto Koellreuter and the Debate over the Nature of the Nazi State', *Cardozo Law Review*, 16, pp. 399–427.
Cristi, Renato. 1984. 'Hegel and Roman Liberalism', *History of Political Thought*, 5, pp. 281–94.
——1989. 'Hegel's Conservative Liberalism', *Canadian Journal of Political Science*, 22, pp. 717–38.
——1994 'La noción de Poder constituyente en Carl Schmitt y la génesis de la Constitución chilena de 1980', *Revista Chilena de Derecho*, 24, pp. 229–50.
Dahm, Georg. 1935. Review of Schmitt's *Über die drei Arten des rechtswissensschaftliche Denkens*, in *Zeitschrift für die gesamte Rechtswissenschaft* 95, pp. 181–8.
Donoso Cortés, Juan. 1970. 'Discurso sobre la dictadura,' in *Obras Completas*, vol. II, edit. by Carlos Valverde, Madrid: Editorial Católica.
Dyzenhaus, David. 1994. '"Now the Machine Runs Itself": Carl Schmitt on Hobbes and Kelsen,' *Cardozo Law Review*, 16, pp.1–19.
——1996. 'The Puzzle of Neo-Conservatism', *Policy Options*, 17, pp. 46–7.
Estévez Araujo, José A. 1989. *La Crisis del Estado de Derecho Liberal: Schmitt en Weimar*, Barcelona: Editorial Ariel.
Fijalkowski, Jürgen. 1958. *Die Wendung zum Führerstaat. Ideologische Komponenten in der politischen Philosophie Carl Schmitts*, Cologne

and Opladen: Wesdeutscher Verlag.

Fraenkel, Ernest. 1941. *The Dual State. A Contribution to the Theory of Dictatorship*, New York: Octagon Books, 1969.

Friedrich, Carl. 1937. *Constitutional Government and Politics. Nature and Development*, New York & London: Harper and Brothers Publishers.

——1950. *Constitutional Government and Democracy. Theory and Practice in Europe and America*, Boston: Ginn and Co.

——1955. 'The Political Thought of Neo-Liberalism', *American Political Science Review*, 49, pp. 509–25.

Friedrichs, Axel. 1939. *Die nationalsozialistische Revolution 1933*, in *Dokumente der Deutschen Politik*, edit. by Paul Meier-Benneckenstein, Berlin: Junker und Dünnhaupt Verlag.

Gierke, Otto von. 1958. *Political Theories of the Middle Age*, translated with an introduction by Frederic William Maitland, Cambridge: Cambridge University Press.

Gissurarson, Hannes H. 1987. *Hayek's Conservative Liberalism*, New York: Garland.

Gottfried, Paul Edward. 1990. *Carl Schmitt: Politics and Theory*, Westport: Greenwod Press.

Gray, John. 1981. 'Hayek on Liberty, Rights and Justice,' *Ethics* 92, pp. 73–84.

Greiffenhagen, Martin. 1979. 'The Dilemma of Conservatism in Germany', *Journal of Contemporary History*, 14, 611–25.

Habermas, Jürgen. 1986. 'Sovereignty and the *Führerdemokratie*', *The Times Literary Supplement*, September 26, pp. 1053–4.

Haselbach, Deiter. 1988. 'Die Wandlung zum Liberalen. Zur gegenwärtigen Schmitt–Diskussion in den USA', in *Carl Schmitt und die Liberalismuskritik*, ed. Klaus Hansen and Hans Lietzmann, Opladen: Leske & Budrich, pp. 119–40.

——1991. *Autoritärer Liberalismus und Soziale Marktwirtschaft. Gesellschaft und Politik im Ordoliberalismus*, Baden-Baden: Nomos Verlaggesellschaft.

——1996. 'Schmittian Economic Liberalism: Post-war West Germany's 'Social Market Economy', paper read at the ISSEI Conference, Utrecht, August 1996.

Hayek, Friedrich. 1944. *The Road to Serfdom*, Chicago and London: The University of Chicago Press.

——1960. *The Constitution of Liberty*, South Bend: Gateway, 1972.

——1967. *Studies in Philosophy, Politics and Economics*, Chicago and London: The University of Chicago Press.

——1973. *Law, Legislation and Liberty*, vol. 1: *Rules and Order*, Chicago: The University of Chicago Press.

Hayek, Friedrich. 1976. *Law, Legislation and Liberty*, vol. 2: *The Mirage of Social Justice*, Chicago: The University of Chicago Press.
——1979. *Law, Legislation and Liberty*, vol. 3: *The Political Order of a Free People*, Chicago and London, The University of Chicago Press.
Hegel, G. W. F. 1991. *Elements of the Philosophy of Right*, edited by Allen W. Wood and translated by H. B. Nisbet, Cambridge: Cambridge University Press.
Heller, Hermann. 1927. *Die Souveränität. Ein Beitrag zur Theorie des Staats- und Völkerrechts*, Berlin and Leipzig: Walter de Gruyter.
——1933. 'Autoritärer Liberalismus?', *Die Neue Rundschau* 44, pp. 289-98.
Henrich, Dieter 1983 'Einleitung,' G. F. W. Hegel, *Philosophie des Rechts. Die Vorlesung von 1819/20 in einer Nachschrift*, edited by Dieter Henrich, Frankfurt am Main: Suhrkamp Verlag.
Herrero, Montserrat. 1996. 'Estudio Preliminar,' in Carl Schmitt, *Sobre los tres modos de pensar la ciencia jurídica*, translated by Montserrat Herrero, Madrid: Tecnos.
Hobbes, Thomas. 1841. *Leviathan*, in *Opera Philosophica* III, ed. by William Molesworth, London: J. Bohn.
——1968. *Leviathan*, edit. with an introduction by C. B. Macpherson, Harmondsworth: Penguin.
Holmes, Stephen. 1993. *The Anatomy of Antiliberalism*, Cambridge: Harvard University Press.
Huber, Ernst Rudolf. 1988. 'Carl Schmitt in der Reichkrise der Weimarer Zeit', in *Complexio Oppositorum. Über Carl Schmitt*, edit. by Helmut Quaritsch, Berlin: Duncker & Humblot, pp. 33-50.
Ilting, Karl-Heinz. 1973. 'Einleitung,' G. W. F. Hegel, *Vorlesungen über Rechtsphilosophie 1818 bis 1931*, edited by Karl-Heinz Ilting, Volume I, Stuttgart: Frommann-Holzboog.
——1983. 'Zur Genese der Hegelschen "Rechtsphilosophie"', *Philosophische Rundschau*, 30, pp. 161-209.
Kaisenberg, Georg. 1933. 'Das Ermächtigungsgesetz', *Deutsche Juristen-Zeitung*, 38 (April 1), pp. 458-61.
Kant, Immanuel. 1957. *Perpetual Peace*, edited and translated by Lewis W. Beck, Indianapolis: Bobbs-Merrill.
Kaufmann, Erich. 1906. *Studien zur Staatslehre des monarchischen Prinzipes. Einleitung; die historischen und philosophischen Grundlagen*, Leipzig: Oscar Brandstetter Verlag.
Kelsen, Hans. 1929. *Vom Wesen und Wert der Demokratie*, Tübingen: J. C. B. Mohr (Paul Siebeck) Verlag.
Kennedy, Ellen. 1985. 'Introduction: Carl Schmitt's *Parlamentarismus* in its Historical Context', in Carl Schmitt, *The Crisis of Parliamentary Democracy*, trans. by Ellen Kennedy, Cambridge, Mass.: MIT Press.

Keohane, Nannerl. 1980. *Philosophy and the State in France. The Renaissance to the Enlightenment*, Princeton: Princeton University Press.
Kervégan, Jean-François. 1992 *Hegel, Carl Schmitt. Le politique entre spéculation et positivité*, Paris: Presses Universitaires de France.
Kierkegaard, Soren. 1967. *Die Wiederholung*, in *Gesammelte Werke*, Düsseldorf: Eugen Diederichs Verlag.
Koellreutter, Otto. 1933. 'Der nationales Rechtsstaat', *Deutsche Juristen-Zeitung*, 38 (April 15), pp. 417–24.
Koenen, Andreas. 1995. *Der Fall Carl Schmitt. Sein Aufstieg zum "Kronjuristen des Dritten Reiches"*, Darmstadt: Wissenschaftliche Buchgesellschaft.
Kondylis, Panayotis. 1986. *Konservativismus. Geschichtlicher Gehalt und Untergang*, Stuttgart: Klett-Cotta.
Krauss, Günther. 1990. 'Erinnerungen an Carl Schmitt – Teil 3: 1933', *Schmittiana*, 1, 55–69.
Krieger, Leonard. 1957. *The German Idea of Freedom*, Boston: Beacon Press.
Lokatis, Siegfried. 1992. 'Hanseatische Verlagsanstalt. Politisches Buchmarketing im "Dritten Reich"', *Archiv für Geschichte des Buchwesens*, 38, pp. 1–189.
Löning, Georg. 1933. 'Frühjahreslang der Deutschen Vereinigung für Staatswissenschaftliche Fortbildung', *Deutsche Juristen-Zeitung*, 38 (May 15), pp. 676–7.
Maistre, Joseph de. 1980. *Considérations sur la France*, critical edition by Jean–Louis Darcel, Geneva: Slatkine.
Mannheim, Karl. 1971. 'Conservative Thought,' *From Karl Mannheim*, (Kurt Wolff, ed.), New York: Oxford University Press.
Marcuse, Herbert. 1967. 'The Struggle Against Liberalism in the Totalitarian View of the State', *Negations. Essays in Critical Theory*, Boston: Beacon Press, pp. 3–42.
Marx, Karl and Friedrich Engels. 1978. *The Marx and Engels Reader*, ed. by Robert Tucker, New York: Norton.
Mathiez, Albert. 1930. 'La place de Montesquieu dans l'histoire des doctrines politiques du XVIIIe siècle', *Annales historiques de la révolution française*, pp. 97–112.
Maus, Ingeborg. 1976. *Bürgerliche Rechtstheorie und Faschismus. Zur sozialen Funktion und aktuellen Wirkung des Theorie Carl Schmitts*, Munich: Wilhelm Fink.
——1986. *Rechtstheorie und politische Theorie im Industriekapitalismus*, Munich: Wilhelm Fink Verlag.
——1994. 'Die Bekenntnisse der Unpolitischen. Zur gegenwärtige Carl-Schmitt-Renaissance aus Anlass einer Biographie', *Frankfurter*

Rundschau, 77, April 2, p. ZB2.
McCormick, John. 1994. 'Fear, Technology and the State. Carl Schmitt, Leo Strauss, and the Revival of Hobbes in Weimar and National Socialist Germany', *Political Theory*, 22, pp. 619–52.
——1995. 'The Dilemmas of Dictatorship: Carl Schmitt and Constitutional Emergency Powers', *Proceedings of the 17th IVR World Congress*, vol. VI, Bologna: Cooperativa Libraria Universitaria Editrici, pp. 112–18.
Mehring, Reinhard. 1989. *Pathetisches Denken. Carl Schmitt Denkweg am Leitfaden Hegels: Katholische Grundstellung und antimarxistische Hegelstrategie*, Berlin: Duncker & Humblot.
——1992. *Carl Schmitt. Zur Einführung*, Hamburg: Junius Verlag.
Meier, Heinrich. 1995. *Carl Schmitt and Leo Strauss. The Hidden Dialogue*, translated by J. Harvey Lomax, Chicago and London: The University of Chicago Press.
Meinecke, Friedrich. 1922. *Historism. The Rise of a New Historical Outlook*, trans by J. E. Anderson, London: Routledge & Kegan Paul
Mises, Ludwig von. 1985. *Liberalism in the Classical Tradition*, trans. by Ralph Raico, Irvington-on-Hudson: The Foundation for Economic Education, Inc.
Montesquieu. 1949. *Mes Pensées* in *Oeuvres Complètes*, ed. Roger Callois, Paris: Gallimard.
Morsey, Rudolf. 1992. *Das 'Ermächtigungsgesetz' vom 24. März 1933. Quellen zur Geschichte und Interpretation des 'Gesetzes zur Behebung der Not von Volk und Reich'*, Düsseldorf: Droste Verlag.
Mouffe, Chantal. 1993. *The Return of the Political*, London: Verso.
Müller, Johann Baptist. 1982. 'Was heisst "Liberalkonservativ"' *Zeitschrift für Politik*, 29, pp. 351–75.
Muth, Heinrich. 1971. 'Carl Schmitt in der Deutschen Innenpolitik des Sommers 1932'. *Historische Zeitschrift*, Beiheft, pp. 75–147.
Neumann, Franz. 1966. *Behemoth. The Structure and Practise of National Socialism 1933–1944*, New York: Harper & Row.
Neumann, Volker. 1980. *Der Staat im Bürgerkrieg. Kontinuität und Wandlung des Staatsbegriffs in der politischen Theorie Carl Schmitts*, Frankfurt/New York: Campus Verlag.
Nicholls, Anthony. 1994. *Freedom and Responsibility: The Social Market Economy in Germany, 1918–1963*, Oxford: Clarendon.
Noack, Paul. 1993. *Carl Schmitt. Eine Biographie*, Frankfurt: Propylaen.
Ottmann, Henning. 1977. *Individuum und Gemeinschaft bei Hegel*, vol. 1, Berlin: de Gruyter.
Pasquino, Pasquale. 1988. 'Die Lehre vom "pouvoir constituant" bei Emmanuel Sieyès und Carl Schmitt', in *Complexio Oppositorum*.

Über Carl Schmitt, edit. by Helmut Quaritsch, Berlin: Duncker & Humblot, pp. 371–85.
Piccone, Paul and G.L. Ulmen. 1987. 'Introduction to Schmitt', *Telos*, 72, pp. 3–14.
Quaritsch, Helmut. 1988. *Positionen und Begriffe Carl Schmitts*, Berlin: Duncker & Humblot.
Raz, Joseph. 1977. 'The Rule of Law and its Virtue', *The Law Quarterly Review*, 93, pp. 195–211.
Röpke, Wilhelm. 1948. *Civitas Humana*, London: Hodge.
Ruethers, Bernd. 1990. *Carl Schmitt im Dritten Reich. Wissenschaft als Zeitgeist-Verstärkung?*, Munich: Beck.
Rumpf, Helmut. 1972. *Carl Schmitt und Thomas Hobbes. Ideelle Beziehungen und aktuelle Bedeutung mit einer Abhandlung über: Die Frühschriften Carl Schmitts*, Berlin: Duncker & Humblot
Rüstow, Alexander. 1932. 'Industrialisierung und Arbeitslosigkeit', *Verhandlungen des Vereins für Sozialpolitik in Dresden 28. und 29. September 1932*, pp. 62–7.
Sandel, Michael. 1996. *Democracy's Discontent: America in Search of a Public Philosophy*, Cambridge, Mass.: Belknap Press of Harvard University Press.
Schelsky, Helmut. 1983. *Politik und Publizität*, Stuttgart: Seewald.
Scheuerman, William E. 1993. 'The Rule of Law under Siege: Carl Schmitt and the Death of the Weimar Republic', *History of Political Thought*, 14, pp. 265–80.
——1995. 'The Unholy Alliance of Carl Schmitt and Friedrich A. Hayek,' *Proceedings of the 17th IVR World Congress*, vol. VI, Bologna: Cooperativa Libraria Universitaria Editrici, pp. 119–28.
——1996. 'Legal Indeterminacy and the Origins of Nazi Legal Thought: The Case of Carl Schmitt', *History of Political Thought*, 17, pp. 571–90.
Schlenker, Max. 1932. 'Vorwort,' *Mitteilungen des Vereins zur Wahrung der gemeinsamen wirtschaftlichen Interessen in Rheinland u. Wesfalen*, 1, pp. 1–2.
Schwab, George. 1970. *The Challenge of Exception. An Introduction to the Political Ideas of Carl Schmitt between 1921 and 1936*, Berlin: Duncker & Humblot.
——1988. 'Progress of Schmitt Studies in the English-speaking World', in *Complexio Oppositorum: Über Carl Schmitt*, ed. Helmut Quaritsch Berlin: Duncker & Humblot, pp. 447–64.
——1990. 'Carl Schmitt Through a Glass Darkly', *Schmittiana* 1, 70–87.
Schwab, Johann Baptist. 1858. *Johannes Gerson. Professor der Theologie und Kanzler der Universität Paris*, New York: Burt Franklin, 1965.

Slagstad, Rune. 1988. 'Liberal Constitutionalism and its Critics: Carl Schmitt and Max Weber', in *Constitutionalism and Democracy*, ed. Jon Elster and Rune Slagstad, Cambridge: Cambridge University Press, pp. 103–29.

Sontheimer, Kurt. 1962. *Antidemokratisches Denken in der Weimarer Republik. Die politischen Ideen des deutschen Nationalismus zwischen 1918 und 1933*, Munich: Nymphenburger Verlagshandlung.

Springorum, Fritz. 1932. 'Eröffnungsprache', *Mitteilungen des Vereins zur Wahrung der gemeinsamen wirtschaftlichen Interessen in Rheinland u. Wesfalen*, 1, pp. 5–12.

Strauss, Leo. 1932. 'Notes on Carl Schmitt, The Concept of the Political', in *Carl Schmitt and Leo Strauss. The Hidden Dialogue*, translated by J. Harvey Lomax, Chicago and London: University of Chicago Press, 1995.

——1963. *The Political Philosophy of Hobbes. Its Basis and its Genesis*, Chicago and London: University of Chicago Press.

Thoma, Richard. 1925. 'On the Ideology of Parliamentarism', in Carl Schmitt, *The Crisis of Parliamentary Democracy*, trans. by Ellen Kennedy, Cambridge, Mass.: MIT Press, 1985.

Tocqueville, Alexis de. 1961. *Democracy in America*, New York: Schocken.

Tommissen, Piet. 1975. 'Over en in zake Carl Schmitt', *Eclectica* 5, 89–109.

——1988. 'Bausteine zu einer Wissenschaftlichen Biographie (Periode: 1888–1933)', in *Complexio Oppositorum. Über Carl Schmitt*, edit. by Helmut Quaritsch, Berlin: Duncker & Humblot, pp. 71–100.

Treitschke, Heinrich von. 1886. *Deutsche Geschichte im Neunzehnten Jahrhundert*, 3rd edition, Leipzig: Verlag von S. Hirzel.

——1916. *History of Germany in the Nineteenth Century*, trans. by Eden & Cedar Paul, New York: McBride, Nast & Co.

Turner, Henry Ashby. 1985. *German Big Business and the Rise of Hitler*, New York and Oxford: Oxford University Press.

Wilms, Bernard. 1988. 'Carl Schmitt – Jüngster Klassiker des Politischen Denkens?', in *Complexio Oppositorum. Über Carl Schmitt*, edit. by Helmut Quaritsch, Berlin: Duncker & Humblot, pp. 577–97.

Ziegler, Heinz O. 1932. *Autoritärer oder Totaler Staat*, Tübingen: Verlag von J. C. B. Mohr (Paul Siebeck).

Zweig, Egon. 1909. *Die Lehre vom Pouvoir Constituant. Ein Beitrag zum Staatsrecht der französischen Revolution*, Tübingen: Verlag von J. C. B. Mohr (Paul Siebeck).

Index

Abraham, David 212
Adler, Alfred 59
Adler, Max 186
Althusius, Johannes 99, 101
Alvarez, Alejandro 123
anarchism 13, 86, 89, 172, 173, 175, 176, 205, 207
Anderson, Perry 3
Anschütz, Gerhard 4, 41, 158, 160
Aquinas 131, 159
Aristotle 131, 159, 191
armed forces 42, 121, 187, 197, 203, 222, 223
authoritarian (or conservative) liberalism 4, 6, 52, 94, 137, 147, 149, 156, 167, 168, 172–5, 194, 207, 210
authoritarianism 23, 147, 166, 168, 173, 196
  see also totalitarianism
autonomous administration (*Selbtsverwaltung*) 33, 34, 167, **197–9**, 201–3, **225–6**, 232

Bakunin, Mikhail 89, 92
balance of powers 83, 85, 106, 126, 131, 136, 174, 191, 192
Barère, Bertrand 205
Barker, Ernest 181
Becker, Josef 39
Beckerath, Erwin von 217
Bendersky, Joseph 2, 3, 4, 11, 12, 27, 30, 37, 38, 40, 43, 64, 92, 143, 181, 196, 214, 232
Beneyto, José María 82
Bentham, Jeremy 79
Bentin, Armen-Lutz 5, 31, 46, 179, 180, 194, 212, 213, 225

Bergson, Henri 89
Beza, Théodore de 83
Bielefeldt, Heiner 18
Bilfinger, Carl 52
Bismarck, Otto von 174
Blumenwitz, Dieter 123
Bluntschli, J. C. 135
Böckenförde, Ernst-Wolfgang 109
Bodin, Jean 110, 111, 131
Bolingbroke, Henry St John, Viscount 85, 131, 132
Bonald, Louis de 13, 20, 56, 59, 61, 62, 67, 68, 96, 116
Boulainvilliers, Henri Comte de 7, 67
Bracher, Karl D. 39
Breuer, Stefan 125, 191, 217
Brodführer 46
Brüning, Heinrich 180
bureaucracy 144, 187, 197, 204, 222, 223, 230, 231
  see also state, bureaucratic state
Burke, Edmund 1, 3, 20, 53, 56, 59, 62, 68, 94, 132

Caesar 88
Caldwell, Peter 3
Calvin 131
capitalism 201, 202, 203, 213, 218
  anti-capitalist rhetoric 29, 203
  capitalists 29, 76, 77, 153
Catholics 12, 20, 21, 36, 53, 54, 55, 59, 61, 71, 72, 90, 91, 92, 108, 113, 114, 198, 230, 232
  Catholic Centre Party 36, 38
  Catholic Church 13, 34, 75, 77, 80, 90, 126, 131, 172, 174, 228

Catholicism 60, 61, 74, 90, 91, 92
Chile 168
civil society 6, 16, 19, 25, 50, 63, 74, 81, 86, 96, 153, 154, 155, 175, 177, 179, 182, 196
  autonomous 5, 94, 150, 151, 166, 167, 190, 193, 206
  depoliticized 167, 168, 176, 184, 194, 197
  Hegelian 18, 22, 97–101, 103, 104, 175
  separation from the state 23, 26, 30, 75, 100, 146, 150, 166, 167, 176, 184, 186, 188, 189, 190, 192, 193, 197, 201, 204, 207, 208, 218, 221
Cole, G. D. H. 174, 181
Commons, John 183
Communist Party 29, 38, 195, 203, 210
concrete order formation 19, 158–61, 164, 165, 204
  see also institutionalism
Condorcet, Nicholas de 67, 84, 85, 208
conservative philosophy 18, 20, 136, 141
  conservative thought 1, 4, 6, 12, 21, 53
conservatism 1, 7, 12, 19, 20, 53, 55, 56, 57, 77, 91, 92
  revolutionary 12, 23, 28, 37, 50, 51, 54, 73, 74, 79, 86, 89, 113, 121, 122, 160, 197
  see also authoritarian liberalism
Constant, Benjamin 96, 105, 137, 168
constituent power (*pouvoir constituant, verfassunggebende Gewalt*) 3, 8, 12, 13, 19, 20, 21, 40–5, 51, 64–71, 72, 93, 102, 104, 109, 114, 116–25, 131–3, 160, 171, 183, 204–6, 208
  constituted power (*pouvoir constitué*) 40, 204, 205, 208

constitution
  abrogation 11, 20, 39, 40, 41, 43, 44, 104, 123, 124, 138, 143, 179
  destruction 40, 44, 51, 109, 117, 123, 124, 138, 160, 204
  elimination 40
  protection 8, 42, 163, 179, 183, 184
  reform 28, 41, 43, 44, 51
constitutional law 39, 40, 41, 44, 119, 123, 159, 160, 205
constitutional positivism 159
constitutional theory 109, 114, 116, 117, 122, 169, 172, 191, 192, 204
continuity thesis 16, 17, 18, 45, 51, 74, 93, 142, 144, 145, 204
  discontinuity 25, 26, 143
corporate order 198, 199, 202
  corporate state 203
corporatism 7, 34, 35, 174
Cristi, Renato 86, 94, 121, 123
critique of liberalism 4, 6, 10–18, 22, 23, 73, 74, 105, 139, 142, 148, 169, 170, 172, 174, 211
  see also liberalism
Cromwell, Oliver 77

Dahlmann, F. C. 132, 135
Dahm, Georg 13, 146
D'Ailly, Cardinal Pierre 5, 65, 71
decisionism 10, 22, 68, 85, 89, 93, 94, 97, 98, 103–5, 107, 112, 113, 147, 156, 158–60, 162–7, 185, 186
  pure or hard 12, 73–4, 97, 98, 103, 104, 107, 114, 115, 162, 165
  soft or moderate 73, 98, 107, 161, 162
democracy 4, 14–17, 23, 24, 77, 80–3, 91, 102, 109, 112–16, 124, 125, 129, 130, 131, 133–5, 137, 142, 149, 166, 174, 175, 180, 181, 185,

INDEX

188, 190–3, 195, 201, 205, 206
absolute 82, 86, 114, 130, 193
democratic principles 14, 18, 117, 120, 135, 186, 193
democratic state-form 129, 130, 134, 135, 140
distinction between democracy and liberalism 14–17, 21, 22, 82, 109, 147, 205
economic democracy 199, 225
Führerdemokratie 15
liberal democracy 10, 127
parliamentary democracy 10, 14–16, 33, 79
participatory democracy 206, 211
plebiscitary democracy 15, 16, 206
proletarian democracy 134
depoliticization 34, 167, 168, 169, 170, 173, 176, 184, 194, 197, 200, 213, 216, 221, 223, 227
see also politicization
Descartes, René 55, 59, 170
dictatorship 4, 40, 63, 65, 73, 79, 80–3, 86, 87, 91, 92, 113, 119, 138, 168, 179, 205
absolute or sovereign 12, 13, 21, 22, 38, 44, 45, 63–70, 89, 93, 95, 113, 119, 138, 145, 165
commissarial 12, 14, 18, 44, 63–70, 93, 119, 138, 145
educational, enlightened or rationalist 68, 86–9
liberal 168
proletarian 3, 67, 68, 88, 90, 94
discussion 61, 62, 72, 73, 79, 80, 83, 86, 87, 105, 106, 185
Dohna, Alexander Graf zu 64
Donoso Cortés, Juan 3, 12, 13, 53, 61, 67, 68, 72, 73, 82, 89–91, 96, 113, 115, 116
Dostoevsky, Fyodor 77
Dyzenhaus, David 3, 168, 186

Dubos, Jean Baptiste 7

economics 32, 75–8, 169, 196, 197, 199, 216, 220, 224, 225
economic libertarianism 201
economic point of view 75–8, 216
see also free economy
either-or 61, 87, 91, 103, 105
emergency 43, 64, 66, 69, 167, 195, 217, 223, 231
enabling act (13 October 1923) 43
enabling act (24 March 1933) 8, 11, 19, 20, 27, 28, 35, 38–45, 47, 48, 51, 137–9, 143, 160, 200
Engels, Friedrich 67
estates (*Stände*) 34, 70, 102, 106, 110, 228
Estévez Araujo, José 64
Eucken, Walter 194
exception, exceptional situations 6, 67, 68, 103, 104, 109, 111, 112, 117, 124, 148, 162

fascism 14, 20, 142, 194, 195, 198, 201, 202, 208, 217
Fénelon, François 7, 67
Fichte, Johann 54, 57, 87
Figgis, J. N. 174
Fijalkowski, Jürgen 10, 190
Fraenkel, Ernest 199
Franco, Francisco 123
free economy 5, 25, 27, 28, 31, 33, 52, 153, 172, 175, 190, 194, 198, 200, 201, 203, 206, 207, 213, 224, 227
see also market economy
French 1814 *Charte* 64–6, 69, 93, 111, 112
French constitution (1830) 130
French revolution 3, 7, 20, 55, 62, 121, 175
Freud, Sigmund 59
Friedrich, Carl 6, 8, 9, 166, 194
Friedrichs, Axel 40
friend/enemy distinction 6, 10,

108, 129, 133, 140, 171, 195, 207, 209, 210, 211, 217
Führer 10, 15, 43, 50, 51, 155, 202
Führergrundsatz 165
Führerprinzip 51, 160
Führertum 202

Gagern, H. W. A. von 132
Gentz, Friedrich von 1, 54, 62, 95, 209
German constitution (1871) 42, 51, 117, 123
German revolution (1918–19) 1, 2, 7, 12, 16, 20, 28, 40, 41, 47, 51, 53, 82, 123, 165, 180, 187, 204, 205
Nazi revolution 25, 41, 50, 51
Gerson, Jean 5, 65, 66, 71, 144
Gierke, Otto von 19, 65, 174
Gissurarson, Hannes 94
Gneist, Rudolph von 135, 154–6, 199, 225
God 55–60, 72, 75, 87, 89, 103, 112, 163, 171
Goebbels, Joseph 49
goodness of humankind 173, 176, 177, 211
Göring, Hermann 48
Gottfried, Paul Edward 3, 12
Gray, John 164
Greiffenhagen, Martin 1
guilds 227, 231
Guizot, François 79, 105, 130
Günther, Albrecht Erich 34

Habermas, Jürgen 14, 15
Haller, Karl von 1
Hamilton, Alexander 85
Hardenberg, Karl August von 96
Hariou, Maurice 164
Hasbach, Wilhelm 135
Haselbach, Dieter 3, 149, 194, 197, 204, 218
Hayek, Friedrich 3, 9, 22, 23, 84, 94, 137, 146–68, 201
Heidegger, Martin 1
Hegel, G. F. W. 3, 17, 22, 56, 57, 86–8, 94, 96–107, 137, 143, 154, 155, 164, 168, 175, 181
Heller, Hermann 6, 31, 66, 93, 111, 149, 186, 193, 218
Henrich, Dieter 104
Henry VIII 181
Hermens, Ferdinand 37
Herrero, Montserrat 159
Hindenburg, Paul von 8, 25, 26, 29, 35, 36, 37, 180, 188, 212, 214
Hitler, Adolf 5, 11, 20, 25, 27–30, 36, 37, 38, 42, 45, 46, 49, 94, 97, 121, 146, 147, 179, 187, 195, 196, 203, 212
Hobbes, Thomas 1, 3, 4, 6, 10, 11, 23, 44, 84, 85, 94, 96, 99, 101, 103, 111, 113, 126, 131, 170–2, 208, 209, 211
Holmes, Stephen 2, 3, 10, 105, 127, 207–9
homogeneity 133, 186, 205
see also identity
Huber, Ernst Rudolf 214
Hugenberg, Alfred 43
Humboldt, Wilhelm von 96
Hume, David 144

identity (principle of) 15, 23, 101, 102, 103, 132–5, 140, 186, 188, 206
Ilting, Karl-Heinz 18, 104
institutionalism 73, 105, 164
see also concrete order formation
intermediate associations 33, 34, 66, 67, 174, 228
irrational 11, 12, 13, 55, 76, 84, 86, 88, 101
irrationalism 75, 78, 84, 85, 89
irrationalist philosophy 89

Jacobins 56, 86
Jellinek, Georg 118
John of Paris 65
judicial review 152, 183
Jünger, Ernst 36, 194

INDEX

Junius Brutus 83

Kaas, Ludwig 36, 37, 38
Kaisenberg, Georg 39, 49
Kant, Immanuel 129, 144, 149
Kapp-putsch 70
Kaufmann, Erich 66, 109, 110, 112, 118, 142, 155
Kautsky, Karl 88
Kelsen, Hans 11, 14, 71, 111, 112, 118, 120, 130, 136, 155, 157–9, 185, 186, 205
Kennedy, Ellen 3, 14, 15
Keohane, Nannerl 7
Kervégan, Jean-François 22, 73, 74, 96–107, 125
Kierkegaard, Søren 3, 162
Koellreutter, Otto 39, 47
Koenen, Andreas 1, 26, 39, 45, 46, 47, 49, 137, 154, 198, 218
Kondylis, Panayotis 67, 161
Krauss, Gunther 52
Krieger, Leonard 94

Laband, Paul 118
Landfried, Friedrich 49
Langnamverein 5, 19, 25, 29, 30, 36, 203, **212**, 213, 232
 see also Schmitt, *Langnamverein Address*
Laski, Harold 17, 174, 181
legal positivism 11, 14, 19, 97, 144, 155–9, 161, 163, 164
legality 21, 41, 46, 63, 97, 157, 186–8, 192, 205, 230, 231
legibus solutus 122, 124
legitimacy 21, 42, 46, 69, 73, 97, 157, 186–8, 192, 230
 democratic 18, 21, 51, 70, 74, 81, 118, 121
 monarchical 1, 3, 4, 6, 16, 18, 51, 70, 74, 82, 121, 206
Lenin, Vladimir 88
liberalism 13, 14, 15, 21, 55, 57, 63, 73, 77, 84, 98, 110, 113, 114, 118, 120, 137, 148, 150, 151, 152, 166, 169, 200, 217
 bourgeois liberalism 72, 144, 172
 classical liberalism 66, 82, 105, 201, 204, 207
 early or old liberalism 135, 144, 149, 156
 German liberalism 7, 85, 106
 Hegel's liberalism 22, 96
 humanitarian liberalism 58, 61, 62, 65, 92, 207, 209, 210, 211
 individualist liberalism 74
 legal, juridical or procedural liberalism 186, 200, 205, 206
 neoliberalism 31, 176–8, 197, 198
 Ordoliberalismus 176, 197, 218
 Schmitt's accommodation to liberalism 16, 17, 23, 73, 74, 82, 86, 89, 92, 94, 105, 108, 115, 126, 136, 147, 169, 173, 175
 see also critique of liberalism; democracy, distinction between democracy and liberalism
Locke, John 3, 149, 151, 153
Lokatis, Siegfried 37, 137, 177
Löning, Georg 46
Louis-Philippe 86, 191
Löwith, Karl 98
Luther, Martin 94

McCormick, John P. 3, 6, 69, 145
Machiavelli, Niccolò 76, 97, 131
Maistre, Joseph de 1, 3, 12, 13, 20, 53–62, 68, 71, 89, 96, 113, 115
Maitland, F. W. 19
Malebranche, Nicolas de 59, 60
Mannheim, Karl 7
Marbury v. *Madison* 183
Marcks, Erich 36, 37
Marcuse, Herbert 96
market economy 20, 23, 27, 94, 100, 153, 203, 210
 social market economy 218

see also free economy
Marshall, John 84, 183
Marsilius of Padua 65
Marx, Karl 3, 59, 67, 68, 87, 88
Marxism 11, 36, 82, 88, 89, 92, 94, 140
Mathiez, Albert 7, 67
Maus, Ingeborg 1, 30, 40, 50, 144, 166, 193, 199, 204
Mazzini, Giuseppe 92
measure 10, 64, 124, 148, 151, 152, 153, 162, 186, 189, 201, 208
Medicus, Franz 39, 49
Mehring, Reinhard 1, 18, 217
Meier, Heinrich, 23, 169–78
Meinecke, Friedrich 7
metaphysics 55, 97, 112
  Christian metaphysics 57
  metaphysical 2, 18, 19, 53, 59, 73, 98, 121, 122, 144, 160, 161, 170, 190, 207, 208
  pantheistic metaphysics 71
  traditional metaphysics 55, 56, 58, 97, 112, 125
Metternich, Klemens von 54
Michael, Horst 37
Mill, John Stuart 79, 105, 149
Mises, Ludwig von 195
Mohl, Robert von 154
monarchical principle 3, 18, 21, 51, 64, 69, 70, 72, 81, 82, 92, 93, 102, 104, 109–13, 118–21, 144, 202
monarchomachists 82–5, 101, 131
  anti-monarchomachists 6
Montesquieu 67, 84, 132, 209, 210
Morsey, Rudolf 39
Mouffe, Chantal 6
Müller, Adam 7, 20, 53, 54, 59–62
Müller, Johann Baptist 94
Mussolini, Benito 10, 12, 208, 209, 217, 218
Muth, Heinrich 163, 191, 214, 230

myth 10, 11, 12, 13, 75, 89, 183, 209, 217

Napoleon 86–8
natura naturans 71, 121, 122, 125, 132, 144
Naumann, Werner 48, 49
Nazi Party 8, 9, 11, 12, 19, 25–7, 29, 37–9, 47–50, 52, 127, 141–3, 146, 154, 159, 165, 169, 179, 187, 195, 196, 202–4, 208, 210, 232
  Nazi regime 9, 18, 26, 137–9, 143, 145, 156, 161, 172, 200, 202, 203
  National Socialist Party 9, 12, 26, 52, 179, 195, 199, 203
Neumann, Franz 43
Neumann, Volker 69, 70, 163
Nicholls, Anthony 5, 195, 218, 219
Noack, Paul 11, 36, 37, 49, 213–15
normativism 10, 85, 94, 97, 98, 120, 159–64, 186
Novalis 68

Oakeshott, Michael 3
occasionalism 20, 59, 60
Oppenheimer, Franz 175
optimistic anthropology 207
Ott, Eugen 37
Ottmann, Henning 96

Paley, William 151
Papen, Franz von 19, 25–7, 29, 30, 34, 38, 47–9, 176, 191, 193, 195, 196, 198, 201, 203, 212–14, 230, 232
Papen-Gayl reforms 30, 34, 35, 47
parliamentarism 55, 79–90, 134, 135
Pasquino, Pasquale 119
Piccone, Paul 3
Pinochet, Augusto 123, 168
Pius XI 198, 202
Plato 161, 209

plenitudo potestatis 65, 66, 71, 93, 119, 144
political, the 6, 10, 13, 19–22, 43, 62, 65, 73–8, 81, 82, 97, 114, 126–8, 132, 153, 169–78, 191, 204–7, 209, 211, 213
political form 80, 81, 82, 91, 127, 130
political party 32, 196, 203, 220, 222, 228
   multi-party system 140, 203, 219
   party politics 27, 30, 181, 191, 192, 204, 220
   total parties 219, 223
political philosophy 12, 17, 22, 99, 101, 129, 154, 168, 172
political romanticism 20, 53, 54, 61, 74, 75
political theology 91, 112, 113, 122, 125, 144, 162, 163, 169, 170, 171, 172, 173
politicization 32, 98, 101, 137, 175, 184, 194, 216, 218, 219, 225, 228
   see also depoliticization
Polybius 77, 131
Popitz, Johannes 5, 36, 45, 47–9, 180, 181, 194, 198, 201, 212, 213, 225
private property 77, 135, 149, 152, 183, 185, 187, 193, 208, 210, 211
Proudhon, Pierre 89
Prussian coup 31, 48, 49, 191, 214
Pufendorf, Samuel 75, 111, 131

Quadragesimo Anno (1931) 34, 198, 202
Quaritsch, Helmut 218

rationalism 36, 75, 76, 78, 84, 94, 122, 209
   absolute 83, 84, 88, 89, 126
   relative 17, 83, 85, 88, 89, 126
Raz, Joseph 164

Recht (law, the juridical) 19, 50, 66, 69, 70, 71, 78, 162, 164, 207, 230
Rechtsverwirklichung (realization of the juridical) 19, 66, 204, 205, 207
Reichspräsident 4, 8, 13, 14, 16, 18, 21, 42, 51, 63, 64, 68, 70, 92, 93, 111, 136, 137, 161, 163, 175, 180, 190, 196, 206
Reichstag 8, 11, 14, 27, 28, 38, 40, 42, 63, 64, 80, 163, 221, 222, 229
representation (principle of) 78, 101, 125, 132–4, 185
   delegate (*Vertretung*) 101, 102, 135, 140
   sovereign (*Repräsentation*) 101–3, 135, 140
Röpke, Wilhelm 168, 194
Roskopf, Veit 37
Rousseau, Jean Jacques 56, 87, 112
Ruge, Arnold 54
Rumpf, Helmut 4
Rüstow, Alexander 25, 31, 194, 201, 218, 219
rule of law (*Rechtsstaat*) 2, 3, 10, 14, 22, 23, 66, 82, 84, 85, 94, 97, 101, 104, 114, 119, **124–32**, 136, 139, **146–68**, 175, 185–7, 191, 192, 204, 217
   formal *Rechtsstaat* 149, 155–8
   substantive *Rechtsstaat* 156, 157, 186

Sandel, Michael 210
Schelling, F. W. J. 57, 59
Schelsky, Helmut 208, 209
Scheuerman, William 3, 142, 145, 148, 153, 154, 201, 202
Schiffer, Eugen 63
Schlegel, Friedrich 7, 20, 53, 54
Schleicher, Kurt von 8, 11, 19, 26, 29, 30, 31, 35, 36, 37, 181, 196, 201, 232

Schlenker, Max 30
Schmitt, Carl *Concept of the Political* 19, 32, 57, 150, 169–78, 210
  Diktatur 2, 5, 7, 12, 17, 19, 20, 41, 44, 45, 63–70, 71, 80, 81, 108, 111, 112, 113, 122, 138, 144, 145, 165, 185, 205, 208
  Gesetz und Urteil 142
  Hüter der Verfassung 20, 23, 30, 33, 41, 147, 176, 177, 179–83, 188–90, 193, 201
  Langnamverein Address 6, 19, 25, 28, 30–5, 36, 52, 179, 180, 188, 193–9, 200–4, 212–32
  Legalität und Legitimität 2, 23, 41, 176, 179, 182, 185–8, 190–5, 198, 201, 206, 218
  Leviathan 11, 200, 209, 212, 228
  Parlamentarismus 13, 14, 16, 17, 21, 40, 79–90, 105–7, 115, 209
  Political Romanticism 7, 14, 20, 53–63, 68, 79, 209
  Political Theology 12, 14, 17, 20, 70–4, 79, 81, 108, 110–14, 121, 124, 142, 145, 148, 162, 165, 171
  Reichsstatthaltergesetz 19, 28, 38, 49–52, 177
  Römische Katholizismus 74–8, 90–2, 126
  Staat, Bewegung und Volk 19, 39, 45, 47, 96, 127, 137–43, 202–3
  Über die drei Arten 19, 94, 97, 104, 158–64
  Unabhängigkeit der Richter 147, 152, 166
  Verfassungslehre 2, 8, 11, 13, 19, 22, 40, 41, 42, 70, 81, 85, 94, 107, 108, 109, 113–25, 126–37, 139, 142, 147, 152, 155, 156, 159, 163, 169, 171, 173, 191, 197, 199, 205, 206, 208, 217, 218, 222, 225
  Wert des Staates 19, 145, 205
Schopenhauer, Arthur 59
Schotte, Walter 31
Schwab, George 2, 3, 9, 14, 27, 36, 38, 63, 64, 138, 143, 161, 198, 200, 208
Schwab, Johann Baptist 65
separation or division of powers 40, 44, 82, 85, 88, 93, 125, 155, 174, 222
Sieyès, Emmanuel 45, 102, 109, 121, 122, 125, 132
Slagstad, Rune 130
Social Democratic Party 118, 195, 203, 210
socialism 4, 86, 87, 88, 92
Sontheimer, Kurt 31
Sorel, Georges 13, 89
sovereignty 5, 6, 10, 22, 63, 65, 66, 69–71, 72, 101, 108–25, 130, 167, 186, 204
  popular sovereignty 3, 18, 56, 70, 72, 100, 102, 113, 116, 121, 125, 175, 193
  substance/exercise 5, 6, 19, 65, 66, 71, 123, 144, 145, 205, 207
Spengler, Oswald 74
Spinoza, Benedict de 122, 125
spontaneous order 100, 157, 158, 165, 167, 186, 190
Springorum, Fritz 30, 34, 196, 198, 212, 213, 227, 232
Stahl, Friedrich Julius 57, 110, 118, 155
Stapel, Wilhelm 34, 37
state
  absolute state 23, 94, 175, 179, 182, 184
  administrative state (*Verwaltungsstaat*) 181, 182, 188, 192, 201
  authoritarian state 8, 20, 23, 24, 166, 179, 180, 193, 195, 207, 218

bureaucratic state
  (*Beamtenstaat*) 143, 144, 154
executive state
  (*Regierungsstaat*) 27, 181,
  182, **184–6**, 188, 189, 191,
  192
feudal state 65, 182
judicial state (*Juridiktionsstaat*)
  181–4, 189
legislative state
  (*Gesetzgebungsstaat*) 6, 98,
  180–2, 184, **186–8**, 189, 190
modern state 65, 74, 174, 179,
  181, 224, 230
neutral state 10, 20, 23, 140,
  154, 179, 181, 189, 190, 217
party state 27, 43, 45, 50, 213,
  214, 215, 218, 223
qualitative total state 20, 24,
  31, 52, 97, 180, 194, 195,
  217
quantitative total state 24, 31,
  97, 177, 180, 194–7, 201,
  218, 220, 222
strong state 1, 5, 6, 8, 9, 19,
  20, 25, 27, 28, 31, 32, 35,
  50, 52, 55, 74, 94, 97, 99,
  115, 153, 154, 168, 172,
  175, 176, 185, 189, 190,
  193–5, 197–9, 200, 202, 204,
  206–8, 212, 213, 218, 221,
  223, 232
stato totalitario 20, 194, 195,
  217, 218
total state 23, 24, 25, 31, 32,
  33, 98, 99, 166, 174,
  179–82, 191, 193–5, 201,
  206, 216, 217, 219
unity of the state 17, 18, 71,
  81, 82, 86, 91, 129, 161
weak state 6, 74, 75, 97, 194,
  214, 218, 219, 221
welfare state 3, 153, 156, 157,
  186, 190, 193
state-forms 77, 80, 129, 130, 132,
  134–6, 173, 175, 184, 189,
  191, 192
status mixtus 16, 21, 22, 55, 77,
  126–8, 131–6, 139–41, 143,
  144, 189, 191, 192, 206
Stein, Heinrich Karl von 96
Stein, Lorenz von 72, 73, 154–6,
  191
Strauss, Leo 3, 13, 23, 90, 98,
  169, 170, 172, 173, 178, 209
substance 11, 55, 57, 58, 66, 71,
  93, 123, 124, 130, 144, 145,
  159, 160
substantive order, 6, 58, 160
substantivist way of thinking
  145
see also sovereignty,
  substance/exercise
Supreme Court at Leipzig 31, 32,
  42, 183, 214, 215
Supreme Court, American 182, 183

Theseus 88
theology 91, 112, 117
theory of the state and the
  constitution 2, 5, 18, 20, 21,
  22, 31, 116, 174, 204, 208
theory of the constitution 2, 22,
  144, 174, 181, 191, 192, 208
theory of sovereignty 103, 116
theory of the state 2, 17, 22,
  65, 71, 116, 173, 208
see also constitutional theory
Thoma, Richard 13, 14, 105
thèse nobiliaire/royaliste 7, 66, 67
Tocqueville, Alexis de 79, 91, 94,
  112, 130, 137
Tommissen, Piet 25, 36, 47, 49,
  51, 52, 194, 200
Tönnies, Ferdinand 209
totalitarianism 5, 9, 22, 23, 27,
  31, 104, 146, 147, 148, 166,
  179
see also authoritarianism
Treitschke, Heinrich von 54, 74,
  75
Trotsky, Leon 88
Turner, Henry Ashby 29, 30, 195,
  212, 213, 232

Ulmen, G. L. 3

Voltaire 67

Weber, Max 163
Weimar constitution 2, 4, 30, 42, 48, 50, 92, 127, 160, 165, 179, 182, 188, 199, 204, 214, 221, 231
  abrogation 20, 39, 40, 43, 44, 138, 179
  contradictions 65, 70, 126, 128, 135, 139
  death 28, 51, 137, 143
  defective 31, 214
  democratic 4, 14, 16, 70, 80, 132, 133, 135, 136, 193, 205
  destruction 20, 40, 43, 45, 137, 143, 146, 160
  genesis 109, 117–19, 121
  integrity 4, 19, 28
  interpretation 22, 27, 146, 173, 206
  liberal 4, 14, 21, 86, 89, 109, 114, 132, 136, 144, 169
  mixed character 21, 139, 140, 143, 206
  political element 115, 120, 130
  superseded 9, 43
  valid/not valid 22, 45, 95, 137, 166
Weimar constitution articles
  art. 3 38
  art. 21 80
  art. 29 80
  art. 48 8, 21, 31, 36, 42, 63, 93, 111, 180, 213, 223
  arts. 68–77 40
  art. 76 4, 11, 28, 40, 41, 137, 183
  art 129 222
  art. 130 222
Wilms, Bernard 1
Wolin, Richard 3

Zehrer, Hans 232
Ziegler, Heinz O. 23, 121, 166, 179, 193, 195, 218
Zweig, Egon 68, 122